Treat Yourself To The Best Cookbook

Compiled by
Junior League of Wheeling, Inc.

Featuring
Tested Recipes

Copies of **Treat Yourself To The Best** may be obtained from

Treat Yourself To The Best
Junior League of Wheeling, Inc.
907½ National Road
Wheeling, West Virginia 26003

Copyright 1984
by
Junior League of Wheeling, West Virginia, Inc.
All Rights Reserved

International Standard Book Number 0-9613428-0-3

First Printing	1984	10,000 copies
Second Printing	1987	5,000 copies
Third Printing	1990	5,000 copies
Fourth Printing	1993	5,000 copies

Manufactured
by
Favorite Recipes® Press
P.O. Box 305142
Nashville, Tennessee 37230
1-800-358-0560

CONTENTS

In the late 19th century when Samuel S. Bloch and his brother, Aaron, organized a tobacco company at Wheeling, West Virginia, it's likely neither would have guessed the venture would produce a genuine slice of Americana. One of their company's products, Mail Pouch chewing tobacco, has been advertised since 1900 in a special way which has become an American tradition. Sides of hundreds of country barns dotting the United States' rural landscape coast-to-coast have been given and still reach out to passers-by with a message urging use of Mail Pouch as a way to "Treat Yourself To The Best." The Junior League of Wheeling has borrowed that Mail Pouch slogan for this cookbook's title.

"Treat Yourself To The Best," an acrylic painting in a transparent technique which produces a unique watercolor effect, is the work of Don Fusco of Hopedale, Ohio. From 1968 to 1979, Cleveland native Fusco was employed by Hallmark Cards, Inc., as a designer. "My paintings try to capture and save part of America that will bring pleasure for years to come," says Fusco.

The pen and ink drawings of West Virginia landmarks which appear throughout this cookbook are the work of members of the Junior League of Wheeling, Inc.

We dedicate this cookbook to those who
have added the best ingredients to our lives.

COOKBOOK COMMITTEE

Co-Chairmen   Sharon Byrd
                                       Jenny Seibert

Art Chairman   De Anna Joel Taylor
Art Committee   Dana Goff
                                       Debbie Kiester
                                       Janet Kropp

Testing Coordinator   Ange Joel

Section Chairmen
  Appetizers   Lin Companion
  Soups, Salads and Sauces   Jean Bailey
  Entrees   Ruth Smith
  Vegetables   Dea Kennen
  Pasta, Rice and Potatoes   Mary Ann Wagenheim
  Breads   Joan Stamp
  Desserts   Linda Morrison
  Nationality and Heritage   Susan Godish
  Potpourri   Dea Kennen
  Special Parties   Jane Altmeyer

Public Relations   Margaret Beltz

Sustaining Liaison   Ann Bopp

Indexing   Vicky Musicaro

Secretary   Cynthia Reasbeck

Treasurer   Linda Thonen

Layout   Julie Squibb

Marketing Chairmen   Jean Bailey
                                       Vicky Musicaro
                                       Mary Ann Wagenheim

FROM THE COOKBOOK COMMITTEE

To do a project of the magnitude of this cookbook requires the help of many people. We thank all the members of the Junior League of Wheeling for the time, talent, and treasured recipes they unselfishly gave. We are equally grateful to League members' relatives and friends who shared their knowledge and recipes as we prepared **Treat Yourself To The Best.** Our book contains hundreds of recipes, many original and others donated by contributors as favorites. We apologize that all of the recipes submitted could not be included due to space constraints.

Our final words of gratitude go to our families. Their encouragement, support, and patience during the two years this cookbook evolved have been without limit.

Proceeds from the sale of **Treat Yourself To The Best** will be returned to the Community through projects of the Junior League of Wheeling, Inc.

Hors d´ oeuvres
and
Appetizers

Capitol Building, Charleston, West Virginia

CRAB CHEESE SPECIAL DIP

1 (6 ounce) package cream cheese, softened
1 teaspoon Worcestershire sauce
2 teaspoons lemon juice
1 teaspoon garlic salt
1 teaspoon onion salt
1 teaspoon pepper

2 teaspoons finely chopped onion
2 teaspoons finely chopped celery
2 teaspoons finely chopped olives
1 (8 ounce) package crabmeat

Mix together well. Chill overnight. **HINT:** Can do ahead and can be doubled. Yield: 4 to 6 servings.

Jean A. Bailey

CRAB MEAT BALLS

1 pound flaked crabmeat
¼ cup melted butter
1 teaspoon salt
1 teaspoon prepared mustard
1 teaspoon lemon juice

⅛ teaspoon nutmeg
⅛ teaspoon cayenne pepper
½ cup soft bread crumbs
2 egg yolks, beaten

Mix all ingredients together and chill until firm enough to hold shape. Form into small balls and dust with flour. Deep fry in hot oil until browned. Drain and place in chafing dish and serve with mustard sauce.

MUSTARD SAUCE

1 tablespoon dry mustard
1 tablespoon dry wine
½ cup mayonnaise
¼ cup Dijon mustard

1 teaspoon Worcestershire sauce
lemon juice to taste

Make a paste of dry mustard and wine and let stand 10 minutes. Stir in remaining ingredients and chill. Yield: 3 dozen.

Betty Harris

CRAB QUICHE SQUARES

Great for a crowd

double piecrust pastry
10 to 12 ounces shredded
  Swiss cheese
2 tablespoons grated
  Romano cheese
3 to 4 tablespoons flour
5 eggs

1 pint half and half
1 (10 ounce) package frozen
  spinach
1 large onion, chopped
1 tablespoon garlic, minced
½ cup butter
1 (12 ounce) can crabmeat

Press double piecrust pastry into a 15x10x1-inch jelly roll pan and come up the sides. Prebake pie shell at 350° for 10 minutes. Remember to puncture crust with a fork. Cool crust. Toss shredded Swiss and Romano cheese with flour. Beat eggs; add half and half. Add spinach that has been well squeezed. Sauté onions in butter and garlic. Add sautéed mixture to eggs and half and half. Add crabmeat. Then add to Swiss and Romano cheese mixture. Bake at 400° for 40 to 45 minutes until brown. **HINT:** This can also be placed into 2 prebaked pie shells. Freezes well. Yield: 60 (1½ inch) squares.

Debbie Marano

CRAB SNACK

3 ounces cream cheese,
  softened
½ cup butter or margarine,
  softened
1 (6 ounce) package frozen
  king crabmeat, thawed,
  drained and flaked

¼ cup finely chopped onion
1 teaspoon lemon juice
20 Pepperidge Farm party
  rolls (bite size), halved
paprika

In medium mixing bowl, cream the cream cheese and butter. Add crabmeat, onion and lemon juice; mix well. Spread mixture on halves of party rolls (40 halves). Broil 8 to 10 minutes until crab mixture is melted and bubbly. Watch so as not to burn. Sprinkle with paprika. Serve immediately. **HINT:** Can be made early in day and refrigerated until needed. Yield: 40 appetizers.

Teddi H. McBee

HOT HOT CRAB DIP

Very spicy

1 (8 ounce) package cream
  cheese, softened
1 (12 ounce) bottle chili sauce
juice of 1 lemon
black pepper

Worcestershire sauce
horseradish
1 (6½ ounce) can crabmeat,
  drained

Set out cream cheese to soften. Put chili sauce in small bowl. Starting with small amounts of lemon juice, black pepper, Worcestershire sauce, and horseradish, add increasing quantities to make mixture hotter or more tangy. Want it hotter? Add more horseradish. More tangy? Add more lemon juice and Worcestershire sauce. Remember to start small, ½ teaspoon or so, and increase to taste. Mix cream cheese and crabmeat. Press this into a flat serving dish. Now pour on the hot! Spread evenly. Serve with crackers. **HINT:** Can be doubled. Yield: 10 servings.

Maralyn Kline

VI'S CRABMEAT CANAPES

1 (6½ ounce) can crabmeat
3 eggs, hard-boiled and
  grated
1 small onion, grated
1 (4 ounce) package shredded
  Cheddar cheese

¼ cup real mayonnaise
¼ cup French dressing
1 loaf party rye bread
paprika

Break up crabmeat in bowl. Add eggs, onion, cheese, mayonnaise and dressing. Mix to blend well. Spread on party rye and sprinkle with paprika. Broil until bubbly, 5 to 10 minutes. **HINT:** May be prepared ahead and ready to pop under the broiler as guests arrive. Yield: 30 servings.

Vi Joel

PEANUT BUTTER PATÉ

½ cup chopped fresh
  mushrooms
2 tablespoons butter or
  margarine
2 tablespoons lemon juice
1 (8 ounce) package cream
  cheese, softened

2 tablespoons creamy
  peanut butter
2 slices bacon
3 green onions (white part
  only), finely chopped
assorted crackers

Sauté mushrooms in butter or margarine for 5 minutes over low heat, stirring frequently. Stir in lemon juice. Remove from heat. Beat cream cheese and peanut butter until fluffy. Stir in mushroom mixture and cover. Refrigerate for at least 1 hour. Fry bacon until crisp; drain and crumble. Shape cream cheese mixture into a ball. Roll ball in bacon and onions. Cover. Refrigerate until serving time. Serve with crackers.

Vicky Musicaro

BRAUNSCHWEIGER PATÉ

1 pound braunschweiger,
  room temperature, broken
  into pieces
4 ounces cream cheese,
  softened

1 tablespoon milk
1 tablespoon grated onion
1 teaspoon sugar
1 teaspoon chili powder

In electric mixer, combine braunschweiger, cream cheese, milk, onion, sugar, and chili powder. Beat until smooth; place on serving plate and form into igloo shape. Cover and chill.

4 ounces cream cheese,
  softened
1 tablespoon milk

⅛ teaspoon bottled hot
  pepper sauce

Whip cream cheese, milk, and pepper sauce until smooth. Spread evenly over igloo. Chill. Garnish with snipped parsley, red caviar, or paprika. Serve with crackers.

Ruth Foose

STUFFED BRIE

1 round brie, small
¼ pound butter, softened
¾ cup cremé fraiche

1 (3¾ ounce) tin black truffles
in juice (reserve juice)

Cut brie while cold, horizontally. Lift off top half. Butter surface of lower half with softened butter. Spread cremé fraiche over butter. Dot with diced truffles. Leave ½ inch around edges. Sprinkle juice over these ingredients. Replace top half of brie and press together. Put back in box and cover with reasonable weight on top. Let soften for 3 hours. Refrigerate for 3 days with weight on top. Bring back to room temperature and serve. **HINT:** Must do ahead.

Dee Dee McCuskey

CLAM ROLLS

Easy and great for a crowd.

1½ loaves sandwich bread
16 ounces cream cheese,
   softened
½ cup heavy cream
2 envelopes dried onion
   cup a soup

1 (16½ ounce) minced clams,
   drained
butter, melted

Mix cream cheese, cream, onion soup, and clams. Remove crusts from bread. Spread clam mixture on one side. Roll up in jelly roll fashion. Cut each roll in three sections. Dot with melted butter. Freeze in plastic bags. Thaw slightly before baking. Bake at 400° for 10 to 12 minutes. **HINT:** Excellent to have in freezer for a quick appetizer. Yield: 125 appetizers.

Carol Kinder

CHOPPED CHICKEN LIVER

½ cup butter
1 cup chopped onion
1 pound chicken livers
2 hard cooked egg yolks
1½ teaspoons salt

⅛ teaspoon pepper
⅛ teaspoon nutmeg
1 teaspoon lemon juice
2 tablespoons chopped
   parsley

Melt ¼ cup of butter in skillet. Add onions and cook until transparent, stirring frequently. Remove onions and set aside. Add remaining butter and chicken livers to skillet. Sauté, stirring frequently until livers are tender (10 minutes). Cool slightly. Blend onion, livers, and egg yolks in blender. Add remaining ingredients and stir well. Spoon into 2-cup greased bowl. Cover and chill. **HINT:** Can do ahead. Yield: 2 cups.

Diana Ihlenfeld

SPECIAL SPINACH DIP

*A chipper sort of dip. It's not only good
but good for you, although not exactly calorie-free.*

1 (10 ounce) package frozen
   chopped spinach, thawed
   & drained
1 package of imported
   vegetable soup
2 cups sour cream

1 cup mayonnaise
1 small onion, chopped
1 (8 ounce) can water
   chestnuts, drained
2 tablespoons Parmesan
   cheese

Combine all ingredients in blender. For party servings, hollow out a round loaf of dark rye bread; cut removed sections into bite-sized pieces and insert cheese dip into hollow center. Surround dip with small pieces of bread to be dipped with toothpicks. Also great with vegetables, potato chips, or crackers. **HINT:** Can be frozen.

Katherine Doepken

ASPARAGUS DIP

1 (15 ounce) can asparagus
1 (8 ounce) package cream
   cheese
½ cup mayonnaise

Worcestershire sauce to taste
TABASCO Brand Pepper
   Sauce
garlic salt or onion salt
   to taste

Drain asparagus and purée in blender until smooth. Add softened cream cheese, mayonnaise, and seasonings. Blend until creamy. Serve with crackers or crudites. May also be served as a vegetable dip. Yield: 3 cups.

Sally Roberts

APPETIZERS

CURRY DIP

2 cups mayonnaise
1½ tablespoons tarragon
  vinegar
1 dash pepper
1 teaspoon salt
½ teaspoon thyme

1 to 3 tablespoons curry
  powder, according to your
  taste
2 tablespoons chili sauce
4 tablespoons grated onion
1 tablespoon snipped chives

Combine all ingredients and chill several hours. Serve with raw vegetables. **HINT:** Can be used as a sauce for shrimp. Yield: 2½ cups.

Diane Montani

FRESH VEGETABLE DIP

1 (8 ounce) package cream
  cheese, room temperature
1 teaspoon prepared
  mustard
1 tablespoon mayonnaise

1 teaspoon garlic salt
¼ cup sugar
2 tablespoons ketchup
2 tablespoons sweet and sour
  French dressing

Beat all ingredients with mixer or in blender until smooth. Chill until ready to serve. Good dip for fresh vegetables. Yield: 1½ cups.

Dan Tonkovich
State Senator

TUNA-CHEESE VEGETABLE DIP

1 (8 ounce) package cream
  cheese, softened
2 tablespoons milk
1 (6½ ounce) can tuna,
  drained
2 teaspoons grated onion

2 beef bouillon cubes,
  crushed
1 cup sour cream
3 tablespoons Thousand
  Island dressing

Combine cream cheese and milk; mix until smooth. Add all other ingredients and mix well. Cover and chill to blend flavors.

Patti Kota

14

MY FAVORITE CHEESE DIP
Great for a party

1 tablespoon butter
1 tablespoon flour
2 tablespoons sugar
3 tablespoons vinegar
1 teaspoon salt
2 egg yolks, beaten
8 ounces cream cheese,
  softened

½ teaspoon paprika
½ teaspoon dry mustard
1 small onion, chopped
1 small green pepper,
  chopped
1 small jar pimentos,
  chopped

Melt butter in double boiler. Add flour, sugar, vinegar, salt, and egg yolks. Cook until thick, stirring constantly. Remove from heat and cool for 10 minutes. Add remaining ingredients and stir until well blended. Chill several hours. Good with corn chips. Yield: 3 to 4 cups.

Diana Ihlenfeld

CHILI CON QUESO

Authentic Mexican recipe. Delicious!

4 or 5 tomatoes (may use
  canned tomatoes)
1 can green chillies
1 teaspoon oregano
1 teaspoon basil
¼ cup onion, chopped

1 pound pasteurized
  process cheese spread
1 tablespoon Worcestershire
  sauce
½ cup mozzarella cheese

Cook tomatoes over medium heat; add green chillies, oregano, basil, and onion. Simmer 10 minutes. Add rest of ingredients; stir until all cheese is melted. Serve with taco chips. MMMMMMM Good! Yield: 20 servings.

Marlene J. Yahn

CHEESE BALL

2 (8 ounce) packages cream
  cheese, softened
1 teaspoon salt
¼ cup green pepper,
  chopped

2 tablespoons grated onion
2 cups pecans, chopped
1 (8½ ounce) can crushed
  pineapple, drained

Mix all ingredients together; save ¾ cup of pecans for garnishing the cheese ball.

Shirley Milton

SHRIMP CHEESE BALL

2 (3 ounce) packages cream
  cheese, softened
1½ teaspoons prepared
  mustard
1 teaspoon onion, grated
1 teaspoon lemon juice

dash of pepper
dash of salt
1 (4½ ounce) can shrimp,
  drained
⅔ cup salted peanuts,
  chopped

Blend mustard, onion, lemon juice, pepper and salt into cream cheese. Break shrimp into pieces; stir into cheese mixture. Chill. Form into ½-inch balls and roll in nuts. **HINT:** Looks nice to put a pretzel stick into each ball before serving. This may also be used as a spread by omitting nuts. Yield: 25 appetizers.

Kitty Hughes

SHRIMP DELIGHT HORS D'OEUVRES

1 (8 ounce) package cream
  cheese, softened
2 tablespoons melted butter
2 tablespoons mayonnaise
2 tablespoons minced onions
1 tablespoon ketchup

1 tablespoon Worcestershire
  sauce
1 teaspoon horseradish
¼ cup dry white wine
5 ounces small cooked
  shrimp

Mix all ingredients except dry white wine and shrimp. Dip shrimp in white wine and add to mixture. Spread on wafer biscuits or butter thin crackers. Garnish with ½ stuffed olive. Refrigerate until ready to serve. Yield: 12 to 14 servings.

Nila Stobbs

MARINATED SHRIMP

3 pounds shrimp, cleaned
and cooked
1 cup French dressing
½ cup green pepper,
finely chopped
¼ cup raw onion, finely
chopped
¼ cup parsley, finely
chopped

1 clove garlic, crushed, or
⅛ teaspoon dried minced
garlic
2 tablespoons prepared
mustard (as hot as you like)
2 tablespoons lemon juice
salt and pepper to taste

Mix all ingredients and chill several hours. Yield: 14 to 16 servings.

Edi Altmeyer

HOT ARTICHOKE SPREAD

1 (14 ounce) can artichoke
hearts, drained
1 cup real mayonnaise

1 cup Parmesan cheese,
grated
paprika

Cut artichoke hearts into pieces. Mix together all ingredients. Put in ovenproof serving dish and bake 20 minutes at 350° or until bubbly. Add a sprinkling of paprika on top for color. Serve with crackers or melba toast. **HINT:** Can do ahead and can be doubled. Yield: 8 servings.

Sherry Hearne

OYSTER SPREAD

2 (8 ounce) packages cream
cheese, softened
¼ cup milk
2 tablespoons mayonnaise
1 tablespoon lemon juice
1 tablespoon Worcestershire
sauce

salt to taste
2 (3.6 ounce) cans smoked
oysters, minced
paprika
parsley, chopped

Combine all ingredients except oysters, paprika and parsley; blend well. Stir in oysters and refrigerate several hours or overnight. Sprinkle with paprika and parsley. Serve with assorted crackers. Yield: 3 cups.

Ann Bopp

HOT MUSHROOM SPREAD
Different and delicious

1 egg yolk
1 teaspoon lemon juice
2 tablespoons white wine
3 small cans mushroom
  pieces, drained

1 medium onion,
  chopped fine
¼ cup butter, melted
½ teaspoon salt
2 tablespoons flour

Combine egg yolk, lemon juice and wine. Brown mushrooms and onion in butter. Add salt and flour. Stir until mixed. Remove from heat. Add egg yolk mixture. Put spread in cheese crock and bake at 350° for 30 minutes. Serve with crackers. Yield: 1½ cups.

Edi Altmeyer

DRIED BEEF LOG

1 (8 ounce) package cream
  cheese
¼ cup grated Parmesan
  cheese
1 tablespoon horseradish

⅓ cup chopped stuffed green
  olives
2 (½ ounce) packages or 1
  cup dried beef, finely
  snipped

Blend together cream cheese, Parmesan cheese and horseradish. Stir in olives. On waxed paper, shape into two 6-inch rolls. Chill several hours or overnight. Roll log in snipped dried beef. Serve with assorted crackers.

Sandy Mendenhall

CHIPPED BEEF DIP

1 (5 ounce) jar chipped beef,
  chopped
2 (8 ounce) packages cream
  cheese, softened
1 pound sour cream

3 tablespoons onion, minced
3 tablespoons green pepper,
  chopped
½ cup chopped walnuts,
  optional

Combine above ingredients in large bowl. Place in ungreased 2-quart casserole dish. Sprinkle walnuts before baking. Bake at 350° for 30 minutes. Serve warm with crackers. Yield: 4 cups.

Claudia Kepner

SAUERKRAUT BALLS

*One of the most colorful of West Virginia politicians
is Farmington native A. James Manchin,
who was elected and reelected as West Virginia
Secretary of State in 1976 and 1980.*

¼ pound lean ham
¼ pound lean pork
¼ pound corned beef
2 tablespoons chopped onion
1 cup milk
½ teaspoon iodized salt
1 tablespoon chopped
    parsley

2 tablespoons shortening
1 cup unsifted flour
½ teaspoon dry mustard
1 (1 pound) can sauerkraut,
    drained well
flour
1 egg, slightly beaten
fine dry bread crumbs

Put meats and onion through food chopper; add parsley. Pan fry in shortening until browned, stirring occasionally. Blend in flour and milk; slowly stir in seasonings. Cook and stir until light and fluffy. Mixture will be thick at first, but becomes fluffy as it cooks. Allow to cool. Add sauerkraut. Put entire mixture through food chopper once more. Return mixture to skillet and cook, stirring constantly, until mixture is quite thick. Cool. Roll into walnut-size balls. Dip in flour then in beaten egg, then coat with fine bread crumbs. Fry in deep fat preheated to 375° until golden brown. Do not fry at lower temperatures or balls may "explode". Serve hot. **HINT:** These can be made ahead of time. Heat just before serving (in ovens or in slow heat of crockpot...not in hot grease again). Yield: 40 to 50 balls.

A. James Manchin

SWEDISH MEATBALLS

Old-time favorite.

1½ pounds fresh ground
   chuck
½ cup cracker crumbs
½ package dried onion
   soup mix
4 tablespoons onion,
   chopped
2 tablespoons green
   pepper, chopped

½ cup condensed milk
1 teaspoon salt
1 teaspoon dry mustard
1 teaspoon poultry
   seasoning
1 teaspoon paprika
flour for dusting
1 cup beef broth
1 tablespoon flour

Mix all ingredients except beef broth and flour. Make into small meatballs. Chill. Roll in flour and brown. Add beef broth and 1 tablespoon flour and simmer for 1½ hours. Yield: 75 meatballs.

Louise Blackmon

HAM BALLS

Easy and great for a crowd

1½ pounds ground ham
½ pound ground pork
⅔ cup cracker crumbs
2 eggs

⅓ cup chopped onion
1¼ cups evaporated milk
¼ teaspon salt
¼ teaspoon thyme

Mix above ingredients well and form into 1-inch balls. Place in 9x13x2-inch baking dish.

GLAZE

1 cup brown sugar
1 teaspoon dry mustard

3 tablespoons vinegar
½ cup water

Mix sugar, mustard, vinegar, and water; bring to a boil. Pour over meat. Bake at 350° for 1 hour. **HINT:** Can do ahead and can be doubled. Freezes well. Yield: 12 servings.

Beth Ann Dague

LACY MUSHROOM CAPS

24 to 28 medium mushrooms
⅔ cup margarine, melted
½ cup cracker crumbs
½ cup finely shredded
  Swiss cheese

1 clove garlic, minced
1 teaspoon dried marjoram
  leaves, crushed
⅛ teaspoon pepper

Remove stems from mushrooms; brush caps with some of margarine. Place mushrooms, rounded side down, on ungreased baking sheet. In small bowl, mix remaining margarine, cracker crumbs, cheese, garlic, marjoram, and pepper. Blend well. Fill each mushroom cap with 1 teaspoon filling, mounding slightly in center. Bake at 375° for 5 minutes. Broil 6 inches from heat source until golden and lacy. Serve hot. **HINT:** The melted cheese give the mushrooms the lacy look! Yield: 24 to 28 servings.

Donna Niess

MARINATED MUSHROOMS

1½ pounds small mushrooms
1½ cups water
1½ cups white or wine
  vinegar

½ cup reserved cooking
  liquid
1 cup Italian dressing
1 teaspoon oregano

Clean and dry mushrooms. Mix water and vinegar; heat to boiling. Add mushrooms and let boil for 2 minutes. Drain; reserve cooking liquid. Cool mushrooms for 1 hour. Mix ½ cup of reserved cooking liquid with dressing and oregano. Pour over cooked mushrooms. They can be eaten immediately, but the flavor gets better after 12 hours. They can be kept for 7 to 10 days. **HINT:** Can do ahead and can be doubled. Yield: 20 servings.

Linda Thonen

APPETIZERS

COCKTAIL MUSHROOMS

6 large cans whole button
mushrooms (not marinated
or pickled)
⅔ cup Durkee's Famous
Sandwich Sauce®

⅓ cup mayonnaise
paprika

Rinse mushrooms and strain. Stir together sandwich sauce and mayonnaise. Stir in mushrooms. Marinate and chill for 24 hours. Serve with toothpicks or on a bib of Boston lettuce. Add a dash of paprika for color. Can store for weeks in the refrigerator. Yield: 10 to 14 servings.

Stephanie Bloch

*Durkee and Famous Sauce are registered trademarks of SCM Corporation

ZUCCHINI SNACKS

vegetable cooking spray or
shortening
3 cups zucchini, unpared,
very thinly sliced
1 cup packaged quick-biscuit
baking mix
½ cup onion, finely chopped
1 clove garlic, finely chopped
2 tablespoons parsley,
snipped (or dried parsley
flakes)

½ cup Parmesan cheese,
grated
¾ teaspoon seasoned salt
½ teaspoon dried marjoram
or oregano or basil or
mixed Italian herbs
dash of pepper
½ cup vegetable oil
4 eggs, slightly beaten

Preheat oven to 350°. With shortening or vegetable cooking spray, grease 13x9x2-inch baking pan. (Smaller pan works; makes thicker product.) Lightly toss all ingredients except oil and eggs. Combine oil and eggs; pour over other ingredients and mix well. Spread mixture in pan. Bake 25 to 30 minutes at 350° until golden. With sharp knife, cut into 2-inch squares for snacks or 1-inch squares for hors d'oeuvres. Good warm or cool. **HINT:** Cut zucchini in halves or quarters lengthwise before slicing if squash is larger than 1½ inches in diameter. Can do ahead and can be doubled. Yield: 24 large or 48 small appetizers.

Susan Conner

COCKTAIL PIZZAS

1 pound hot sausage
1 cup chopped onion
½ cup sharp Cheddar cheese, shredded
½ cup Parmesan cheese

1½ teaspoons oregano
1 teaspoon garlic salt
8 ounces tomato sauce
6 ounces tomato paste
3 cans flaky biscuits

Fry, crumble, and drain hot sausage. Combine all ingredients except biscuits. Separate each biscuit into 3 pizza rounds. Spread each with mixture and place on cookie sheet. Freeze. Store in plastic bags in freezer until ready to bake. Bake in preheated oven at 425° for 10 minutes. Yield: 90 appetizers.

Linda Thonen

PIZZA PAN DIP

2 (8 ounce) packages cream cheese, softened
1 bottle chili sauce
1 pound hot sausage
1 small sweet purple onion, chopped

1 small green pepper, chopped
1 small can pitted black olives, sliced
1 (4 ounce) package shredded mozzarella cheese

Spread cream cheese on round pizza pan and refrigerate until firm. Spread chili sauce on cream cheese. Brown sausage in skillet; drain and crumble. After sausage cools, spread it on chili sauce. Layer remaining ingredients in order given. Serve with crackers. Yield: 12 to 15 servings.

Joyce McFarland

CHEESE SPINACH SQUARES

Easy and great for a crowd

3 eggs
1 cup flour
1 teaspoon baking powder
1 (1 ounce) package Original
  Ranch Salad Dressing Mix
¼ pound unsalted butter,
  melted

¾ pound Monterey Jack
  cheese, shredded
2 (10 ounce) packages frozen
  chopped spinach, thawed
  and well drained

Beat eggs. Add flour, baking powder, and dressing mix. Stir in melted butter. Add shredded cheese and spinach. Mixture will be very thick; blend well. Spread evenly in 13×9×2-inch greased baking pan. Bake for 30 minutes at 350°. Cool at least 30 minutes and then cut into squares. Serve warm or at room temperature. **HINTS:** After cutting, the squares may be placed on a cookie sheet and flash frozen. Store in freezer bags in freezer until needed. Heat frozen square 10 to 12 minutes at 350°. Yield: 50 appetizers.

Ange Lavy Joel

CHEESE PUFFS

2 eggs, beaten
⅛ teaspoon nutmeg
1 cup crumbled feta
  cheese
1 cup small curd cottage
  cheese

1 (3 ounce) package cream
  cheese
2 tablespoons uncooked
  Cream of Wheat
½ pound phyllo dough

Beat eggs well. Add nutmeg and blend. Then add feta cheese, cottage cheese, cream cheese, and Cream of Wheat to the egg and nutmeg mixture, mixing well (mix by hand). Cut phyllo dough into 3-inch strips. Keep dough covered so it does not dry out. Working with one 3-inch strip at a time, place approximately 1 teaspoon of cheese mixture on one end of dough and roll flag fashion to end of strip. You should end up with a small, filled triangle of dough. Bake at 350° for approximately 12 minutes. **HINT:** Can do ahead. Yield: 8 to 10 servings.

Mary Lou DeFillippo

SUPER TACO

Guests will rave.

1 (10½ ounce) can bean dip
2 to 3 avocados, mashed
1 tablespoon lemon juice
½ cup mayonnaise
1 cup sour cream
1 bunch green onions, chopped
3 medium tomatoes, cored and chopped
1 (3¼ ounce) can ripe olives, drained and sliced
8 ounces Cheddar cheese, shredded

Cover a 12-inch round serving plate with a layer of bean dip. Layer will be thin. In a small mixing bowl, mash avocados; stir in lemon juice. Spread avocados over bean dip. Combine mayonnaise and sour cream; spread evenly over avocados. Sprinkle with green onions, chopped tomatoes, sliced ripe olives, and top with shredded cheese. Serve cold or at room temperature with your favorite crackers or tortilla chips. Yield: 12 to 14 servings.

Margaret Altmeyer

LAYERED MEXICAN DIP

1 pound ground chuck
1 (16 ounce) can refried beans
1 (16 ounce) can chili without beans
1 (1¼ ounce) envelope taco seasoning mix
3 tablespoons picante sauce
3 medium-size ripe avocados
2 tablespoons lemon juice
½ teaspoon garlic salt
⅛ teaspoon pepper
2 cups dairy sour cream
3 cups shredded iceberg lettuce (about ½ medium-size head)
2 medium-size tomatoes, cored, halved, seeded, and coarsely chopped
¾ cup shredded Cheddar cheese
¾ cup shredded Monterey Jack cheese
corn chips

Grease shallow serving platter or 13x9x2-inch glass baking dish. Brown meat in medium-size skillet; drain excess fat. Stir in refried beans, chili, and taco seasoning mix. Spoon evenly into prepared platter. Spoon picante sauce over top. Peel, pit, and mash avocados in medium-size bowl with lemon juice, garlic salt, and pepper. Stir in sour cream. Spread avocado mixture over meat, leaving a narrow border. Sprinkle with lettuce, tomatoes and cheeses. Serve with corn chips. Yield: 20 servings.

Pat Kramer

SCALLION FLOWERS

Very pretty!

8 ounces whipped cream
  cheese
2 tablespoons chopped
  chives
25 paper-thin slices of
  good, hard salami
  (3 inches in diameter)

25 scallions, trimmed to
  about 5 inches long

Combine cream cheese and chives (and any seasoning you like, pepper, paprika, etc.) in a small bowl. Lightly cover each slice of salami. Place scallion in center of each salami slice and roll into cornette. (It should stick shut!) Refrigerate. Makes 25 "flowers". Arrange in a fan-shaped fashion or around edge of platter like a green wreath. Crunchy and cold!

Stephanie H. Bloch

COCKTAIL CREAMPUFFS
A favorite at parties

½ cup margarine
1 cup water
1 cup flour

dash of salt
4 eggs

Boil margarine and water together in saucepan until margarine is melted. Add flour and salt all at once. Beat with mixer until it sticks together. Cool. Then add eggs one at a time—beating after each. Grease a cookie sheet. Drop by teaspoons onto sheet. Bake at 425° for 10 minutes and then lower oven to 350° for ½ hour or until a deep golden brown. Cool on racks. Then cut in half and allow center to dry out. Just before serving, fill with chicken salad or tuna salad. Fill with cream if using them for dessert and top with chocolate or powdered sugar. **HINT:** Freezes well. Yield: 6 to 8 dozen.

Lin Companion

Sandwiches
and
Soups

Covered Bridge, Philippi, West Virginia

SOUPS AND SANDWICHES

BROCCOLI-CHEDDAR CHEESE SOUP

¼ cup butter
1 onion, chopped
¼ cup flour
3 cups chicken broth
3 cups milk
1 pound or 4 cups Cheddar
   cheese, shredded

1 large bunch broccoli,
   cooked, drained and
   chopped, or 2 (10 ounce)
   packages frozen chopped
   broccoli, cooked and
   drained

In large saucepan, melt butter; add onion and cook until tender, about 5 minutes. Stir in flour, blending well. Add chicken broth slowly, while stirring. Cook until mixture starts to thicken; add milk. Heat until just boiling. Add broccoli and cheese. Heat, stirring, until cheese melts and soup is hot. Yield: 6 to 8 servings.

Joan Stamp

GOLDEN CAULIFLOWER SOUP

2 (10 ounce) packages frozen
   cauliflower
2 cups water
½ cup onion, chopped
¼ cup butter
½ cup flour

2 chicken bouillon cubes
2 cups Cheddar cheese,
   shredded
2 cups milk
¼ teaspoon nutmeg
chopped parsley for garnish

In medium saucepan, cook cauliflower in 1 cup water. Cook 4 minutes after reaching full boil. Drain. Reserve liquid. Reserve 1 cup cauliflower flowerettes. Blend or mash thoroughly remaining cauliflower. In large saucepan, cook onion in butter until tender. Stir in flour. Gradually add remaining water and dissolved bouillon cubes. Stir in mashed cauliflower and cheese. Cook until cheese melts. Add milk, nutmeg and flowerettes. Heat through—do not boil. Serve hot. **HINT:** Recipe is easy and can be done ahead of time. Yield: 6 to 8 servings.

Alyce B. Squibb

CHEESE CHOWDER

1¾ cups chicken broth
2 tablespoons butter
¼ cup onion, finely chopped
¼ cup all-purpose flour
2 cups milk

dash of salt
dash of pepper
¼ cup carrots, finely diced
¼ cup celery, finely diced
½ cup sharp cheese, cubed

Boil chicken broth in large pan. In skillet, melt butter; add onion and sauté until tender. Add to broth. Blend in flour; add remaining ingredients except cheese. Stir until thick and bubbly. Reduce heat and add cheese. Stir to melt. Simmer 15 minutes. **HINT:** Recipe can be doubled. Yield: 4 servings.

Shellie Goss

CORN CHOWDER KATHLEEN

4 slices bacon, chopped
2 tablespoons butter
½ pound yellow onions
½ tablespoon flour
1 cup cream
12 ounces chicken broth

1 (1 pound) can pumpkin
1 (1 pound) can creamed corn
dash of ginger
dash of cinnamon
dash of nutmeg

Fry bacon and drain. Sauté onions in butter until tender; add flour and broth. Blend in pumpkin and transfer to soup pot. Add corn, cream and seasonings. Top with crisp bacon when serving. Yield: 6 to 8 servings.

Kathleen Gibbs
The Shed, Wheeling, W.VA.

RICH SEAFOOD CHOWDER

1 (11 ounce) can New
  England clam chowder
1 (4 ounce) can mushrooms
1 (7½ ounce) can tuna fish or
  1 (8 ounce) can crabmeat or
  1 (8 ounce) package
  langostine

1 (13 ounce) can evaporated
  milk
dot of butter for each serving
parsley, chopped

Mix all ingredients and heat slowly. Pour into soup bowls and dot butter and parsley on top. Yield: 4 servings.

Ann Gleason

QUICK BISQUE

2 (6½ ounce) cans lobster or
   crabmeat, shell removed
1 (11 ounce) can turtle soup
1 (10½ ounce) can condensed
   tomato soup
1 (10½ ounce) can beef
   bouillon

1 teaspoon instant minced
   onion
1½ cups heavy cream
½ cup sherry
fresh pepper

Combine all ingredients except sherry, and heat until blended and almost boiling. Stir in sherry. Add freshly ground or coarse pepper, if desired. Yield: 6 servings.

Stephanie H. Bloch

CREMÉ DE FRANCE

2 (10 ounce) packages frozen
   peas
2 (10 ounce) packages frozen
   fordhook lima beans
10 to 12 shallots, finely
   chopped

1 quart heavy cream
½ pound butter
1 tablespoon bovril
   (meat extract)
salt

Cook peas, beans, and shallots in 2 quarts water until very soft. Drain vegetables and strain through sieve, reserving pulp and keeping skins. Scald heavy cream and pour over remaining skins until all remaining pulp is flushed clear. Combine heavy cream with pulp and place in double boiler. Add meat extract and butter. Heat slowly, stirring, until butter is melted. Salt to taste. Serve immediately. Yield: 6 servings.

Toni Clawson

CREAMY ONION SOUP

2½ cups Bermuda onion
   slices
1 (10¾ ounce) can beef
   bouillon soup
½ cup beer
2 tablespoons margarine

2 tablespoons flour
1 cup milk
½ pound Swiss cheese,
   shredded
seasoned croutons

Heat oven to 425.°Cook onions with beef bouillon in covered, medium-sized saucepan for 20 minutes, then add beer. In large saucepan, melt margarine. Stir in flour; then gradually add milk. Cook over low heat until thickened. Stir in cheese. Slowly add soup mixture to cream sauce. Pour into 4 to 6 individual oven proof bowls. Sprinkle with croutons. Bake 15 minutes or until bubbly and lightly browned. **HINT:** This recipe can be done ahead of time and can be doubled. Yield: 4½ cups.

Penelope Ault

LAMB AND GREEN BEAN STEW

¼ cup margarine
1 onion, chopped
1 to 2 pounds lamb chunks, cubed
3 pounds fresh green beans, washed and snapped

1 (6 ounce) can tomato paste
⅛ teaspoon cinnamon
5 or 6 potatoes, peeled and cut
water
salt and pepper to taste

Brown onion and lamb in margarine in 6- or 8-quart pot. Do not drain. Add green beans with just enough water to cover. Simmer 1 hour, covered, until almost tender. Add tomato paste, cinnamon, potatoes; cover with water. Salt and pepper to taste. Simmer another hour until potatoes are tender. **HINT:** Potatoes may be eliminated and stew may be served over rice; however, still cook stew extra hour. Also, round steak may be used in place of lamb. Yield: 8 servings.

Cynthia Reasbeck

CUCUMBER SOUP

1 cup sour cream or plain yogurt
1 cucumber, peeled, seeded and sliced
¼ teaspoon dry mustard

½ teaspoon instant chicken bouillon
1 tablespoon snipped chives or 1 chopped green onion
dill or chives for garnish

Put all ingredients into blender. Blend until cucumber is finely chopped but not smooth. Chill. Serve. Serve in old-fashioned glasses. Garnish with dill or chives. **HINT:** Recipe is easy and can be doubled. Yield: 2 to 4 servings.

Susan Jones

POTATO SOUP I

4 slices bacon, chopped
⅓ cup celery, chopped
⅓ cup onion, chopped
5 or 6 medium red potatoes,
   peeled and diced
4 potatoes for mashing

1 cup milk
2 tablespoons butter
1 tablespoon sugar
salt
pepper
water

Cook bacon, celery and onion in large pot until tender. Add diced red potatoes and enough water to cover. Simmer, covered, until potatoes are semi-soft. Meanwhile, cook 4 potatoes in separate pot with water for mashing; when soft, drain, peel and mash with no liquid. Add mashed potatoes to soup (this is the thickening). Add milk, butter, sugar, salt and pepper to taste. Stir well and simmer 2 hours. Stir occasionally. **HINT:** This recipe can be done ahead of time and can be doubled. It also freezes well. Yield: 8 servings.

Janet Kropp

POTATO SOUP II

4 slices lean bacon,
   diced
2 or 3 leeks, sliced
   thin
½ cup chopped onion
2 tablespoons flour
4 cups beef bouillon

3 large potatoes,
   sliced thin
2 eggs, beaten
1 cup sour cream
1 tablespoon minced
   parsley
1 tablespoon chervil

In 3-quart saucepan, sauté bacon for 5 minutes. Add sliced leeks (green tops may be used) and chopped onions and continue to sauté for 5 minutes. Stir in flour until uniformly moistened. Add bouillon slowly while stirring constantly. Add potatoes and simmer, covered, for 1 hour. Combine eggs and sour cream, mixing thoroughly. Stir into soup. Simmer for 10 minutes while stirring constantly. Do not boil. Add spices and serve hot. **HINT:** Chervil may be deleted but adds a special zest. Also, recipe can be done ahead of time and can be doubled. Yield: 6 servings.

Barbara J. Sterling

FRESH MUSHROOM SOUP

1 pound fresh mushrooms	1 cup water
¼ cup plus 2 tablespoons margarine	1¾ cups chicken broth
	1 cup dry vermouth
2 cups minced onion	¼ teaspoon pepper
½ teaspoon sugar	½ teaspoon salt
¼ cup all-purpose flour	

Slice one-third of mushrooms and finely chop the remainder. Melt butter; add onion and sugar, sautéing until onion is tender. Add mushrooms; cook 5 minutes, stirring often. Stir in flour; cook 2 minutes, stirring constantly. Stir in water; then add all the remaining ingredients. Bring soup to a boil; reduce heat and simmer, uncovered, 10 minutes. Yield: 8 cups.

Nancy M. Nuzum

COLD PEACH SOUP

"King of the Road" Bill Rodgers, four-time winner of the Boston Marathon, endures as one of the United State's premiere distance runners of the 1980s. Rodgers won the 20-K Wheeling race in 1977, 1979 and 1981.

1½ pounds peaches, peeled, pitted and sliced	½ cup dry sherry
	1 tablespoon fresh lemon juice
2 cups sour cream	sugar, optional
1 cup fresh orange juice	
1 cup fresh pineapple juice	

Purée peaches in food processor until smooth. Add all remaining ingredients except sugar (in batches, if necessary) and blend well. Pass soup through fine strainer. Add sugar to taste. Serve chilled. Yield: 8 servings.

Bill Rodgers

GAZPACHO

3 pounds fresh tomatoes
1 cucumber, peeled
1 green pepper, quartered
1 clove garlic
½ onion

1 tablespoon oil
3 tablespoons vinegar
3 slices bread
croutons for garnish

Soak bread in water for several minutes and then squeeze dry. Add soaked bread and all other ingredients into a blender and purée. Garnish with croutons or chopped eggs. Yield: 4 to 6 servings.

Dottie Stobbs

MEDITERRANEAN BROILED SANDWICHES

Great with soups

1 cup Swiss cheese, shredded
4 slices bacon, fried, drained,
  and crumbled
¼ cup mayonnaise
¼ cup ripe olives, chopped
  and pitted

2 tablespoons green onions,
  chopped
4 slices bread, toasted

Mix all ingredients together except bread. Spread on toasted bread. Broil 4 inches from flame for 2 minutes or until cheese melts. Yield: 4 open-face sandwiches.

Jean Bailey

HOT CHIPPED HAM SANDWICHES

Easy and great for a crowd

½ pound chipped ham
½ pound shredded cheese
  (your preference)
1 small onion, chopped
5 ounces pickle relish

6 ounces chili sauce
2 hard-boiled eggs, chopped
2 tablespoons mayonnaise
1 dozen buns

Fill 10 to 12 buns with mixture and wrap tightly in foil. Heat 10 minutes at 400.° **HINT:** May be prepared ahead of time and frozen but allow 20 minutes to heat. This recipe can be doubled. Yield: 10 to 12 servings.

Barbara Whitehead

PEPPERONI ROLLS

Great for a crowd

1 package dry yeast	1 egg
1½ cups lukewarm water	1 teaspoon salt
½ cup dry milk	5 cups unbleached flour
¼ cup sugar	1½ pounds stick pepperoni
¼ cup corn oil	

In a large bowl, combine first 7 ingredients plus 2 cups unbleached flour. Beat with an electric mixer until smooth. Stir in additional flour until dough pulls away from sides of bowl. Turn onto floured surface and knead, adding just enough flour to make a soft dough. Place in a buttered bowl and cover; let rise 1 hour. Slice pepperoni stick lengthwise and then cut into thin slices. Use about 3 pieces for each roll. When dough has risen, separate into 4 pieces. Roll each into a long rope and cut off 2-inch sections and wrap around 3 slices of pepperoni, punching to seal. Place on greased cookie sheet to rise 20 minutes. Bake in preheated oven 450° for 5 to 6 minutes. Serve warm or cold. Great for lunch boxes! Yield: 2 dozen.

Charl Kappel

HOT SAUSAGE ROLLS

2 loaves frozen white bread	1 egg yolk
2 pounds hot sausage, loose	1 cup shredded mozzarella
1 green pepper, chopped	cheese
1 small onion, chopped	
½ pound fresh mushrooms or 1 small can	

Thaw frozen bread. Fry sausage and drain off fat; add green peppers, onions, and mushrooms. Simmer for 10 minutes. Roll out each loaf of bread on a floured surface into a rectangle (approximately ½ the size of a jelly roll pan). Place the 2 rolled rectangles on a greased 15x10x1-inch jelly roll pan and add sausage mixture. Top with cheese and roll up from long side. Baste rolls with a mixture of egg yolk and water to brown crust. Bake at 350° for 30 minutes. Slice and serve. Great with soups. Yield: 2 loaves.

Jody Wharton

SOUPS AND SANDWICHES

SHREDDED BEEF SANDWICHES

1 (4 to 5 pound) inexpensive
  beef roast
1 small onion
¼ teaspoon garlic salt
¼ teaspoon oregano

½ teaspoon parsley
1 teaspoon salt
¼ teaspoon pepper
water

Sprinkle meat with seasonings. Add enough water to cover meat. Cover with tight lid and bake at 400° for 1 hour. Turn oven to 325° and bake 3 hours. Cool meat; then shred apart. If juice has too much fat, remove it. Reheat in juice when ready to serve. Serve on hard rolls. **HINT:** Freezes well. Yield: 12 servings.

Connie Krzysiak

CHEDDAR CHEESE SPREAD FOR SANDWICHES

½ pound mild Cheddar
  cheese, shredded
1 small onion, chopped fine

½ green pepper, chopped fine
½ cup mayonnaise or salad
  dressing, more if desired

Combine all ingredients. Spread on bread to make sandwiches; butter sandwiches to toast on griddle. Cook on low heat so cheese melts. Yield: 2 cups.

Janet Kropp

DEVONSHIRE SANDWICHES

⅓ cup margarine
1 cup flour
2 cups chicken broth
2 cups hot milk
¼ pound Cheddar cheese,
  shredded
1 teaspoon salt

6 slices toast, crusts
  trimmed off
18 slices bacon, fried
sliced turkey breast
  (about 4 thin slices for
  each sandwich)

Melt margarine and slowly blend in flour. Blend in hot milk and chicken broth. Add Cheddar cheese and salt and cook cheese sauce for 20 minutes. To assemble sandwiches, toast bread and remove crusts. Place bacon on bread. Top with turkey. Put all 6 sandwiches in 9x13-inch pan. Pour cream sauce over top and sprinkle with melted butter, Parmesan cheese and paprika. Bake 15 minutes at 450.°**HINT:** This recipe can be done ahead of time. Yield: 6 servings.

Diana Davis

Salads
and
Salad Dressings

Birthplace of Pearl Buck, Hillsboro, West Virginia

APRICOT SALAD

1 (17 ounce) can apricots
1 (3 ounce) package apricot
   gelatin
½ cup celery, finely chopped
½ cup pecans, chopped

½ cup miniature
   marshmallows
1 cup frozen whipped
   topping, thawed

Drain apricots reserving syrup. Add water to syrup to make 1 cup liquid. Heat to boiling. Add gelatin, stirring to dissolve. Cool. Chop apricots and combine with remaining ingredients. Stir into cooled gelatin. Pour into mold and chill. Yield: 8 servings.

Mrs. Herbert Kuehn

STRAWBERRY FLUFF

1 (6 ounce) package
   strawberry gelatin
1 envelope unflavored gelatin
2 cups boiling water
1 (8 ounce) package cream
   cheese, softened

1 (10 ounce) package frozen
   strawberries, thawed
1 (8 ounce) carton frozen
   whipped topping, defrosted
1 dozen fresh strawberries

Stir gelatins together. Add boiling water and stir until thoroughly dissolved. Place cream cheese and thawed strawberries with juice in blender. Blend well. Pour blended mixture into gelatin mixture. Fold in whipped topping. Pour into 13x9x2-inch pan. Chill until set. Decorate top with sliced fresh strawberries. Yield: 12 servings.

VARIATIONS

1 (13 ounce) can crushed
   pineapple with juice
lemon gelatin

pineapple pieces for
   decoration

or

1 (1 pound) can peeled
   apricots with juice

apricot gelatin
apricot pieces for top

Margaret Ann Beltz

PETITE FROZEN CRANBERRY-ORANGE SALAD

Delicious with turkey or chicken

2 cups whipped topping
¼ cup sugar
dash of salt
2 tablespoons mayonnaise
3 ounces frozen orange juice,
    unthawed

1 (11 ounce) can mandarin
    oranges, drained
1 (1 pound) can jellied
    cranberry sauce, diced

To whipped topping, add sugar and salt. Fold in mayonnaise, then orange juice. Mix thoroughly. Add mandarin oranges and diced cranberry sauce. Line muffin pans with paper baking cups. Fill each with mixture. Freeze until firm. Remove from freezer 5 minutes before serving. Place on lettuce leaf. Yield: 9 to 12 servings.

Alyce B. Squibb

RAINBOW SALAD

6 (3 ounce) boxes of different
    flavored gelatin
1 (24 ounce) container dairy
    sour cream

water

Dissolve 1 box of gelatin in 1 cup of boiling water. Divide mixture in half. To one half, add 4 ounces of sour cream. Mix well with a fork or whisk. Pour into a 9x13-inch pan. Refrigerate 20 minutes. Add 2 tablespoons of cold water to the other half of gelatin. Pour on top of the first layer and chill 20 minutes. Repeat above with each box of gelatin. After all layers are complete, chill well before serving. Cut in squares to serve. Makes a colorful summer dish. **HINT:** Must be made ahead. Yield: 12 to 14 servings.

Leigh Longenette

SALADS AND SALAD DRESSINGS

CRANBERRY SALAD

1 orange, sectioned
½ cup cranberries
½ cup celery, chopped
1 apple, chopped
½ cup nuts (walnuts or
  pecans)

1 (3 ounce) package lemon
  gelatin
1½ cups water
½ cup sugar

Grind orange sections with cranberries and add celery and apple. Mix gelatin, water, and sugar together and add cranberry mixture. Pour into 12x8x2-inch glass baking pan and chill. Yield: 9 to 12 servings.

Pauline Taylor

BEET AND HORSERADISH MOLD

3 (12 ounce) cans beets,
  shoestrings or cubes
1 (6 ounce) package lemon
  gelatin
½ cup sugar
½ cup cider vinegar

2 tablespoons prepared
  horseradish
lettuce
½ cup mayonnaise
½ tablespoon prepared
  horseradish

Drain beets, reserving juice. Combine juice with enough water to make 3 cups. Heat in saucepan to boiling. Combine gelatin and sugar in heat proof bowl and add boiling liquid. Stir to dissolve. Add beets, vinegar and 2 tablespoons horseradish. Wet inside of 6-cup mold, pouring out excess water. Pour beet mixture in and chill until firm. Unmold onto lettuce lined platter just before serving. Combine mayonnaise and remaining horseradish to serve alongside as topping for salad. **HINT:** Best done day before. Yield: 12 to 16 servings.

Joan Stamp

BETTY'S BUTTERBEAN SALAD

2 (10 ounce) packages frozen
  baby lima beans
1 (10 ounce) can shoepeg
  corn, drained

1 bunch green onions,
  chopped with tops
1 cup real mayonnaise

Cook beans according to package directions and drain. Add corn, onions and mayonnaise. Mix well and chill. **HINT:** If doubling, don't quite double mayonnaise. Yield: 8 servings.

Betty Worls

BROCCOLI MEDLEY

Attractive salad

DRESSING

½ cup salad oil	1 teaspoon garlic salt
¼ cup wine vinegar	salt and pepper

Mix salad oil, vinegar, garlic salt and salt and pepper to taste.

1 head broccoli	
1 medium onion, sliced in rings	1 pint cherry tomatoes
1 (15 ounce) can pitted black olives	½ pound fresh mushrooms

Separate broccoli into flowerettes and cut up stalks. Combine broccoli, onion rings, olives and tomatoes. Cover with dressing. Cover dish and refrigerate overnight. Before serving, slice and add fresh mushrooms. Toss and serve. Yield: 6 to 8 servings.

Carol R. Copenhaver

ITALIAN POTATO SALAD

6 potatoes, unpeeled	¼ cup black olives, sliced
½ cup olive oil	¼ cup wine vinegar
¼ cup celery, chopped	salt
2 tablespoons green onions, chopped	

Boil unpeeled potatoes in salted water until tender. Do not overcook. Peel potatoes immediately without cooling and dice into 1-inch cubes. Coat potatoes with oil and allow to cool. Toss cooled potatoes with remaining ingredients and salt to taste. Serve warm or cold. Yield: 4 to 6 servings.

Country Road Inn
Mrs. E. L. Jarroll

MEX-A-CORN PUFF SALAD

1 pound ground beef
1 (8 ounce) can kidney beans,
  drained
½ cup water
1 (1¼ ounce) package
  taco mix seasoning
4 cups lettuce, shredded
2 cups spinach, shredded
3 tomatoes, cut into thin
  wedges
1 small avocado, peeled and
  pitted

1 cup shredded Cheddar
  cheese
½ cup sliced pitted ripe
  olives
1 (8 ounce) can chick peas
  (garbanzo beans), drained
⅓ cup chopped onions
⅓ cup mayonnaise
¼ cup chili sauce
4 cups tortilla chips

Cook and stir ground beef in 10-inch skillet until brown; drain. Stir in kidney beans, water, and seasoning mix. Heat to boiling; reduce heat. Simmer uncovered, stirring occasionally, 10 minutes. Cool 5 minutes. Mix lettuce, spinach, tomatoes, avocado, cheese, olives, chick peas, and onions in very large salad bowl. Mix mayonnaise and chili sauce; toss gently with salad mixture. Pour beef mixture over salad mixture; toss gently. Crush tortilla chips and add at the last minute; toss and serve immediately. Yield: 6 servings.

Shirley Milton

CHICKEN SALAD

Great served on lettuce or in pockets of warm pita bread

2 to 3 cups cooked and
  diced chicken
1 cup diced celery
2 tablespoons lemon juice
1 tablespoon minced onion
1 teaspoon salt
⅓ cup mayonnaise or slaw
  dressing

1 cup seedless green grapes,
  halved
1 (11 ounce) can mandarin
  oranges, halved
½ cup toasted slivered
  almonds

Combine chicken, celery, lemon juice, onion and salt. Chill well. Add salad dressing, grapes, oranges and almonds to chicken mixture; toss until well mixed. Yield: 6 servings.

Sue Mendenhall

CAESAR SALAD

3 medium heads romaine
  lettuce, chilled

Break romaine leave into bite-size pieces. Top with blender caesar salad dressing (Page 47). Toss with croutons.

CAESAR CROUTONS

6 slices white bread	3 cloves garlic
½ cup butter	grated Parmesan cheese

Place cloves of garlic in solid butter. Let sit at room temperature for 1 hour. Cut each slice of bread in 5 strips one way, then across 5 times to make squares. Toss bread squares with butter in a large bowl with your hands. Spread out on baking sheet. Heat in slow oven, 225°, for 2 hours. Sprinkle with grated Parmesan cheese. Store covered in jar in refrigerator.

Janie Altmeyer

SPINACH SALAD

1 pound spinach, washed and drained	1 cup oil
4 hard-boiled eggs	¾ cup sugar
½ pound bacon, fried and crumbled	1 small onion, diced
1 (8 ounce) can water chestnuts	¼ cup white vinegar
½ pound mushrooms (optional)	⅓ cup ketchup
	2 tablespoons Worcestershire sauce
	⅛ teaspoon salt

Tear spinach; add chopped eggs, bacon, sliced water chestnuts, and sliced mushrooms (optional). Blend oil, sugar, onion, vinegar, ketchup, Worcestershire sauce, and salt. Refrigerate at least 1 hour before pouring over spinach mixture. **HINT:** Recipe must be done ahead and can also be doubled. Yield: 6 to 8 servings.

Ruth Smith

POST RACE COOLER

Tom Fleming, one of America's outstanding distance runners, twice won the New York City Marathon. He has had two second place and one third place finishes in the Boston Marathon and has run in several Wheeling Elby's Distance Races.

1 head lettuce, shredded
1 large banana, peeled and chopped
1 large apple, cored and chopped
lemon juice
1 large orange, peeled and segmented

½ cantaloupe, peeled and cubed
3½ ounces Roquefort cheese, cubed
yogurt and honey dressing (below)
finely chopped pecan nuts

Place lettuce in salad bowl and sprinkle cubed apple with lemon juice. Then mix all fruit together and place on lettuce. Add cheese; mix lightly.

DRESSING

juice of ½ lemon
1 teaspoon melted honey
12 tablespoons plain yogurt
1 garlic clove, crushed

salt
pepper
1 tablespoon finely chopped mint

Combine lemon juice, honey, and yogurt, blending well. Stir in garlic and season to taste with salt and pepper. Stir in chopped mint and let stand in refrigerator until chilled. To serve, top salad with dressing and sprinkle with nuts. Yield: 4 servings.

Tom Fleming

STRAWBERRY-SPINACH SALAD

juice of large lemon or 3 scant tablespoons
¼ cup sugar
1 egg yolk

6 tablespoons vegetable oil
1 (10 ounce) package fresh spinach
1 quart strawberries

In medium bowl, mix lemon juice and sugar. Add egg yolk and whisk until sugar is dissolved. Add oil, 1 tablespoon at a time, and whisk until thick. Cover and chill. When ready to serve, toss spinach and strawberries with dressing. Yield: 6 to 8 servings.

Jody Wharton

ROQUEFORT MOUSSE

1 envelope unflavored gelatin
¼ cup lemon juice
1 cup boiling water
¼ pound Roquefort cheese
1 cup grated cucumber,
  drained
4 tablespoons minced
  parsley

2 tablespoons minced
  pimento
1 tablespoon minced capers
1 teaspoon grated onion
1 teaspoon salt
black pepper, freshly ground
1 cup heavy cream, whipped
paprika

Soften gelatin in lemon juice. Add 1 cup boiling water and stir until gelatin is dissolved. Mash cheese. Add cucumber, parsley, pimento, capers, onion, salt and pepper and mix well. Combine with gelatin mixture. Chill for 20 minutes or until mixture is slightly thickened. Fold in whipped cream. Pour into mold and chill for at least 4 hours or until firm. Sprinkle paprika on top for color. **HINT:** Must be done ahead of time and can be doubled. Pretty in a ring on watercress with mayonnaise in center. Especially good with cold, sliced meats or birds. Yield: 6 servings.

Stephanie H. Bloch

SHRIMP LUNCHEON SALAD

1 (4¼ ounce) can shrimp,
  chilled and drained
1 cup shredded carrots
1 cup diced celery
½ cup mayonnaise

1½ tablespoons grated onion
1 teaspoon lemon juice
1 cup shoestring potatoes,
  canned

In medium bowl, mix shrimp, carrots, celery, mayonnaise, onion and lemon juice. Chill for at least 3 hours. Just before serving, add shoestring potatoes. Toss lightly. **HINT:** It is important that you don't add shoestring potatoes until you are ready to serve salad. Otherwise, shoestring potatoes become soggy. This recipe must be done ahead of time and can be doubled. Yield: 6 servings.

Donna Niess

SHRIMP SALAD ROVIGO

¼ pound fresh mushrooms
2 tablespoons tarragon
  vinegar
1 pound fresh small shrimp,
  cooked and peeled
juice of 1 lemon
1 sprig parsley

2 bay leaves
1 cup mayonnaise
2 tablespoons chili sauce
1 mashed garlic clove
2 tablespoons finely chopped
  scallions

Do not wash mushrooms, simply wipe with a damp paper towel. Remove stems. Slice mushrooms finely and place in a bowl. Sprinkle with vinegar, a pinch of salt and pepper, and marinate for at least 1 hour. Place shrimp in another bowl and sprinkle with lemon juice. Add sprig of parsley and bay leaves. Let shrimp marinate, covered, for at least 2 hours. To mayonnaise, add chili sauce, garlic, and scallions. Drain both shrimp and mushrooms. Remove parsley and bay leaves. Combine shrimp and mushrooms in a glass serving dish. Add mayonnaise and carefully blend it into salad. Be sure not to break mushroom slices. Refrigerate salad for 1 or 2 hours before serving. Correct seasoning. **HINT:** For a more elegant presentation, serve this salad on marinated artichoke hearts. Serve with thinly sliced, buttered pumpernickel. Yield: 6 servings.

Carolyn B. Keagler

CUCUMBERS IN SOUR CREAM

1 tablespoon sugar
1½ teaspoons salt
1 cup sour cream
3 tablespoons grated onion

2 tablespoons white vinegar
4½ cups cucumbers, thinly
  sliced and peeled (about
  6 medium cucumbers)

Blend together sugar, salt, sour cream, onions and vinegar. Stir in cucumbers. Chill for at least 2 hours. Yield: 6 servings.

Jenny Seibert

POPPY SEED DRESSING

1½ cups sugar
2 teaspoons dry mustard
2 teaspoons salt
3 tablespoons onion juice
  or 3 tablespoons finely
  chopped onion

⅔ cup vinegar
2 cups vegetable oil
3 tablespoons poppy seeds

Mix everything but poppy seeds in blender (just enough to mix). Add poppy seeds and give blender 1 or 2 more whirls. **HINT:** Half of this recipe makes 8 to 10 servings. Will keep in refrigerator for 2 weeks. It will separate so must be mixed again. May be used over fruit or green salad. Yield: 16 to 20 servings.

Mrs. Fontaine B. Hooff

BLENDER CAESAR SALAD DRESSING

1 teaspoon salt	1 egg
dash of ground pepper	½ cup salad oil
1 teaspoon Worcestershire	¼ cup lemon juice
sauce	1 cup freshly grated
¼ teaspoon garlic powder	Parmesan cheese
¼ cup salad oil	anchovies (optional)

Put first 5 ingredients in blender. Place raw egg in boiling water for 1½ minutes. Break open egg and scrape into blender. Turn motor on. Immediately remove cover and add ½ cup more salad oil. Turn off and add lemon juice and cheese. Give blender one more flick. Refrigerate. Add anchovies to salad when you make it (Will taste too strong if put in the dressing). **HINT:** Do not double recipe but make twice instead. Should be done ahead to blend flavors. Yield: 2 cups.

Lou Crawford

SESAME SEED SALAD DRESSING

¾ cup sugar	¾ tablespoon instant minced
¼ teaspoon dry mustard	onion
½ teaspoon paprika	1 cup salad oil
½ teaspoon salt	½ cup red wine vinegar
¼ teaspoon TABASCO Brand	¼ cup toasted sesame seeds
Pepper Sauce	
¼ teaspoon Worcestershire	
sauce	

Toast sesame seeds at 350° for 10 minutes. Place all ingredients in blender. Blend until smooth. **HINT:** This must be prepared in blender or it will not be properly mixed. This is an excellent spinach salad dressing. Yield: 1 pint.

Patti Kota

SALADS AND SALAD DRESSINGS

FRENCH DRESSING
Excellent on tossed salad

3 hard-boiled eggs
3 medium onions
1 cup vinegar
1 cup ketchup

1 cup salad oil
1 cup sugar
1 teaspoon salt

Grate eggs and finely chop onions. Combine all ingredients in order listed. Yield: 1 quart.

Alyce B. Squibb

POTATO SALAD DRESSING

3 eggs, well beaten
6 tablespoons sugar
12 tablespoons vinegar
1 cup mayonnaise

1 teaspoon prepared
mustard

Combine eggs, sugar, and vinegar; cook for 2 minutes. Add mayonnaise and mustard, then stir. Yield: 1½ cups.

Olive W. Bigelow

FRENCH DRESSING II

Saves Well

1 (10¾ ounce) can tomato
  soup
¾ cup vinegar
1 cup oil
1 teaspoon horseradish

1 teaspoon salt
1 teaspoon pepper
1 cup sugar
2 small onions, chopped

Blend tomato soup, vinegar, oil, horseradish, salt, mustard and pepper. Mix sugar and chopped onions. Combine all ingredients and shake well. Yield: 1 pint.

Olive W. Bigelow

"MOM BESS" SALAD DRESSING

2 eggs, beaten
½ cup sugar
6 ounces prepared mustard

¼ pound butter or margarine
2 ounces vinegar

Combine all ingredients in small saucepan. Stir over low heat, just to boiling point. Cool. Refrigerate. **HINT:** Can be used in potato, macaroni or tossed salad. Excellent over fruit salad, too. Yield: 1½ cups.

Libby Messerly

MAYONNAISE

This is excellent for potato salad or deviled eggs

2 eggs
½ teaspoon prepared
  mustard
¾ cup vinegar
1 cup water

1 cup sugar
1 tablespoon butter
2 tablespoons flour
¼ cup water

Beat eggs well and add mustard, vinegar, 1 cup water, sugar, and butter. Thicken with flour mixed with ¼ cup water. Cook and stir constantly over low heat until thick. Yield: 2½ cups.

Mrs. Donald Burkle

GOLDEN GATE DRESSING

1 egg yolk
2 tablespoons tarragon
  vinegar
½ teaspoon salt
1 cup olive oil
¼ cup light cream

1 tablespoon lemon juice
1 teaspoon onion salt
2 tablespoons chopped
  chives
2 tablespoons chopped
  parsley

In bowl, combine egg yolk, vinegar and salt. Beat in oil, 2 tablespoons at a time. Add remaining ingredients; blend well. Refrigerate until ready to use. **HINT:** Very good on greens and avocados. Yield: 1 cup.

Mrs. W. L. Harris

SALADS AND SALAD DRESSINGS

MUSTARD VINAIGRETTE DRESSING

Great for greens of all kinds

¼ cup mustard, Dijon
  style
1¼ teaspoons coarse, crystal
  salt or 1 teaspoon regular
  salt
black pepper, freshly ground
  (12 grinds of pepper mill)
½ teaspoon Worcestershire
  sauce

2 drops TABASCO Brand
  Pepper Sauce
½ cup white wine vinegar
¼ cup water
1½ cups vegetable oil or
  peanut oil
½ cup olive oil

Fit food processor with steel blade or use large container of blender. Put all ingredients in container and process (use low blender speed) for about 10 seconds until well blended. Store in covered jar in refrigerator. **HINT:** Great for spinach salad with orange sections and red onion rings. Yield: 3 cups.

Joan Stamp

CREAMY BACON DRESSING

2 tablespoons cider vinegar
½ cup real mayonnaise
1 tablespoon light corn syrup
⅛ teaspoon salt

4 slices bacon, fried crisp
  and crumbled
2 tablespoons green onions,
  chopped

Gradually stir vinegar into mayonnaise. Add remaining ingredients. Serve immediately on tossed green salad. **HINT:** It is especially good on fresh spinach. Yield: ¾ cup.

Jenny Seibert

SWEET AND SOUR SALAD DRESSING

6 tablespoons mayonnaise
2 tablespoons prepared
  mustard
1 teaspoon salt
2 heaping tablespoons sugar

1 teaspoon celery seed
⅛ cup white vinegar
2 hard-boiled eggs, chopped

Mix all ingredients together except for eggs. Add chopped eggs. Chill. **HINT:** Very good on sliced fresh tomatoes and lettuce salad. Yield: ½ cup.

Mrs. Robert Hazlett

Sauces

Old Main, Marshall University, Huntington,
West Virginia

SAUCES

MEAT MARINADE

¾ cup oil
½ cup soy sauce
2 tablespoons Worcestershire
  sauce
¼ cup lemon juice

1 tablespoon dry mustard
1 teaspoon salt
1 teaspoon pepper
¼ cup wine vinegar
garlic powder to taste

Combine all ingredients and blend well in blender. Marinate steak, pork chops, or chicken several hours or overnight in a non-metallic container. Drain meat and cook on grill. **HINT:** Marinade is reusable if kept in refrigerator. Yield: 2 cups.

Mrs. Edith Kropp

STEAK MARINADE

1 (10 ounce) bottle steak
  sauce
⅓ cup oil

⅓ cup Worcestershire
  sauce

Combine all ingredients. Marinate overnight. Sirloin steak cut to 1½ inches thick is great with this. Yield: 1½ cups.

Susan Eismon

HORSERADISH SAUCE FOR BEEF

½ pint heavy cream, whipped
1 (6 ounce) bottle
  horseradish, drained

1 tablespoon vinegar
½ teaspoon dry mustard

Beat together all ingredients and serve cold with roast beef or corned beef. **HINT:** This recipe is easy to do and can be prepared ahead of time. Yield: 1½ cups.

Cookbook Committee

HOT MUSTARD SAUCE

Very hot!

1 cup dry mustard
1 cup tarragon vinegar

3 eggs
1 cup sugar

Mix mustard and vinegar; soak overnight. Beat eggs; add sugar and mustard mixture. Cook in double boiler until thick. Yield: 1½ cups.

Ruth P. Polack

ORANGE SAUCE

Excellent with ham

5 tablespoons sugar
1½ teaspoons cornstarch
¼ teaspoon salt
¼ teaspoon cinnamon

10 whole cloves
2 teaspoons orange rind
½ cup orange juice
4 orange slices

Combine all ingredients except orange slices. Stir over low heat until thick and clear. Add orange slices to garnish. **HINT:** Can be served warm or cold. Can also be reheated and served with leftover ham.

Janie Altmeyer

HAM SAUCE

1 (8 ounce) jar currant jelly
4 ounces horseradish

¼ cup walnuts, broken
  by hand

Combine and heat until jelly melts. Serve hot over ham. Yield: 1 cup.

Shirley Milton

CURRANT–BRANDY GLAZE

½ cup orange juice
½ cup brandy
2 tablespoons currant jam

1 tablespoon dry mustard
1 teaspoon ground ginger

Combine all ingredients in blender and blend until smooth. Spoon over baking ham 30 minutes before the end of cooking time. Yield: 1 cup.

Dee Dee McCuskey

MINT SAUCE

½ cup sugar
¼ cup white wine vinegar
1 cup fresh mint,
  chopped, or ½ cup
  dried mint

Combine sugar and vinegar in saucepan. Let boil for 5 minutes. Pour over mint leaves. Let stand 1 to 2 hours. Strain into bottle and cap. Refrigerate or serve warm over lamb. Yield: 8 servings.

Joan Corson

SAUCES

CHEESE SAUCE

2 tablespoons butter
  or margarine
2 tablespoons flour
¼ teaspoon salt

1 cup milk
¾ cup sharp Cheddar cheese,
  shredded
⅛ teaspoon dry mustard

Melt butter in saucepan over medium heat. Blend in flour and salt; stir well. Gradually add milk, stirring well until thickened and bubbly. Add Cheddar cheese and dry mustard. Stir until cheese melts. Serve over broccoli, cauliflower or your favorite vegetable. Yield: 1¼ cups.

Ann Diotti

HOT FUDGE SAUCE

2 squares unsweetened
  chocolate
6 tablespoons water
½ cup sugar

pinch of salt
3 tablespoons butter
¼ teaspoon vanilla

Over low heat, melt chocolate in water, stirring until smooth. Add sugar and salt. Cook and stir until slightly thickened. Add butter and remove from heat. Stir in vanilla. Serve. **HINT:** For extra flavor, add 1 tablespoon orange liqueur. Leftovers may be refrigerated and warmed over low heat to reserve. Yield: 1 cup.

Joan Corson

FRUIT SAUCE TOPPING

Fantastic!

2 egg yolks
1 cup powdered sugar
3 tablespoons rum

1 cup whipped cream
1 teaspoon vanilla

Beat egg yolks. Add powdered sugar and then mix in rum. Beat until well blended. Fold in whipped cream and vanilla. Serve with fresh strawberries or mixed fruit. Yield: 1 pint.

Judi Hendrickson

Entrees

Oglebay Mansion, Oglebay Park, Wheeling,
West Virginia

BEEF WELLINGTON

3 pounds beef tenderloin	brown sauce
2 tablespoons soft butter	3 single piecrusts
1 teaspoon salt	(frozen or homemade)
½ teaspoon pepper	1 egg
mushroom filling	1 tablespoon water

Heat oven to 425° Tie tenderloin with heavy string; place meat on rack in a shallow pan. Spread butter over top and sides of meat; sprinkle meat with salt and pepper and bake for 20 minutes. Remove meat and rack to cool (about 30 minutes). Remove strings and pat dry with paper towels. Roll piecrusts on well-floured surface, crimping edges to get one rectangle about 16x14 inches; trim edges evenly. Preheat oven to 400° Place meat on longer side of pastry. Spread mushroom filling on remaining surface of pastry, leaving margin for crimping. Roll meat and pastry. Crimp edges, sealing by moistening with water. Carefully place pastry-wrapped meat seam side down on baking sheet. Mix egg and water; brush on pastry for golden brown crust, if desired. Bake tenderloin for 30 minutes or until pastry is browned. If one cooks 2 Wellington recipes in the same oven, the cooking time is often fifteen minutes longer.

MUSHROOM FILLING

1 pound fresh mushrooms, finely chopped	¼ cup real butter
½ cup chopped onion	¼ cup snipped parsley
½ cup dry sherry	pinch of salt

In a skillet, melt butter and cook onions until clear. Add all other ingredients and cook until all liquid is absorbed.

BROWN SAUCE

2 bouillon cubes	2 sprigs of parsley
2 cups water	1 bay leaf, crumbled
½ cup sherry	⅛ teaspoon crushed thyme
3 tablespoons finely chopped onion	leaves
1 tablespoon finely chopped celery	3 tablespoons sherry
	2 tablespoons butter

In saucepan, boil water and dissolve bouillon cubes. Add next 6 ingredients and simmer for 30 minutes. Strain mixture through fine sieve and discard vegetables. Stir in 3 tablespoons dry sherry and simmer 5 minutes more. Stir in butter. When melted, sauce is ready to serve. Brown sauce is served over Beef Wellington. Yield: 8 servings.

Laura Carter

FILET MIGNON MOUTARDE FLAMBE

*From boyhood in Wheeling, Morgan Paull has gone
on to a thriving career as an actor and producer.*

4 filets, 1¾ inch thick
¼ teaspoon salt
¼ teaspoon pepper
¼ teaspoon rosemary
¼ teaspoon sage
⅓ cup cognac

5 teaspoons Dijon mustard
**3 tablespoons Gulden's®
   mustard**
2 tablespoons sour cream
½ cup cream

Sauté filets in butter for about 5 minutes on each side for medium rare. During this process, sprinkle filets with combination of salt, pepper, rosemary, and sage. Pour off any excess fat from skillet and pour cognac over filets. Light with match. When flame goes out, remove filets and keep warm. Add the mustards, sour cream, and cream to skillet and cook for 1 minute. Pour over filets and sprinkle with paprika. Yield 4 servings.

Morgan Paull

BEEF TENDERLOIN

1 (3½ to 5 pound) beef
  tenderloin
Kitchen Bouquet®
meat tenderizer
garlic (fresh or salt)

thyme
dehydrated onions
dehydrated parsley
coarse black pepper
2 bay leaves

Trim meat well and remove excess fat and tendons. Tie roast with string
to keep shape. Place roast in pan. Brush meat with Kitchen Bouquet.
Sprinkle meat liberally with meat tenderizer. Rub on garlic; season
with thyme, onions, parsley, and pepper. Place bay leaves on top. Allow
to stand until roast is at room temperature. Place meat thermometer
in thickest part of meat. Roast uncovered at 325° until thermometer
registers rare. Take meat out of oven and wrap in foil. It will continue
to bake for ½ hour to medium. Slice thin and serve. **HINT:** It turns out
perfect and delicious. Yield: 8 servings.

Alfred Ihlenfeld

LOBSTER STUFFED TENDERLOIN

Elegant!

3 to 4 pounds beef tenderloin
2 (4 ounce) frozen lobster
  tails
1 tablespoon margarine,
  melted
1½ teaspoons lemon juice

6 slices bacon, partially
  cooked
½ cup sliced green onion
½ cup margarine
¼ to ½ cup dry white wine
⅛ teaspoon garlic salt

Cut tenderloin lengthwise to within ½ inch of bottom. Boil lobster tails
and remove from shells. Place lobster inside beef. Combine melted
margarine and lemon juice. Drizzle over lobster. Tie roast together every
2 inches with string. Place partially cooked bacon over roast. Place roast
on rack in roasting pan. Preheat oven to 500° and roast tenderloin for
5 minutes. Reduce heat to 350°. Cook roast 10 minutes per pound for
rare, 15 minutes for medium. Sauté onion in margarine. Add wine and
garlic salt. Slice roast and remove string. Spoon on wine sauce and serve.
HINT: Tenderloin may be stuffed and tied ahead of time. If made in
advance, remove from refrigerator at least 2 hours before roasting. Yield:
8 servings.

Karen Recht

ROAST PRIME RIB OF BEEF

1 (4 to 5) rib roast (9 to 12 pounds)	flour salt and pepper

Preheat oven to 500°. Rub roast well with flour and salt and pepper to taste. Place roast bone side down on a rack in a shallow roasting pan. Place in the oven and cook 15 minutes per rib. (Example, 3 ribs, 45 minutes; 4 ribs, 60 minutes.) Turn off heat and do not open oven door for 2 more hours. Then carve and serve. This produces a rare roast with a crusty outside. If you want medium beef, add 15 minutes to roasting time. Oven will smoke. **HINT:** Responsible for entree at a dinner party? Cook a 5-pound standing rib roast for 1 hour at 325°. Remove from oven, wrap in foil and transport to destination. One hour before eating, place roast in a 325° oven and bake 1 additional hour. Will be medium rare. Yield: 6 to 8 servings.

Joan Stamp
Jenny Seibert

STEAK DIANE

4 (10 to 12 ounce) sirloin
  steaks
salt to taste
freshly ground pepper
butter
½ cup cognac
2 tablespoons shallots,
  chopped
	2 tablespoons parsley,
	  chopped
	2 tablespoons chives,
	  chopped
	⅓ cup sherry

On a cutting board, pound each steak with a meat mallet until it is no thicker than ¼ inch. Season with salt and pepper. Add enough butter to skillet to completely cover bottom and place over high heat. Very quickly brown steaks on both sides, turning only once. Pour in cognac, allow to warm, ignite, and blaze. Remove steaks to heated platter. Add additional butter, shallots, parsley and chives to skillet and sauté lightly. Add sherry, mix well, and pour hot sauce over steaks. Serve immediately. Yield: 4 servings.

Tom Briley
Editor, The Intelligencer

BEEF ROULADEN

*The chef says you don't even have to
be a football player to enjoy it.*

*Oliver Luck, quarterback for the Houston Oilers of the
National Football League, is one of West Virginia
University's all-time athletic greats.*

4 thin slices beef	**pepper**
4 strips bacon	**flour**
4 small pickles	**fat**
salt	**½ onion, chopped**

Beat and tenderize beef with meat mallet. Place one strip of bacon and one pickle on each slice of meat (larger pickles may be halved or quartered). Roll up strips (whence comes the name Rouladen), starting at narrow end and secure with skewer. Cover entire roll with seasoned flour (pepper and salt are seasoning; other spices can be used depending on individual taste). Brown well in heated fat in a heavy skillet or pot. Add chopped onion and brown alongside meat. Add ½ cup water to pot and simmer slowly for 2 to 2½ hours (pot should be closely covered). Regularly replace any water lost during cooking. When ready, thicken gravy with flour and season to taste (the addition of a little red wine is recommended). Pour gravy over rolls and serve with rice, noodles, or mashed potatoes. One roll is usually sufficient for someone with an average appetite (a football player may need two or three). Yield: 4 servings.

Oliver Luck

MARINATED FLANK STEAK

flank steak	**2 tablespoons onion,**
¾ cup oil	**chopped**
¼ cup soy sauce	**½ clove garlic**
1 cup honey	**1½ teaspoons ginger**
2 tablespoons vinegar	

Blend all ingredients except steak in blender; pour over steak. Marinate 10 to 12 hours or overnight. Grill on outdoor grill 5 to 8 minutes on each side. Slice against grain. Meat will be pink inside. **HINT:** Sauce may be doubled if marinating several steaks. Recipe must be done ahead.

Marlene Yahn

STEAK CONTINENTAL

2 pounds flank steak
1 clove garlic, quartered
1 teaspoon salt
¾ teaspoon pepper

2 tablespoons soy sauce
1 tablespoon tomato paste
1 tablespoon vegetable oil
1 teaspoon oregano

Score both sides of steak. Mash garlic with salt. Then add remaining ingredients. Mix well and rub into steak. Wrap steak in waxed paper and let stand in refrigerator 5 to 6 hours or overnight. Broil 5 to 8 minutes on each side. **HINT:** Must be done ahead. Yield: 4 servings.

Pam Warfield

CHINESE PEPPER STEAK

Easy and Economical

1 pound round steak,
  ½ inch thick
1 tablespoon paprika
2 tablespoons butter
2 cloves garlic, crushed
1½ cups beef broth
1 cup green onions, sliced

2 green peppers, seeded
  and sliced into strips
2 tablespoons cornstarch
¼ cup water
¼ cup soy sauce
hot cooked rice to
  accompany

Cut round steak into ¼- to ½-inch strips. Sprinkle paprika over meat and toss lightly to distribute evenly. Let stand while preparing onions and peppers, about 15 minutes. Melt butter in a large skillet and brown meat; add garlic and broth. Simmer covered for 30 minutes or until meat is tender. Add onions and peppers and continue to cook 10 minutes until peppers are becoming tender. Mix cornstarch, water, and soy sauce together. Add to meat and peppers, stirring constantly, while sauce thickens. Serve over hot cooked rice. Yield: 4 servings.

Cookbook Committee

BEST BRISKET EVER

1 (4 pound or larger) beef
  brisket
1 package onion soup

1 cup ketchup
1 cup ginger ale
¼ cup water

Trim brisket as much as possible. Mix onion soup, ketchup, and ginger ale in large roasting pan or dutch oven. Place brisket in pan coating well on both sides. Place fat side up. Heat on top of stove until sauce is bubbly. Add water. Roast covered in 350° oven for 1½ to 2 hours. Turn roast after 1 hour, if desired. Be sure to check roast after 1½ hours to see if it is done. The time on this cut can vary from 1½ to 2½ hours. Slice thinly across the grain. Remove fat from sauce, if necessary. Pour sauce over sliced beef. **HINT:** Excellent cold with horseradish and mayonnaise on a toasted roll. Yield: 6 servings.

Karen Recht

EASY BEEF BRISKET

1 lean beef brisket,
  3 to 4 pounds
2 to 3 tablespoons
  Worcestershire sauce

salt and pepper to taste
1 cup ketchup
1 medium onion, chopped

Heat ketchup, Worcestershire sauce, chopped onion, and salt and pepper in saucepan. Place brisket in baking dish and pour sauce over meat. Cover tightly and bake at 300° for 3 to 4 hours. When cool, slice thin. **HINT:** Best when cooked day before and reheated. Yield: 6 to 8 servings.

Anne Lamb

BAKED SWISS STEAK

2 tablespoons shortening
2 pounds round steak,
  2½ inches thick
½ cup flour
salt and pepper
½ green pepper,
  finely chopped

½ onion, thinly sliced
2 cups boiling water
½ package onion soup mix,
  optional

Season flour with salt and pepper. Flour meat that has been cut in large pieces. Pound meat with a mallet. Brown steak in heated shortening. Add onions, green pepper, and water (onion soup mix, if desired). Put in a covered casserole and bake at 350° for 1 to 1½ hours. Vegetables may be added. Serve over rice or noodles. Yield: 6 servings.

Louise Blackmon

ROAST SIRLOIN OF BEEF WITH MADAGASCAR PEPPERCORNS AND COGNAC

1 (4 pound) sirloin roast
2 tablespoons oil
1 tablespoon crushed,
   green peppercorns
1 tablespoon salt

3 cups heavy cream
2 tablespoons cognac
½ cup rinsed, green
   peppercorns

Heat oil in skillet and brown sirloin on all sides. Place fat side down in skillet and season top with crushed green peppercorns and salt. Roast at 375° to desired doneness. Remove meat from skillet and allow to rest in a warm place. Pour off excess fat from skillet and deglaze with heavy cream; add all drippings collected from roast (several times, if necessary). Allow cream to cook and reduce to point when it will coat the back of a spoon moderately. Finish with cognac and peppercorns. Adjust seasoning. Carve roast "English cut style" and serve with sauce. Yield: 6 to 8 servings.

The Greenbrier

SAUCY MEAT LOAF

1½ pounds lean ground beef
1 (1¼ ounce) package
   onion soup
1½ cups soft bread crumbs
½ cup ketchup

½ cup chopped green pepper
2 eggs, beaten
1 (8 ounce) can tomato sauce
parsley, optional

Preheat oven to 350.° In large bowl, combine all ingredients except tomato sauce and parsley, mixing well. Shape into loaf in shallow baking pan. Bake 1 hour. Remove from oven; pour off fat. Pour tomato sauce over loaf; bake 15 minutes longer. If desired, garnish with parsley. Yield: 6 servings.

Mayor William Muegge

BEEF

MEAT LOAF STUFFED WITH SOUR CREAM

MEAT MIXTURE

1 pound ground round
½ cup sour cream
¼ cup chopped green pepper
1 tablespoon chopped
    parsley

½ teaspoon salt
¼ teaspoon pepper

Mix together ground round, sour cream, green pepper, parsley, salt and pepper. Set aside.

STUFFING

½ cup chopped celery
½ cup chopped onion
1½ cups fresh bread crumbs
½ cup sour cream

2 eggs, slightly beaten
2 tablespoons melted butter
    or margarine
½ teaspoon salt

Sauté celery and onion in butter or margarine until soft. Add bread crumbs, sour cream, eggs, and salt. Add ⅓ of stuffing mixture to meat mixture. Put ½ of meat mixture in bottom of an 8x8-inch baking dish. Spread remaining stuffing over meat and top with remaining meat mixture. Bake at 350° for 45 minutes. **HINT:** Recipe can be done ahead of time and can also be doubled. Yield: 4 servings.

Debbie Kiester

SAUCY MEATBALLS

1 pound ground beef
½ cup applesauce
½ cup bread crumbs
1 teaspoon salt
1 teaspoon pepper
1 egg, beaten

1 carrot, sliced
1 green pepper, sliced
1 onion, sliced
1 stalk celery, sliced
1 (10¾ ounce) can tomato
    soup

Mix ground beef, applesauce, bread crumbs, salt, pepper, and beaten egg together and shape into balls. Roll in flour and brown in skillet. Place sliced carrot, green pepper, onion, and celery over top of meatballs. Pour tomato soup over top and add ½ can of water. Cook for 40 minutes or until vegetables are done. **HINT:** Freezes well. Recipe can be prepared ahead of time and can also be doubled. Yield: 12 to 15 meatballs.

Mary Ann Wagenheim

REUBEN MEAT LOAF

1 egg, beaten
1 cup rye crackers,
 finely crushed
½ cup onion, chopped
¼ cup sweet pickle relish
¼ cup Russian salad
 dressing
1 tablespoon Worcestershire
 sauce

1 teaspoon salt
¼ teaspoon pepper
1½ pounds ground beef
1 (8 ounce) can sauerkraut,
 drained
1 cup shredded Swiss cheese

In a large mixing bowl, combine egg, cracker crumbs, onion, relish, salad dressing, Worcestershire sauce, salt and pepper. Add ground beef and mix well. On waxed paper, pat mixture to a 12x8 rectangle; spread sauerkraut over meat mixture and then sprinkle cheese over sauerkraut. Using waxed paper to lift rectangle, roll up meat jelly-roll style, beginning with short side. Press ends to seal. Place roll, seam side down, in a 13x9x2-inch baking pan. Bake in a 350° oven for 50 minutes. Yield: 8 servings.

Cheryl Cox

LASAGNA

Great for a crowd

½ pound lasagna noodles,
 cooked
1 pound ground beef
½ cup chopped onions
1 (6 ounce) can tomato paste
1 garlic clove, minced
¾ teaspoon oregano
1½ cups water

2 teaspoons salt
¼ teaspoon pepper
1 pound cottage cheese
12 ounces mozzarella cheese,
 sliced
½ cup Parmesan cheese,
 optional

Cook lasagna noodles according to directions on package. Brown meat and add onion, cooking until onion is tender. Stir in tomato paste, garlic, oregano, water, salt and pepper. Simmer for 30 minutes. In a 12x8x2-inch glass baking pan, layer noodles, meat sauce, cottage cheese, and mozzarella. Repeat layers. Sprinkle with Parmesan cheese. Bake at 375° for 30 minutes. Let cool slightly in pan. **HINT:** Freezes well. Yield: 8 to 10 servings.

Linda Morrison

BEEF STROGANOFF

U.S. Senate Democratic Leader since 1977,
Robert C. Byrd was the Senate Majority Leader
in the 95th and 96th Congress.

1½ pounds round steak
¼ cup butter
1 cup sliced mushrooms or
  1 (3 ounce) can, drained
1 garlic clove, minced

½ cup chopped onion
1 can tomato soup
1 cup sour cream
salt
pepper

Cut beef into long thin strips. Brown well in ¼ cup butter in heavy skillet. Add mushrooms, chopped onion, and garlic. Cook until lightly browned. Blend in tomato soup, sour cream, salt and pepper. Cover and simmer about 1 hour, or until beef is tender. Stir occasionally. Serve with hot cooked rice. Yield: 4 servings.

Robert C. Byrd

CABBAGE ROLLS

1 medium head cabbage
1 pound ground beef
1 cup cooked rice
1 onion, finely chopped
¼ cup milk

1 teaspoon salt
¼ teaspoon pepper
1 cup bouillon
1 cup tomato sauce

With a sharp knife, remove core from cabbage, leaving the head in one piece. Cook in a large pot of boiling, salted water just until large outer leaves can be peeled off easily without tearing. Drain and cool cabbage. Set aside 10 or 12 leaves for rolls. Chop rest of head coarsely and place in shallow, greased baking dish. Place meat in a bowl with rice, onion, milk and seasonings. Mix very thoroughly. Trim stalks from large cabbage leaves, if needed, so they can roll easily. Spoon a portion of filling in center of each leaf. Fold in sides of each leaf to enclose filling. Roll up firmly. Arrange filled rolls close together with seam side down, on top of chopped cabbage in baking dish. Combine bouillon with tomato sauce and pour over cabbage rolls. Bake in a 350° oven for 1½ hours. Cover with foil, if necessary, during baking. If you like, serve rolls with a dollop of sour cream. **HINT:** If preparing this dish ahead for later baking, cover it with foil and either freeze or refrigerate. Yield: 4 to 5 servings.

Hali Exley

BREAST OF CHICKEN VERONIQUE

*Hovah Hall Underwood served as West Virginia's First
Lady from 1957 to 1961 when her husband, Cecil
H. Underwood, served the State as its 25th governor.*

9 tablespoons butter
3 large chicken breasts,
  split
18 medium mushrooms,
  quartered (caps only)
3 tablespoons flour

1½ cups coffee cream
¾ cup white wine
1 cup diced ham
salt and pepper to taste
1½ cups seedless grapes

Melt 6 tablespoons butter in large heavy pan and brown chicken breasts.
Remove to casserole. Melt 3 tablespoons butter in same pan and sauté
mushrooms over high heat for 3 minutes. Remove with slotted spoon
and scatter over chicken. Reduce heat and stir flour into skillet. Cook
the roux 1 minute. Gradually add cream and wine, stirring constantly.
Cook until thick. Add diced ham. Season with salt and pepper and pour
sauce over chicken. Bake covered in a 350° oven 35 to 40 minutes.
Uncover and scatter grapes over chicken and bake another 10 minutes.
HINT: I usually add some herbs to the sauce. I don't measure, but my
guess is ¼ to ½ teaspoon of thyme, rosemary and tarragon mixed, or
alone. This can be prepared ahead and refrigerated, but grapes should
not be added until the last ten minutes of cooking. Yield: 6 servings.

Hovah Underwood

CHICKEN BREASTS WITH DRIED BEEF

1 (2½ to 3 ounce) package
  dried chipped beef
3 chicken breasts, split,
  skinned and boned
  (6 pieces)

6 slices bacon
1 (10½ ounce) can cream of
  mushroom soup
1 (8 ounce) carton sour cream

Butter a 9x13x2-inch pan and line with pieces of dried beef. Wrap each
piece of boned chicken with a piece of bacon and place over chipped beef.
Mix mushroom soup and sour cream together and pour over chicken.
Bake at 250° for 3 hours. Yield: 6 servings.

Mary Jane Amos

COMPANY CHICKEN BREASTS

6 boneless chicken breasts
  (3 whole)
1 cup flour
1 teaspoon basil
1 teaspoon garlic salt
salt and pepper to taste
1 cup homogenized milk

1½ cups Parmesan cheese
½ cup *fine* white bread
  crumbs
1 teaspoon parsley
1 cup margarine
½ cup cooking oil

Bone and skin chicken. You will need 3 bowls for the ingredients. In bowl number 1, mix flour, basil, garlic salt, salt and pepper. In bowl number 2, put milk. In bowl number 3, combine Parmesan cheese, bread crumbs, and parsley. Dip chicken into each bowl in order beginning with bowl number 1. Sauté chicken in margarine and oil in electric frying pan. Fry until golden brown, turning only once. Bake at 375° for 15 minutes on cookie sheet. Yield: 4 to 6 servings.

Elizabeth M. Day

ELEGANT CHICKEN

4 double breasts of chicken,
  skinned, boned and split
2 tablespoons hot Marsala
  wine
½ teaspoon tomato paste
1 tablespoon flour

½ cup chicken stock
1 to 1½ cups warm cream
salt and pepper to taste
1 tablespoon Parmesan
  cheese

Dust chicken breasts with flour. Brown in frying pan. Pour on hot marsala. Remove chicken to 13x9x2-inch baking pan or casserole. In frying pan, stir in tomato paste, flour, and chicken stock. Stir until thickened. Add warm cream slowly and carefully, stirring continuously. Season with salt, pepper, and Parmesan cheese. Return chicken to frying pan; cover and cook for 20 minutes. Arrange chicken in casserole and cover with sauce. Before baking, sprinkle liberally with Parmesan cheese. Bake at 350° for ½ hour. **HINT:** Above can be done 1 day ahead and refrigerated. Can also be doubled. Yield: 4 to 6 servings.

Marianne L. Hazlett

CHICKEN KIEV

¾ cup soft butter
1 teaspoon cut chives
⅛ teaspoon salt
1 tablespoon chopped
  parsley
1 tablespoon finely
  minced green onion

⅛ teaspoon pepper
6 chicken breasts
flour
1 egg
1 tablespoon water
bread crumbs

Mix first 6 ingredients and shape into 6 sticks. Place on aluminum foil and freeze about 40 minutes. Bone and skin 6 chicken breasts. Place breasts between waxed paper and pound to about ¼ inch thickness. Roll breasts around sticks and secure with toothpicks. Dredge with flour. Dip in mixture of egg beaten with water. Roll in bread crumbs to coat well. Fry in hot oil, about ½ inch deep, for about 4 to 5 minutes. Bake at 350° for 30 minutes. Yield: 6 servings.

Bonnie Roberts

COQ AU VIN

Elegant look and taste

4 chicken breasts, split
  and boned
4 slices bacon
1 small onion, chopped
1 carrot, thinly sliced
1 small clove garlic, minced
2 tablespoons flour
2 tablespoons parsley flakes

1 teaspoon marjoram
½ bay leaf
½ teaspoon thyme
1 teaspoon salt
¼ teaspoon pepper
1½ cups dry red wine
1 (3 ounce) jar sliced
  mushrooms

Brown bacon, onion and vegetables. Place this mixture aside and brown chicken in juices. Add all seasonings and stir well. Add wine and simmer chicken for about 45 minutes, covered. Add mushrooms during last 5 minutes. Serve chicken on toast points with sauce. Yield: 4 servings for dinner, 8 servings for lunch.

Jeanne Neff

JANE'S 10-MINUTE CHICKEN DISH

Jane Blalock is a gallery favorite in Wheeling where she won the West Virginia LPGA Classic in 1976 and again in 1978.

1 whole chicken breast, boned and halved	¼ cup plain or flavored bread crumbs
1 egg, slightly beaten	flour for dredging
½ tablespoon water	salt and pepper
2 to 3 tablespoons butter	½ cup white or red wine
¼ cup Parmesan cheese	

Remove skin from chicken. Jane suggests that you cut away any tough strands and remove all fat. Place chicken between two sheets of waxed paper and pound. Rinse chicken and pat dry. In a bowl, lightly beat egg and water together. On a plate, mix Parmesan cheese and bread crumbs. Salt and pepper chicken and lightly dredge with flour. Dip chicken breasts in beaten egg, then into cheese/bread crumb mixture. Shake off excess. Melt butter in frying pan and sauté chicken over medium heat for 2 minutes. Be careful not to overheat pan, as butter will burn. Chicken breasts should be golden brown. Add wine. Jane prefers white wine. Simmer over low heat 4 to 5 minutes more. The wine will evaporate quickly. Serve immediately on warm plates. Pour remaining sauce over chicken. Yield: 2 servings.

VARIATIONS

Substitute red wine for white. Add fresh sliced mushrooms during the last 5 minutes of cooking. Add ¼ cup fresh chopped parsley during the last 5 minutes of cooking.

COPYRIGHT, Dale Danenberg 1983—Excerpts from soon to be published official LPGA Cookbook, "COOKING ON COURSE".

Jane Blalock

QUICK ITALIAN CHICKEN

12 pieces of chicken,   salt
  skin removed   pepper
¼ cup butter, cut into   paprika
  pieces
½ cup (or more) of Italian
  dressing

Place chicken on broiler pan; lightly salt and pepper. Sprinkle with paprika. Place a pat of butter on each piece. Pour half of the dressing over the pieces of chicken and place under broiler. Turn each piece of chicken several times while cooking, basting as you go with remaining dressing. Remove when chicken is brown, 20 to 30 minutes. Yield: 4 servings.

David J. Joel

CHICKEN BITS N' PIECES

8 chicken wings   Italian herb seasoning
4 chicken breast halves   seasoned salt
flour
bacon grease or vegetable
  oil
1 small onion, chopped
  several stuffed olives,
  sliced
  1 small green pepper,
  chopped

Wash chicken wings; discard tips, and cut at joint to have sixteen pieces. Wash chicken breast halves; remove bone and skin, and cut in half to have eight pieces. Heat bacon grease or vegetable oil in frying pan. Roll each piece of chicken in flour. Place single layer of chicken in frying pan; sprinkle with chopped onion, pepper, and olives; sprinkle with herbs and seasoned salt to preference. When chicken is brown and crusty, arrange in baking dish. (Repeat frying process for any pieces not fitting into the first frying.) Place in 300° oven for 30 minutes or more to let flavor develop. Yield: 4 servings.

Betty Samuels, Food Editor
The Parkersburg Sentinel

BACKYARD CHARCOAL GRILLED
BARBECUED CHICKEN

1½ cups tomato juice
½ cup water
⅓ cup lemon juice
¼ cup butter, soft
1 medium onion, finely
  chopped
2 tablespoons ketchup
1 tablespoon paprika
1 tablespoon Worcestershire
  sauce

1 teaspoon sugar
1 teaspoon salt
½ teaspoon pepper
2 quartered broiler chickens
1 charcoal grill, greased
  when chicken charcoaling
  begins

To make barbecue sauce, mix tomato juice, water, lemon juice, butter, onion, ketchup, paprika, Worcestershire sauce, sugar, salt and pepper. Bring just to boil. Marinate 2 quartered broiler chickens with barbecue sauce while preparing fire. Spread hot coals apart with tongs once fire is well underway. Brush grill with oil or butter to keep meat from sticking. Drain chicken of excess sauce before grilling. Set chicken on grill 6 to 8 inches from coals. Watch carefully to avoid burning. Turn chicken every 5 minutes while basting with sauce. Cook 30 to 60 minutes depending on size of chicken pieces. Keep sauce hot while basting. (Add ketchup for desired thickness.) Yield: 8 to 10 servings.

Harry Hamm
Editor, Wheeling News Register

ROAST CHICKEN WITH POTATO SALAD STUFFING

1 large roasting chicken,
  cleaned and drained
4 to 6 potatoes, boiled
  and peeled
¼ teaspoon rosemary
8 to 10 stuffed olives,
  chopped

3 to 4 tablespoons parsley,
  chopped fine
1 clove garlic, minced
1 teaspoon capers
¼ cup olive oil
salt and pepper to taste
anchovies, optional

After potatoes have been boiled and peeled, dice and place in large bowl. Add all other ingredients and mix throughly with hands. Stuff chicken with potato mixture. Rub chicken skin with butter. Bake 1 hour at 375°. When done and ready to serve, cut all the way through like a plus sign. Roll out four sections. Each serving will be a piece of chicken with potato salad on top. Yield: 4 to 6 servings.

Mrs. George Stimac

CHICKEN AND FRUIT CUP

3 cups cooked, diced chicken
1 apple, diced
½ cup coarsely chopped,
  toasted almonds (salted)

½ cup white seedless grapes,
  cut into halves
1 tablespoon lemon juice
1 cup mayonnaise

Mix all ingredients lightly, but thoroughly. Chill. Place mixture in biscuit cups.

BISCUIT CUPS
1 package buttermilk
  flaky biscuits

Roll or pat each biscuit to 3½- to 4- inch circle. Fit this circle over back of well-greased muffin tin. Bake 8 to 9 minutes at 400°. Remove from tin and you will have biscuit cups. Yield: 6 to 8 servings.

Magdalene Foster

ROAST DUCKLING WITH BURGUNDY AND PEACH SAUCE

*As Executive Food Director of the Greenbrier,
Rod Stoner is responsible for maintaining the famed resort's
celebrated reputation for food preparation and presentation.
The Greenbrier's fine cuisine has pleased the palates of countless
guests—including presidents, prime ministers and
royalty—from throughout the world since the 19th century.*

1 (4 pound) duckling,
  seasoned and trussed
2 tablespoons oil
6 tablespoons brown sugar
½ teaspoon red wine vinegar
1 cup burgundy wine

1 cup brown sauce
2 whole peaches, peeled and
  sliced thinly, or 4
  Greenbrier peach halves,
  sliced thinly
2 tablespoons brandy

Heat oil in heavy skillet and brown breasts of duck. Place duck on back and roast for 1½ hours at 400°, basting frequently. When duck is finished, place on warming tray and pour excess fat from skillet. Add sugar and cook to a light carmel. Deglaze pan with vinegar and red wine; allow to reduce to ½ volume. Add brown sauce and bring to simmer. Add peaches that have been flamed in brandy. Carve duck and serve with sauce and wild rice. Yield: 2 servings.

The Greenbrier

CHESTNUT STUFFING

6 cups bread crumbs in
large bowl
2 eggs, beaten
3 pounds chestnuts
1½ cups chopped onions

1½ cups chopped celery
¾ cup butter, melted
2 tablespoons poultry
seasoning
salt and pepper to taste

Make gash in flat side of each chestnut. Place several at a time in hot skillet with ½ to ¾ cup oil. Shake back and forth over burner for 5 minutes. (Be very careful; hot oil splatters and chestnuts will crack). Remove chestnuts from skillet and put on cookie sheet. Place in hot (400°) oven for 10 minutes. Remove, let cool, and shell. Sauté onions and celery. While doing this, add beaten eggs to bread crumbs. Add shelled chestnuts, which have been cut up, to mixture. Combine onions, celery, melted butter, salt, pepper and poultry seasoning with bread mixture. Mix well. **HINT:** Recipe can be done ahead of time and can be doubled. Yield: 6 cups dressing.

Alison L. Bowman

CLASSIC CHICKEN DIVAN

2 (10 ounce) packages frozen
broccoli spears
¼ cup butter or margarine
2 tablespoons all-purpose
flour
½ teaspoon salt
dash of pepper

2 cups chicken broth
½ cup whipping cream
3 tablespoons dry white wine
3 chicken breasts, halved
and cooked
¼ cup grated Parmesan
cheese

Cook broccoli according to package directions; drain. Melt butter; blend in flour, salt and pepper. Add chicken broth; cook and stir until mixture thickens and bubbles. Stir in cream and wine. Place broccoli crosswise in 12x7½x2-inch baking dish. Pour half sauce over broccoli. Top with chicken. To remaining sauce add cheese; pour over chicken; sprinkle with additional Parmesan cheese. Bake at 350° for 20 minutes or until heated through. Broil just until sauce is golden - about 5 minutes. **HINT:** Recipe can be done ahead and can be doubled. Yield: 6 to 8 servings.

Phyllis Duncan

VEAL SCALOPPINE MARYLAND

8 (2 ounce) scaloppine of veal
¼ cup softened butter
juice from ½ lemon
¼ teaspoon Worcestershire
  sauce
1 tablespoon chopped
  parsley
1 tablespoon white wine

½ teaspoon Dijon mustard
1 cup backfin crabmeat
  (picked for shell and
  cartilage)
2 ounces proscuitto ham, cut
  into thin, julienne strips

Knead first 6 ingredients together.

¼ cup clarified butter,
  for sautéing

Heat butter in sauté pan until it just starts to smoke. Season and flour veal and sauté quickly, allowing light brown color to form on veal. Arrange on platter. Pour off excess oil from pan and add kneaded butter mixture. When mixture is hot, add ham and crabmeat and toss until all is heated through. Serve over scaloppine. **HINT:** May be served with hollandaise or bearnaise sauce. Yield: 4 servings.

The Greenbrier

VEAL IN VERMOUTH

Excellent served with Noodles Alfredo!

1½ pounds thin veal steak
2 tablespoons flour
¼ cup butter or margarine
1 clove garlic, minced
½ pound mushrooms, sliced
½ teaspoon salt

dash of pepper
1 tablespoon lemon juice
⅓ cup dry vermouth
2 tablespoons snipped
  parsley

Flatten veal to ¼ inch thick. Cut into 2-inch squares and flour. Melt butter and sauté veal, a little at a time, until golden brown on both sides. Return all meat and garlic to skillet and heap mushrooms on top. Sprinkle with salt, pepper, and lemon juice. Pour on vermouth, cover, and cook over low heat for 20 minutes or until veal is fork tender. Add a little more vermouth, if needed. Sprinkle with parsley just before serving. **HINT:** This dish can be prepared ahead and reheated in the oven. Yield: 4 servings.

Mary Lou DeFillippo

VEAL FRANCIS

Easy and great for a crowd

1 pound veal cutlets, cut thin	1 cup Italian bread crumbs
flour for dusting	2 tablespoons Parmesan cheese
2 eggs, beaten	¼ cup white dry wine
½ teaspoon salt	1 cup beef broth or bouillon
¼ teaspoon pepper	2 tablespoons olive oil
2 tablespoons milk	2 tablespoons butter
¼ teaspoon lemon juice and/or rind	1 lemon, cut into very thin slices

Pound cutlets until very thin. Sprinkle with flour and dip into eggs beaten with salt, pepper, milk, and lemon juice or rind. Mix bread crumbs with Parmesan cheese and dip cutlets in this mixture. Heat frying pan until hot. Add olive oil and butter. Brown cutlets on both sides. Place cutlets in serving casserole and garnish with lemon slices. Add wine and broth to frying pan, scraping well. Pour over cutlets. May put aside until ready to finish. To serve, bake, covered, in slow oven, 325° to 350°, for 30 to 35 minutes. Uncover and cook down juices for 10 minutes. **HINT:** Especially good with Riz Pilaf a la Valencienne. Recipe can be done ahead of time and can be doubled. Yield: 4 servings.

Anne Clark

VEAL SCALOPPINE

2 pounds veal, thinly sliced	1 (10 ounce) can sliced mushrooms or ½ pound fresh mushrooms
½ cup butter	
½ cup sherry	
½ tablespoon flour	dash of salt
1 cup beef bouillon	dash of pepper

Pound veal slightly and brown in 6 tablespoons of butter. Add sherry. Cook a few seconds and remove from heat. Melt remaining butter in small saucepan. Stir in flour. Add bouillon to flour mixture and stir vigorously with wire whip until smooth and thick. Add sliced mushrooms, salt and pepper. Bring to boil, stirring constantly. Pour sauce over veal and simmer 15 minutes or until thick. Serve over rice. **HINT:** Recipe can be doubled. Yield: 4 to 6 servings.

Jo Kepner

SCALOPPINE AL MARSALA

1½ pounds veal scallops, sliced 3/8 inch thick and pounded to ¼ inch salt pepper	flour 2 tablespoons butter 3 tablespoons olive oil ½ cup dry Marsala ¼ cup chicken stock

Season veal scallops with salt and pepper, dip in flour, and shake off excess. In heavy skillet melt butter with oil over moderate heat. Brown scallops about 3 minutes on each side. Transfer from skillet to plate. Pour off most of fat from skillet, leaving thin film on bottom. Add marsala and chicken stock. Boil briskly over high heat 1 or 2 minutes. Return veal to skillet. Cover pan and simmer over low heat 10 to 15 minutes. Transfer scallops to heated platter. Pour sauce from pan on top. Serve. Yield: 4 servings.

Helen Ann Grammen

VEAL ROAST WITH MUSTARD

Any leftovers make great sandwiches!

1 (3 to 4 pounds) veal roast, boned and rolled ¼ cup butter, melted	8 ounces Dijon wine mustard 1 (10½ ounce) can consommé ¼ cup sherry

Place roast in a shallow pan. Mix melted butter and mustard and coat roast with all the mixture. Roast veal in a preheated 300° oven for 3 hours. For last 30 minutes, baste with a combination of sherry and consommé. Test roast for doneness. If not tender and done through, continue roasting for another 20 to 30 minutes. Blend pan juices well to use over carved roast. Allow roast to rest before slicing thinly. **HINT:** This is good served with corn pudding which is slightly sweet and a good contrast to the mustard's tartness. Yield: 6 to 8 servings.

Cookbook Committee

VEAL

BARBECUED LOIN OF VEAL WITH CITRUS SAUCE

Mark J. Cox, the son of Dorothy and Harry Cox of Wheeling's Warwood neighborhood, is Executive Chef of Brennans of Houston.

4 to 5 ounces veal loin
  medallion
1½ ounces OPEN PIT®
  Barbecue Sauce, Hickory
  Smoke Flavor
Juice of ½ lemon,
  ½ lime and ½ orange

salt and pepper to taste
1 teaspoon freshly chopped
  rosemary
1 teaspoon freshly chopped
  thyme
½ tablespoon horseradish

GARNISH

Place ½ inch thick onion slice and ½ inch slice completely peeled orange topped with 1 tablespoon honey in foil and wrap tightly. Place on barbecue grill. Rotate ¼ turn every 8 minutes. Edges of onion and orange should be lightly caramelized. Unwrap.

Prepare barbecue grill. Season veal with salt and pepper. Brush with sauce; place on grill along with prepared garnish. Barbecue veal 8 minutes on each side, checking for doneness. Baste as needed. Remove veal and garnish, placing veal on plate and garnish on top. Yield: 1 serving.

Mark J. Cox

SCALOPPINE BURGERS

1½ pounds ground veal
1 cup soft bread crumbs
1 egg, beaten
2 tablespoons milk
½ teaspoon salt
dash of pepper
¼ cup cooking oil
1 (8 ounce) can tomato sauce

1 (3 ounce) can mushrooms,
  chopped
¼ cup white wine
1 tablespoon parsley,
  finely snipped
¼ teaspoon dried oregano,
  crushed

Combine veal, crumbs, egg, milk, salt and pepper; shape into 6 patties. Coat lightly with flour. Brown in hot cooking oil in skillet. Drain fat. Combine tomato sauce, undrained mushrooms, wine, parsley, and oregano; pour over meat. Cover; simmer 20 to 25 minutes. Serve on hot cooked noodles; sprinkle with grated Parmesan cheese. **HINT:** The veal patties can be made ahead and frozen. Yield: 6 servings.

Ann R. Bopp

BUTTERFLIED LEG OF LAMB

1 leg of lamb, butterflied
(allow ½ pound bone—in
weight for each person)

MARINADE

½ cup vegetable oil
¼ cup red wine vinegar
½ cup chopped onion
2 cloves garlic, minced
1 bay leaf
½ teaspoon dry basil or
1 teaspoon fresh basil

½ teaspoon dry oregano or
1 teaspoon fresh oregano
2 teaspoons Dijon mustard
salt and pepper to taste

Butcher can butterfly leg of lamb. Combine ingredients for marinade. Put leg of lamb into large glass baking dish or in plastic storage bag (which will be set in large bowl to prevent leakage) and add marinade. If using bag, seal it and place in a bowl. Refrigerate marinating meat for 24 hours minimum (up to 2 days), turning it over occasionally. When ready to cook, remove lamb from marinade and grill on barbecue grill 15 minutes per side, basting frequently with marinade, until done as desired. (Well done—allow 20 minutes per side). If done in the oven, broil 4 inches from heat, 10 minutes per side. Then reduce heat to 425° and bake another 15 minutes or to desired doneness. Lamb is best when pink inside and crusty outside. Serve any remaining marinade, heated, over lamb. **HINT:** Must be done ahead of time. Yield: 10 to 12 servings.

Joan Stamp

LEG OF LAMB ZINFANDEL

MARINADE

½ cup tamari or light soy
sauce
¼ cup olive oil
¼ cup sesame oil
½ cup parsley leaves
2 cloves garlic

1 tablespoon thyme
1 teaspoon rosemary
1 teaspoon dry mustard
½ teaspoon mace
½ teaspoon oregano

LAMB

Prepare marinade by combining all ingredients in food processor or blender until smooth. Reserve ½ cup.

1 boned leg of lamb **1 cup zinfandel wine**

Have your butcher bone the leg of lamb and remove as much fat as possible. Arrange lamb in glass baking dish. Pour marinade (except the reserved ½ cup) over lamb. Cover and refrigerate overnight. Preheat oven to 450°. Bake lamb for 10 minutes. Reduce heat to 325°. Bake 20 minutes per pound for medium doneness, 25 to 30 minutes for well done. Add zinfandel to reserved marinade. Simmer 10 minutes. Serve as a sauce with lamb. **HINT:** Must be done ahead of time. Yield: 12 servings.

Charl Kappel

GRILLED LEG OF LAMB WITH MUSTARD COATING

leg of lamb (boned and tied) **1 tablespoon soy sauce**
¾ teaspoon rosemary **¾ cup Dijon mustard**
2 cloves garlic, minced **5 tablespoons olive oil**

PAN VEGETABLES
½ cup sliced carrots **2 cups brown lamb**
½ cup sliced onions **stock or beef bouillon**
2 cloves garlic

Mix rosemary, garlic, soy sauce, and mustard in a small bowl with a wire whip. Beat in oil by droplets to make a thick sauce. Put lamb in aluminum foil roasting pan. Coat all sides with mustard coating, reserving 2 to 3 tablespoons. Insert meat thermometer into thickest part of lamb. Strew pan vegetables around lamb. Prepare a kettle-type barbecue grill for indirect cooking, putting coals on sides of grill. Put roasting pan in center of grill. Roast lamb until meat thermometer reads 140°, about 1 hour and 30 minutes. To bake in oven, adjust oven rack to lower middle and bake 1½ hours at 350°. Remove lamb to warm plate. Spoon fat out of roasting pan. Pour in stock or bouillon and boil for several minutes scraping up coagulated juices. Remove from heat, stir in reserved mustard, and strain sauce into a warm bowl. Serve sauce over sliced lamb. Yield: 10 to 12 servings.

Elaine Sherman
Community Advisor

CROWN PORK ROAST

crown of pork (16 to   garlic salt and pepper
  24 ribs)

Rub garlic salt and pepper over crown of pork. Fill cavity in crown with fruit stuffing. Cover each rib bone with foil and protect stuffing with aluminum foil. Roast crown on a metal rack in an open roasting pan. Time it 35 minutes per pound or until meat thermometer registers 170°. Remove foil and place paper frills on each rib bone. Carve in between rib bones, serving a double rib to each person.

FRUIT STUFFING

1 (20 ounce) can pie-   1 teaspoon ground
  sliced apples   cinnamon
1 egg   ¼ teaspoon ground allspice
9 slices dry raisin bread,   3 tablespoons butter
  cut in ½-inch cubes (6 cups)

Drain apples, reserving juices; finely chop apples. Add water to reserved juice to equal 1 cup. Melt butter in skillet. Stir in bread crumbs, cinnamon, allspice, egg, and chopped apples. Spoon stuffing into center of pork roast. (Use aluminum foil to line metal rack.) Spoon remaining stuffing into 1-quart casserole. Bake, uncovered, with roast during last 40 minutes of cooking time. Mix two stuffings together. **HINT:** Cover stuffing in roast with aluminum foil if it starts to get too brown. Yield: 12 servings.

Janie Altmeyer

PORK CHOPS MONTEREY

6 pork chops, 1 inch   ⅛ teaspoon pepper
  thick   1½ teaspoons lemon
⅓ cup brown sugar   juice
¾ teaspoon salt   ⅓ cup chili sauce
6 large onion slices

Trim chops of excess fat. Arrange in baking pan. Top each chop with onion slice. Combine remaining ingredients and pour over chops. Cover tightly and bake in oven at 350° for 1 to 1½ hours or until tender. Yield: 6 servings.

Bonnie Roberts

PORK

PORK CHOP SUPREME

potatoes as desired
1 (10¾ ounce) can cream
of mushroom soup or
1 (10¾ ounce) can golden
mushroom soup
½ soup can of milk

1 cup sour cream
5 or 6 pork chops
⅛ teaspoon garlic
powder
⅛ teaspoon onion
powder

Peel and slice as many potatoes as desired. Place in a 13x9x2-inch baking dish. Combine mushroom soup and milk. Heat to remove lumps. Remove from heat and add sour cream, garlic powder, and onion powder. Combine and pour over potatoes. Brown chops and arrange on top of potatoes. Bake uncovered at 350° for 1½ to 2 hours or until potatoes are done. Yield: 6 servings.

Linda Neuhart

STUFFED PORK CHOPS

6 pork chops, 2 inches
thick
1 teaspoon salt
⅛ teaspoon pepper
1½ tablespoons butter
2½ tablespoons onion,
chopped
1½ cups crumbled stale
bread

1 large green apple, peeled,
cored and thinly sliced
5 tablespoons raisins
½ teaspoon nutmeg
¼ teaspoon cinnamon
2 to 4 tablespoons water

Cut a pocket in pork chop along meat edge almost in to bone. Spread meat open and pound thin with a mallet; sometimes butcher will do this. Season chops using ½ teaspoon salt and pepper. Make the stuffing by sautéing onion and crumbs in butter in a heavy skillet. Add apple, raisins, ½ teaspoon salt, nutmeg, cinnamon, and water. Use only enough water to moisten well. Mix together. Divide into 6 equal portions and spread on chops. Fold over and fasten at edge with toothpicks. Put chops in a shallow roasting pan. Bake at 350° for about 1½ hours or until tender. Turn chops once during baking. Yield: 6 servings.

Joan Corson

WINE PORK CHOPS

Great for company since it just bakes unsupervised.

8 pork chops, ½ inch thick or thinner	⅓ cup red wine or red wine vinegar
½ cup ketchup or tomato paste	⅓ cup water
	3 tablespoons brown sugar

Brown pork chops in heavy pan. Salt and pepper to taste. Meanwhile, mix ketchup, wine, water, and brown sugar in bowl. Place chops in baking dish, preferably in 1 layer. Pour sauce over chops and cover baking dish with lid or foil. Bake at 325° about 2 hours until sauce thickens and chops are tender. Bake uncovered for last 30 minutes and turn chops once during 2-hour period to cook evenly. **HINT:** Sauce is good over rice. Yield: 4 servings.

Terry Magro

STIR FRY PORK

1 pound lean pork, cut in strips	2 tablespoons oil
3 tablespoons cornstarch	2 cloves garlic, minced
1½ cups cold water	2 cups broccoli, sliced on diagonal
⅓ cup soy sauce	2 medium onions, sliced on diagonal
⅓ cup light corn syrup	2 carrots, sliced on diagonal
¼ teaspoon crushed red pepper	½ pound mushrooms, sliced

Mix cornstarch, water, soy sauce, syrup, and pepper. Set aside. In wok or large skillet, heat oil. Add pork and garlic. Cook, stirring often, for 5 minutes or until pork is tender. Remove pork from skillet. Add to skillet broccoli, onion, and carrots. Cook 2 minutes, stirring often. Add mushrooms and cook 1 minute more. Add pork to vegetables, stirring constantly. Add cornstarch mixture and cook 1 minute or until mixture thickens and becomes somewhat transparent. Serve at once with rice. Yield: 4 to 6 servings.

Pat Kramer

BAKED HAM

1 ham, size is your
   choice

prepared mustard
ground cloves

Rub prepared mustard all over ham. Then sprinkle ground cloves all over mustard on ham.

SAUCE

½ cup lemon-lime soda
½ cup pineapple juice
¾ teaspoon prepared
   mustard

1 cup brown sugar

Mix sauce ingredients for basting. Bake ham at 225° for 15 minutes per pound. Baste ham every 15 minutes. Suggested garnish: pineapple slices, cherries and whole cloves. Garnish as you put in the oven. May be served with Orange Sauce found in the sauce section.

Debbie Marano

HAM LOAVES

1 pound ground veal
1 pound ground pork
2 pounds ground ham
1 small loaf of bread,
   cubed

1 cup milk
1 teaspoon dry mustard

BASTING SAUCE

2 cups brown sugar
¾ cup water

¼ cup vinegar

Make paste of bread, milk, and mustard. Add to ground meats and shape into individual loaves. Place in large baking dish. Bake at 350° for 1 hour. Baste often. **HINT:** Have butcher mix meats. This can be done ahead of time and can be doubled. Yield: 8 to 10 servings.

Diana Ihlenfeld

COQUILLE MARSEILLE

Absolutely elegant

9 tablespoons butter
6 tablespoons flour
2 teaspoons salt
¼ teaspoon white pepper
4 cups cream or half and half
1 pound scallops
½ pound small shrimp

½ pound crabmeat
3 tablespoons butter
½ cup finely chopped onion
1 cup mushrooms, sliced
¼ cup sherry
Italian bread crumbs
pimento

Place 9 tablespoons of butter and flour in a large saucepan or dutch oven. Cook on very low flame until smooth. Add salt, pepper, and cream. Remove pan from heat when adding cream. Stir over low flame until bubbling, not boiling. Be very careful not to burn. Cook 5 to 10 minutes. Next, add scallops, shrimp, and crabmeat. In separate saucepan, sauté onions and mushrooms in 3 tablespoons butter. Add this to cream sauce. Then add sherry. Stir together and chill. This is better to be made day before serving. Reheat in saucepan. May need to add a little more cream. Place in chafing dish and serve with rice. **HINT:** May also be served as an appetizer. Place in real seashells and sprinkle with seasoned bread crumbs. Bake at 400° for 10 to 15 minutes or until golden brown. Top with pimento. Yield: 10 to 12 servings.

DeAnna Joel Taylor

CRAB IMPERIAL

Delicious and worth every calorie

1 to 1½ cups mayonnaise
1 teaspoon dry mustard
1 teaspoon chopped chives
½ teaspoon Worcestershire sauce

2½ cups fresh backfin lump crabmeat
lemon wedges
watercress or parsley for garnish

Mix mayonnaise, dry mustard, chives, and Worcestershire sauce together. Reserve ¼ cup sauce. Mix remaining sauce with crabmeat. Salt to taste. Pile into individual scallop shells or dishes. Coat each serving with small amount of extra sauce to smooth tops of servings. Broil until golden brown. Garnish with lemon wedges and watercress or parsley sprigs. **HINT:** Easy to do and can be doubled. Yield: 4 to 6 servings.

Joan C. Stamp

SHRIMP SCAMPI

Nice for a special occasion

1½ pounds raw medium-size shrimp
¼ cup margarine
½ cup olive oil
¾ cup shallots, finely chopped
4 cloves garlic, finely minced

1 cup canned tomatoes
½ cup sliced mushrooms
1 teaspoon salt
dash of pepper
⅓ cup lemon juice
¼ cup chopped parsley

Shell and devein shrimp; butterfly, then set aside. In a large skillet, using olive oil and margarine, sauté shallots and garlic. Add tomatoes and mushrooms; cook, stirring, about 5 minutes. Add salt, pepper, lemon juice, 2 tablespoons parsley, and shrimp. Mix well. Divide shrimp mixture into 6 individual baking dishes. Broil 4 to 5 inches from heat for 10 minutes or until shrimp are tender. Sprinkle with remainder of parsley before serving. Yield: 6 servings.

Becky Stevenson

HELEN'S SHRIMP CREOLE

½ cup onion, chopped
½ cup celery, chopped
1 clove garlic, minced
3 tablespoons cooking oil
1 (16 ounce) can tomatoes
1 (16 ounce) can seasoned tomato sauce
1½ teaspoons salt
1 teaspoon sugar

1 teaspoon chili powder
1 tablespoon Worcestershire sauce
dash of TABASCO Brand Pepper Sauce
2 teaspoons cornstarch
1 pound raw shrimp, cleaned
1 cup green pepper, chopped

Sauté onions, celery and garlic in cooking oil. Cook until tender but not brown. Add tomatoes, tomato sauce, salt, sugar, chili powder, Worcestershire sauce, and Tabasco to taste. Simmer, uncovered, for 45 minutes. Mix cornstarch with 2 tablespoons water and stir this into tomato mixture. Cook and stir until this thickens. Add green pepper and shrimp. Cover and simmer about 5 minutes. Serve with rice. Yield: 6 servings.

Becky Stevenson

SHRIMP WITH SNOW PEAS

Easy, colorful dish

1 pound shrimp, shelled,
cleaned and deveined
1 clove garlic, minced
4 green onions, chopped
½ pound snow peas, fresh
or frozen
½ pound mushrooms, sliced

⅓ cup salad oil
2 tablespoons cornstarch
2 tablespoons sherry
1⅓ cups chicken broth
1 tablespoon soy sauce
½ teaspoon sugar

In a large skillet or wok, heat the oil to very hot. Add shrimp, garlic, onions, snow peas, and mushrooms. Stir constantly until shrimp curl and turn pink, about 3 minutes. Combine cornstarch and sherry, stirring to dissolve. Then add broth, soy, and sugar. Add to shrimp, stirring until thickened. Serve with hot cooked rice. **HINT:** You can do all the cleaning, slicing and chopping in the morning and refrigerate, then quickly put together before serving. Recipe can be doubled. Yield: 4 servings.

Cookbook Committee

SUPER SEAFOOD NEWBURG

1½ to 2 cups shrimp, Alaska
king crab, lobster, or
scallops cooked
¼ cup butter
2 tablespoons flour
1 teaspoon salt
¼ teaspoon paprika

dash of cayenne pepper
2 cups coffee cream
2 egg yolks, beaten
2 tablespoons sherry
toast points or cooked
rice

Melt butter. Blend in flour and seasonings. Add cream gradually and cook until hot and smooth. Stir a little hot sauce into egg yolks. Add to remaining sauce, stirring constantly. Add seafood, heat. Remove from heat and slowly stir in sherry. Serve immediately over toast points or rice. **HINT:** Recipe can be doubled. Yield: 4 servings.

Kathie Briley
Editor, People Page
The Intelligencer

LOBSTER IN PHYLLO

6 tablespoons butter
1 tablespoon chopped onion
6 (6 ounce) whole lobster
  tails, shelled
2 tablespoons sweet
  vermouth, heated
6 tablespoons butter,
  softened

1 tablespoon fresh lemon
  juice
1 clove garlic, minced
12 phyllo pastry shells
¼ cup butter, melted
½ cup whipping cream
¼ cup brandy
fresh lemon juice

Melt 6 tablespoons butter in large skillet over low heat. Add onion and cook until translucent. Increase heat to medium and add lobster. Add sweet vermouth and ignite, shaking pan gently until flames subside. Continue to cook until lobster is almost cooked through, about 3 minutes. Remove lobster and set aside. Reserve cooking liquid. Preheat oven to 375°. Whip 6 tablespoons butter, softened with lemon juice. Spread each lobster tail with lemon butter. Brush 1 phyllo sheet with melted butter. Sit lobster tail in center and fold phyllo over, enclosing lobster completely. Brush another phyllo sheet with melted butter. Sit phyllo package in center and wrap again. Arrange seam side down on baking sheet. Repeat with remaining phyllo and lobster tails. Lightly brush top of each package with melted butter. Bake until phyllo is golden, about 20 minutes. While baking, warm reserve lobster cooking liquid over medium heat. Add cream, garlic and ¼ cup brandy. Increase heat to high and cook until sauce is reduced to ¾ cup, about 2 minutes. Stir in lemon juice to taste. Arrange lobster package on individual plates. Top with sauce and serve immediately. Yield: 6 servings.

Janie Altmeyer

SAUTÉED SCALLOPS

2 tablespoons flour
½ teaspoon salt
½ teaspoon onion powder
¼ teaspoon white pepper
¼ teaspoon garlic powder
¼ teaspoon thyme

1 to 1¼ pounds scallops
3 tablespoons butter
1 tablespoon olive oil
¾ cup vermouth
3 tablespoons parsley,
  finely snipped

Combine flour with salt, onion powder, white pepper, garlic powder, and thyme in paper bag. Heat oven to 250°. Rinse scallops with cold running water, drain, and pat dry on paper towels. Heat butter and oil over medium heat. Shake scallops in flour mixture. Increase heat to high. Sauté scallops until lightly brown, 3 to 4 minutes. Remove and put on a platter in oven. Cook pan drippings over high heat. Add wine and cook, stirring constantly, about 1 or 2 minutes. Pour over scallops and sprinkle with parsley. Yield: 3 to 4 servings.

Kara Franklin

SALMON MOUSSE

1 envelope gelatin
¼ cup cold water
½ cup boiling water
½ cup mayonnaise
1 tablespoon lemon juice
1 tablespoon grated onion
½ teaspoon TABASCO Brand Pepper Sauce
¼ teaspoon paprika

1 teaspoon salt
2 cups finely chopped, cooked salmon
1 tablespoon finely chopped capers
½ cup heavy cream, whipped
2 cups drained cottage cheese

Soften gelatin in cold water. Add boiling water; mix and let cool. Add to gelatin the mayonnaise, lemon juice, onion, Tabasco, paprika, and salt. Mix well and chill until it begins to thicken. Add salmon and capers. Mix well and fold in whipped cream. Put in an oiled 1-quart mold. When firm, spoon the cottage cheese on top and push it down to pack it. Chill several hours or overnight. Unmold on a chilled plate and serve with dill sauce. Yield: 6 to 8 servings.

DILL SAUCE

1 egg
½ teaspoon salt
pinch of pepper
pinch of sugar
4 tablespoons lemon juice

1 teaspoon grated onion
2 tablespoons finely cut, fresh dill or 1 tablespoon dry dill
1½ cups sour cream

Beat egg until fluffy and lemon colored. Add salt, pepper, sugar, lemon juice, onion, and dill; mix well. Add sour cream and mix well. Serve cold with mousse or hot with baked salmon.

Donna Glass

STUFFED FLOUNDER

¼ cup onions, chopped
¼ cup butter or margarine
1 (7½ ounce) can crabmeat,
   drained and cartilage
   removed
½ cup coarse cracker crumbs
2 tablespoons snipped
   parsley
½ teaspoon salt
2 pounds flounder fillets
   (8 fillets)

3 tablespoons butter
3 tablespoons flour
¼ teaspoon salt
1½ cups milk
½ teaspoon lemon juice
⅓ cup dry white wine
1 cup or 4 ounces processed
   Swiss cheese, shredded
½ teaspoon paprika

In skillet, cook onion in butter until tender but not brown. Stir into skillet flaked crab, crackers crumbs, parsley, salt and dash of pepper. Spread mixture over flounder fillets. Roll fillets and place seam side down in a 12x8x2- inch baking dish. In saucepan, melt 3 tablespoons butter. Blend in flour and ¼ teaspoon salt. Add milk and lemon juice. Add with wine to saucepan. Cook and stir until mixture thickens and bubbles. Pour over fillets. Bake in a 400° oven for 25 minutes. Sprinkle with cheese and paprika. Return to oven. Bake 10 minutes longer or until fish flakes easily with a fork. **HINT:** Easy and freezes well. Yield: 8 servings.

Christine Doepken

SOLE ITALIANO

3 pounds fresh sole fillets
2 tablespoons shortening
1 cup flour
2 cups Italian style fine
   bread crumbs

1 teaspoon nutmeg
2 eggs
2 tablespoons lemon juice

Combine flour, bread crumbs, and nutmeg and spread on large piece of waxed paper. Mix eggs and lemon juice. Dip sole first into egg mixture and then into flour mixture. Fry fillets quickly, about 3 to 5 minutes on each side, in a large skillet in which you have heated shortening. Fish should be well browned. May be served with tartar sauce. Yield: 6 to 8 servings.

Maureen Barte

FRITTATA

Superb as the entree for breakfast or brunch

1 tablespoon butter
1 tablespoon oil
2 shallots, chopped
2 green onions, chopped
1 garlic clove, chopped
4 large mushrooms, sliced
6 asparagus stalks, sliced
1 small zucchini, thinly sliced
½ cup chopped proscuitto
½ cup sliced pepperoni or
  1 cup chopped, cooked
  beef, pork or ham

6 eggs, well beaten
6 slices mozzarella cheese
3 tablespoons grated
  Parmesan cheese
2 tablespoons chopped
  parsley
1 tablespoon oregano
salt and pepper to taste
1 tomato, sliced

Melt butter in oil over medium heat. Add shallots, green onions, garlic, mushrooms, asparagus, zucchini and cook until asparagus is tender. Add proscuitto and pepperoni. Continue to cook over low heat until meat is heated through and slightly browned. Add beaten eggs. Top with cheeses, parsley, oregano, salt and pepper. Cover. When omelet is lightly browned underneath, top with tomato slices and place under broiler to lightly brown surface. Serve at once. Yield: 6 servings.

Bradley H. Thompson

CHRISTMAS BREAKFAST

7 slices white bread
8 ounces shredded Cheddar
  cheese
6 eggs
3 cups milk

½ teaspoon salt
½ teaspoon pepper
1 teaspoon dry mustard
4 slices bacon

Trim crusts from bread. Cube bread. Mix bread and cheese. Place in a greased 7½x12-inch baking pan. Mix eggs and milk; stir in salt, pepper, and mustard. Pour over bread cubes and cheese. Lay bacon on top. Refrigerate overnight. Christmas morning bake, uncovered, at 350° for 50 to 55 minutes, while opening gifts. **HINT:** Serve promptly, as it tends to sink. Can also add crabmeat or ham. Yield: 6 servings.

Karen DiOrio

CREAM CHEESE AND CASHEW OMELET

1 tablespoon butter or
  margarine
2 eggs
1 ounce cream cheese, cut in
  ½-inch cubes
1 tablespoon of coarsely
  chopped cashew nuts

dollop of sour cream
dash of celery salt, optional
dash of dried green onion
  tops, optional

Use a well-seasoned 8-inch iron skillet. Preheat over medium heat. While skillet is heating, crack eggs into a small bowl, and scramble with fork or whisk (do not beat too much and do not add either water or milk to eggs). To season eggs, add a dash of celery salt and/or the shredded dried green onion tops for flavor. Test the heat in the skillet by letting a drop of water fall from your finger into the skillet. When the drop of water dances merrily about the pan, it is properly heated. Put butter into pan and move it around to coat entire pan. Do not add eggs until butter is light to medium brown. Add eggs. As they cook, gently lift the edges and let the uncooked portions run out of the center into the pan. Do not overcook. When eggs are almost firm, sprinkle cubes of cream cheese across half of omelet. When they are about half melted, sprinkle chopped cashew nuts across same half. Fold the omelet and slide out of pan onto a warm plate. Top omelet with a generous dollop of sour cream. **HINT:** For a change of pace, try bleu cheese and black walnuts. After making a few omelets, you will be able to gauge how much cream cheese, how many nuts, and how much sour cream you prefer. Yield: 1 serving.

Joe Hoffman

SPINACH QUICHE

1 (9 inch) unbaked pie shell
1 pound spinach, cooked
1 tablespoon butter
½ cup chopped green
  onions
1 clove garlic, minced
1½ cups or 6 ounces
  shredded Swiss cheese
3 eggs, lightly beaten

¾ cup milk
1 teaspoon salt
1 teaspoon basil, crumbled
½ teaspoon celery salt
2 medium tomatoes, thinly
  sliced
1 tablespoon bread crumbs
1 tablespoon grated
  Parmesan cheese

Press excess water out of cooked spinach; chop finely. Sauté oinions and garlic in butter until golden. Add spinach; cook over medium heat, stirring constantly until all moisture is evaporated. Combine all ingredients except tomatoes, bread crumbs, and cheese in large bowl. Pour into pastry shell. Arrange tomato slices around edge. Bake at 425° for 15 minutes. Lower heat to 350° and bake for 10 minutes. Combine cheese and bread crumbs. Sprinkle over tomatoes and bake an additional 10 minutes. Let stand 10 minutes before cutting. Yield: 6 servings.

Diane Montani

FRENCH STYLE CHEESE OMELET

2 large eggs	1 ounce thinly sliced cheese,
pinch of marjoram	Cheddar or Swiss
pinch of salt	1 slice diced onion, optional
pinch of pepper	2 mushrooms, boiled and
1 tablespoon butter	chopped, optional

Beat eggs with fork in a cup for 30 seconds. Add marjoram, salt and pepper. Add onion or mushrooms, if desired. In an 8-inch skillet over moderately high heat, melt butter until golden brown. Pour seasoned egg mixture into pan and tilt pan from side to side 5 times to build up edges of omelet. Holding pan with one hand and fork with the other, shake pan moderately while whipping egg surface with fork until egg thickens throughout. Add cheese. Fold ½ of omelet over the other in pan and lower heat and cook for another minute or so until omelet rises to a puff and cheese melts. Serve with love. Yield: 1 serving.

William M. Coombe
Times Leader Editor

CHICKEN AND DRESSING EN CASSEROLE

Good for a luncheon

1 (7 ounce) package cubed
  stuffing mix
2 (13 ounce) cans french cut
  green beans, drained
2 (4 ounce) package slivered
  almonds

5 whole chicken breasts,
  cooked, boned, and cut
  into large pieces

Place a thin layer of dry dressing on bottom of a buttered 9x13x2-inch baking pan. Prepare remaining dressing according to package directions. Set aside. Spread an even layer of green beans over dry dressing. Sprinkle with slivered almonds. Layer chicken pieces over almonds, then pour sauce evenly over all. Top with remaining prepared dressing mix. Bake for 45 to 50 minutes at 375° until bubbly and brown on top. **HINT:** Freezes well. Can be doubled. Yield: 8 servings.

SAUCE

2 (10½ ounce) cans cream of
  mushroom soup
½ cup milk
1 cup mayonnaise
½ tablespoon curry powder

1 teaspoon lemon juice
½ cup sharp Cheddar cheese,
  shredded
3 tablespoons white wine

Mix together all ingredients.

Jeanne Hicks

CRISS-CROSS CHICKEN PIE

2 cups cooked chicken
  breasts, chopped
1 (10 ounce) package frozen
  Deluxe or English peas
1 cup shredded sharp
  Cheddar cheese
1 cup diced celery
½ cup soft bread crumbs

¼ cup chopped onion
¼ teaspoon salt
⅛ teaspoon pepper
1 cup mayonnaise
3 dashes hot sauce
1 (8 ounce) can crescent
  dinner rolls
2 teaspoons sesame seeds

Combine chicken, peas, cheese, celery, bread crumbs, onion, salt, pepper, mayonnaise, and hot sauce in a large mixing bowl. Mix well. Spoon mixture into ungreased 12x8x2-inch baking dish. Separate crescent dough into 2 rectangles; press perforations to seal. Cut into 4 long and 4 short strips of equal width. Arrange strips into lattice design across top of casserole. Sprinkle with sesame seeds. Bake at 350° for 30 to 35 minutes. **HINT:** If preparing ahead, do not put lattice strips or sesame seeds on until immediately before baking. Yield: 4 to 6 servings.

Genny S. McIntyre

CHICKEN RICE CASSEROLE

2 cups cooked chicken, diced
1½ cups chopped celery,
  sautéed in butter
2 cups cooked rice
1 (10¾ ounce) can cream of
  chicken soup

1 cup mayonnaise
½ cup milk
1 teaspoon minced green
  onion
1 cup fine bread crumbs
2 tablespoons butter

Mix first 7 ingredients. Place in 2-quart buttered casserole. Sprinkle with bread crumbs. Dot with butter. Bake 40 minutes at 350°, uncovered. Yield: 6 to 8 servings.

Diana Ihlenfeld

CREAMY CHICKEN-RICE CASSEROLE

2 cups wild rice
½ cup chopped onion
½ stick butter
¼ cup enriched flour
1 (6 ounce) can sliced
  mushrooms
chicken broth
1 cup light cream

3 cups diced, cooked chicken
¼ cup diced pimento
2 tablespoons snipped
  parsley
1½ teaspoons salt
¼ teaspoon pepper
½ cup slivered, blanched
  almonds

Prepare wild rice according to package. Sauté onion in butter until tender; remove from heat; stir in flour. Drain mushrooms, reserving liquid. Add enough chicken broth to liquid to measure 1½ cups; gradually stir into flour mixture. Add cream. Cook and stir until thick. Add wild rice, mushrooms, chicken, pimento, parsley, salt and pepper. Place in 2-quart casserole. Sprinkle with almonds. Bake at 350° for 25 to 30 minutes. Yield: 8 servings.

Jenny Seibert

CASSEROLES

CORN PIE WITH HAM

Good one-step meal

3 large eggs
1 (8 ounce) can cream style
  corn
1 (10 ounce) can whole corn,
  drained
½ cup butter, melted
½ cup yellow corn meal
1 (8 ounce) package sour
  cream

8 ounces Cheddar cheese,
  shredded
½ teaspoon salt
4 ounces ham, chopped
  small, or crumbled bacon,
  optional
1 (4 ounce) can chopped,
  mild green chili peppers,
  optional

Beat eggs in a large bowl and add remaining ingredients. Mix well. Pour into greased 10-inch round glass dish. Bake uncovered at 350° for 55 minutes. **HINT:** Leave out meat and it is a great side dish. If you don't like spicy foods, remember that chilies mentioned above are very mild. If made ahead, it will keep well in refrigerator for up to a week. It also freezes well. Yield: 4 to 6 servings.

Kathleen Gibbs

KIELBASA AND FRIED CABBAGE

1 to 1½ pounds kielbasa
1 medium head cabbage
3 tablespoons butter
2 to 3 tablespoons
  Italian dressing

salt and pepper to
taste

Slice kielbasa very thin; place in large frying pan with a little butter and cook until meat begins to curl and brown. Remove from pan and drain. Chop cabbage in fairly small pieces. Put kielbasa and rest of butter in frying pan. Add chopped cabbage and Italian dressing. Cover pan and let stand over medium heat for about 5 to 7 minutes. Remove cover; stir. Add salt and pepper, if needed. Stir continuously for about 5 more minutes or until most of cabbage is translucent. Serve immediately or turn into casserole to keep warm in oven. Yield: 4 to 6 servings.

Kathleen Gibbs

SPARONI

*Arch A. Moore, Jr. was the 28th governor of West Virginia
from 1969 to 1977 and was the first to serve two four-year
terms. The State's 1st Congressional District sent Moore
to the U.S. House of Representatives six times.*

½ cup butter
flour
milk
1 (2 pound) can peeled
  tomatoes, not stewed

dash of salt and sugar
1 medium-size onion
1 pound ground chuck
¾ small package of spaghetti,
  cooked as directed

Mix flour with butter to make a thick paste and add just enough milk
to thin paste a little. Chop tomatoes very fine. Pour chopped tomatoes
and juice into cream sauce and add salt and sugar. Chop onion very fine
and brown in butter or oil; add meat and brown. In buttered casserole,
alternate layers starting with spaghetti, meat, and then tomato sauce.
Top with shredded Cheddar cheese, cover, and bake 350° for 45 minutes.
HINT: You may want to add a little milk around edges of casserole before
baking to keep from getting too dry. Yield: 4 servings.

Arch A. Moore, Jr.

FIESTA CASSEROLE

For Mexican food lovers

1 large onion, chopped
1 clove garlic, minced
2 tablespoons cooking oil
1 pound ground beef
1 (1 pound 12 ounce) can
  tomatoes
1 (16 ounce) can enchilada
  sauce, mild

1 (15½ ounce) can kidney
  beans, undrained
2 teaspoons salt
¼ teaspoon pepper
chili powder to taste
Cheddar cheese, at least
  1 cup
1 (11 ounce) can corn tortillas

In large skillet, brown ground beef, leaving in chunks, with oil, onion,
and garlic. Add tomatoes, enchilada sauce, kidney beans, salt, pepper,
and chili powder to meat mixture. Heat to boiling. Place corn tortillas,
overlapping, in a long baking dish. Add layer of meat sauce. Continue
these layers until you have used most of sauce. Have meat sauce on top
layer and sprinkle with Cheddar cheese. I think the more cheese the
better. Bake for 30 minutes in a 400° oven. Cool before serving. **HINT:**
May be made ahead of time and heated when ready. Yield: 8 servings.

Becky Stevenson

CASSEROLES

SEAFOOD CASSEROLE

2 cups cooked white rice
½ cup milk
½ cup minced onion
¼ cup minced green pepper
1 cup mayonnaise (not salad dressing)
½ pound fresh backfin crabmeat
½ pound fresh cooked shrimp
1 (5½ ounce) can tomato juice
3 to 6 ounces slivered almonds
10 butter crackers, crumbled

Butter a 1½-or 2-quart baking dish. Sauté onions and green peppers in 2 tablespoons butter or margarine until limp. Fold all ingredients together, except crackers, gently, so as not to break up crab lumps. Fill casserole and top with crumbs; dot with butter. Bake at 350° for 30 minutes until hot and bubbly at edge. **HINT:** Can be done ahead, early in day, and can be doubled. If made ahead and refrigerated, increase baking time to 45 minutes to 1 hour. Yield: 4 to 6 servings.

Joan C. Stamp

LANGOSTINO CASSEROLE

2 pounds frozen langostino
½ cup chopped celery
2 tablespoons chopped green pepper
¼ cup butter
2 tablespoons flour
1 cup milk,
1 egg yolk, beaten
2 tablespoons lemon juice
½ teaspoon salt
dash of pepper
2 tablespoons dry white wine
1 tablespoon butter, melted
½ cup dry bread crumbs

Thaw and rinse langostino; drain. Cook celery and green pepper in butter until tender. Blend in flour. Add milk gradually and cook until thick, stirring constantly. Stir a little of hot sauce into egg yolk; add to remaining sauce, stirring constantly. Add lemon juice, seasonings, langostino, and wine. Place in well-greased, 1-quart casserole. Combine butter and crumbs; sprinkle over casserole. Bake in a moderate oven, 350°, for 20 to 25 minutes or until brown. Yield: 4 generous servings.

Mary Ellen Harmon

Pasta, Rice and Potatoes

The Bavarian Inn, Shepherdstown,
West Virginia

PASTA, RICE AND POTATOES

SPAGHETTI PIE

6 ounces spaghetti
2 tablespoons butter or
 margarine
⅓ cup grated Parmesan
 cheese
2 well-beaten eggs
½ pound ground beef
½ pound Italian sausage,
 sweet or hot sausage
1 medium onion, chopped
½ medium green pepper,
 chopped
1 (8 ounce) can whole
 tomatoes

1 (6 ounce) can tomato paste
1 teaspoon sugar
1 teaspoon leaf oregano
1 clove garlic, crushed
½ teaspoon salt
few twists freshly ground
 black pepper
1 cup small-curd cottage
 cheese
½ cup shredded mozzarella
 cheese

Cook the spaghetti according to package directions and drain. While
hot, mix spaghetti with butter, Parmesan, and eggs. Butter a 10-inch
quiche dish or pie pan with 2-inch rim. Spread spaghetti over bottom
and up sides of pan with back of spoon to form a crust. Cook sausage
and ground beef over moderate heat until it loses red color. Add onion
and green pepper during last 5 minutes of cooking time. Drain grease.
Cut tomatoes in small pieces. Add tomatoes and their liquid, tomato
paste, sugar, oregano, garlic, salt and pepper to meat mixture. Cook until
hot. Spread cottage cheese over bottom of crust. Spoon meat mixture
on top of cheese. Bake, uncovered, at 350° for 20 minutes. Sprinkle mozzarella cheese in center of pie. Bake 5 minutes (until cheese melts). Let
stand at room temperature for 5 minutes. Cut into wedges. **HINT:** Recipe
can be done ahead and can be doubled. Freezes well. Yield: 4 to 6 servings.

Mrs. Fontaine B. Hooff

COLD SPAGHETTI SALAD

Excellent for cookout

1 pound spaghetti
2 large green peppers,
 chopped
3 red tomatoes, chopped
3 green onions (stems
 included), chopped

12 ounces creamy Italian
 salad dressing
1½ ounces salad seasoning,
 about ½ jar
3 ounces grated Parmesan
 cheese

Cook spaghetti according to directions on package. Drain and rinse with cold water. Spaghetti can either be broken into 1-inch pieces before cooking or cut into bite-size pieces after cooking. Add green peppers, tomatoes, and green onions. Mix in salad dressing, salad seasoning, and Parmesan cheese. This will now be an orange colored mixture. Chill well. Mixture improves more if it stands a few hours before serving. Keeps 2 days. Yield: 8 servings.

Jackie Boury

SPAGHETTI WITH WHITE CLAM SAUCE

linguine or spaghetti, 1 to 2 pounds, depending on serving size and/or appetite
½ cup olive oil
4 large cloves of garlic, mashed
3 (6½ ounce) cans minced clams
¼ teaspoon black pepper

½ teaspoon dried basil
½ teaspoon thyme
¼ teaspoon oregano
½ cup finely chopped parsley or 2 tablespoons dried parsley
2 tablespoons butter
grated Parmesan cheese
lemon juice, optional

Add linguine or spaghetti to salted water and cook until done, but still firm. Start sauce after spaghetti is added to boiling water as the clams should not overcook. Heat olive oil in saucepan and add garlic. Cook until soft. Add clams with their juice and remaining spices. Bring to a simmer. Drain spaghetti. Pour into bowl and mix with butter. Add sauce to individual servings. Sprinkle with Parmesan cheese. Squeeze lemon juice over clam sauce before adding Parmesan cheese, if desired. Yield: 4 to 6 servings.

Becky Stevenson

QUICKEY CARBONARA

¼ pound bacon
2 tablespoons olive oil
2 tablespoons butter
1 clove garlic, pressed
2 cups ham strips
1 (8 ounce) package spaghetti, cooked and drained

⅓ cup grated Parmesan cheese
¼ cup chopped parsley
½ teaspoon salt
½ teaspoon pepper
3 eggs, beaten
¼ cup ripe olives
2 pimentos, sliced

Brown bacon in pan. Drain, crumble, and reserve bacon. Pour off fat; add oil, butter, garlic and ham to pan. Sauté slightly; add spaghetti, bacon, cheese, parsley, salt and pepper. Stir well. Turn off heat; pour eggs over and toss to coat spaghetti evenly. Add olives and pimentos; toss. Decorate with parsley. Yield: 4 servings.

Jo Clarke

PASTA PRIMAVERA

A colorful dish!

½ cup broccoli flowerets
½ cup sliced mushrooms
½ cup red pepper, cut in strips
½ cup zucchini, sliced
4 tablespoons unsalted butter

1 cup light cream, warmed
freshly ground black pepper
1 pound linguine
grated Parmesan cheese

Lightly cook broccoli, mushrooms, red pepper, and zucchini in butter until everything is crisply tender. Add cream and pepper; cook down briefly. Cook pasta according to package directions. Drain. Toss with sauce. Sprinkle generously with freshly grated Parmesan cheese. Yield: 4 servings.

Marie Daley

SPINACH FETTUCINI WITH SCALLOPS

2 (8 ounce) packages sour cream
1 cup cream or milk
1 package hollandaise sauce mix
½ teaspoon minced garlic
1 tablespoon chives

¼ teaspoon pepper
¼ cup lemon juice
1 pound Bay scallops, blanched and drained
2 (8 ounce) packages spinach fettucini
Parmesan cheese

In large saucepan, combine sour cream and milk; heat until almost boiling. Add dry hollandaise mix, a little at a time, and blend with whisk. Add garlic, chives, and pepper. Add lemon juice, if needed, to thin sauce. Add scallops and reduce heat to simmer, stirring often. Cook and drain fettucini. Toss with Parmesan and spoon sauce over noodles. Yield: 4 to 6 servings.

Kathleen Gibbs

FETTUCINI

¼ pound bacon
1 (12 ounce) box fettucini
¼ cup butter or margarine, softened
½ cup heavy cream, room temperature
½ cup grated Parmesan cheese

2 eggs, slightly beaten
2 tablespoons snipped parsley
¼ pound fresh mushrooms, optional

Sauté bacon until crisp; drain well, crumble, and set aside. Reserve bacon drippings. Slice mushrooms and sauté in the drippings. Drain well and set aside. Cook fettucini according to package directions. Drain well and place in warm serving dish, large enough for tossing. Add crumbled bacon, sliced mushrooms, butter, heavy cream, grated cheese, eggs, and snipped parsley. Toss until fettucini is well coated. Salt and pepper to taste. Yield: 4 to 6 servings.

Ann Diotti

MOSTACCIOLI ALFRONO

Salad, bread and wine complete this meal

1 (10 ounce) package frozen spinach
1 (15 ounce) package ricotta cheese
3 eggs, slightly beaten
⅔ cup grated Parmesan cheese
1 cup shredded mozzarella cheese

⅓ cup dried parsley
1 teaspoon salt
¼ teaspoon pepper
8 ounces mostaccioli
3 cups spaghetti sauce
2 tablespoons grated Parmesan cheese

Combine spinach, ricotta cheese, eggs, ⅔ cup Parmesan cheese, ⅔ cup mozzarella cheese, dried parsley, salt and pepper. Set aside. Cook mostaccioli for 12 minutes and drain. Add 2 cups spaghetti sauce to mostaccioli. Arrange half of pasta on the bottom of a 9-inch square baking dish. Layer spinach mixture over pasta. Cover with remaining pasta. Spread on 1 cup of spaghetti sauce. Sprinkle on ⅓ cup mozzarella cheese and 2 tablespoons Parmesan cheese. Bake uncovered at 350° for 35 to 40 minutes. Yield: 6 servings.

Debbie Gallagher

NOODLES SOUFFLÉ

1 (8 ounce) package cream
cheese
8 ounces cottage cheese
1 cup sour cream
½ cup butter or margarine
½ cup sugar

1 teaspoon vanilla
6 eggs, separated
6 ounces medium-size
noodles, cooked and
drained

Have all ingredients at room temperature. Cream together cream cheese, cottage cheese, sour cream and butter. Add sugar, vanilla, and egg yolks (add egg yolks one at a time and beat after each addition). Beat egg whites until stiff, but not dry. Fold them into cheese mixture. Carefully fold in noodles. In a slightly greased 13x9x2-inch baking pan, bake at 375° for 45 minutes until puffed and lightly brown. **HINT:** Freezes well. Yield: 6 servings.

Becky Rivlin

WILD RICE DELIGHT

⅓ cup oil
¼ cup chopped parsley
½ cup minced green onion
½ cup chopped celery
1½ cups wild rice
1 (10 ounce) can chicken
stock

1½ cups boiling water
1 teaspoon salt
½ teaspoon basil
½ teaspoon margarine
½ cup white wine

Heat oil in skillet. Add parsley, onion and celery. Cook until tender. Wash rice very well. Add rice, chicken stock, water, salt, basil and margarine to skillet. Cover and cook over low heat for 45 minutes. Stir rice every few minutes. If it becomes too dry, add a little more boiling water. When rice is tender and water absorbed, stir in white wine. Leave uncovered and cook 3 to 5 minutes longer. Yield: 6 servings.

Nancy Ellen O'Leary

SPICY RICE

Great with lamb

1 cup uncooked rice	¼ cup green onion, chopped
2 cups chicken broth	2 tablespoons butter
¼ cup green pepper, chopped	salt to taste
¼ cup red pepper, chopped	dash red pepper sauce

Cook rice according to package directions, using chicken broth in place of water. Sauté peppers and onions in butter. Mix sautéed vegetables with rice. Add salt and red pepper sauce to taste. Yield: 4 servings.

Dee Dee McCuskey

RIZ PILAF A LA VALENCIENNE

½ cup butter	2 teaspoons pimento, chopped
1 cup peeled eggplant, diced	1 cup rice
1 small zucchini, diced	1 (13¾ ounce) can chicken broth
3 to 4 mushrooms, sliced thin	salt and pepper to taste
1 clove garlic, mashed	
1 large tomato, seeded, peeled, and chopped	

Melt butter in large saucepan. Add eggplant, zucchini, mushrooms, garlic, tomato, and chopped pimento. Salt and pepper to taste. Cook over medium heat for 10 minutes, stirring occasionally. Add the rice and chicken broth. Bring to a boil, cover, and cook over low heat for 30 to 35 minutes. Check for seasoning. **HINT:** May be cooked in oven also. Yield: 4 servings.

Anne Clark

CHEESE AND RICE CASSEROLE

2 cups water
1 cup uncooked rice
1 teaspoon salt
½ teaspoon dry mustard
½ teaspoon red pepper sauce
¼ teaspoon pepper
1 medium onion, chopped

2 cups or 8 ounces shredded
  mozzarella or Cheddar
  cheese
4 eggs, slightly beaten
2½ cups milk
½ cup grated Romano cheese

Heat water, rice, salt, mustard, red pepper sauce, and pepper to boiling, stirring once or twice. Reduce heat. Cover and simmer 14 minutes. Do not lift cover or stir. Remove from heat. Fluff with fork. Cover. Let steam for 5 minutes. Layer half the rice mixture, onion and mozzarella cheese in a greased 11x7x1½-inch baking dish. Repeat. Mix eggs and milk; pour over rice mixture. Sprinkle with Romano cheese. Casserole can be covered and refrigerated up to 24 hours. Cook uncovered at 325° until set, approximately 45 to 50 minutes. Let stand 10 minutes. Cut into squares. **HINT:** Freezes well after cooking. Yield: 6 servings.

Mary Leibold

DISGUSTINGLY RICH POTATOES

6 large potatoes
½ to ¾ cup butter
2 teaspoons salt
1 cup heavy cream
1 teaspoon freshly ground
  black pepper

4 ounce Gruyere cheese,
  shredded (or Swiss or
  Cheddar)

Bake potatoes. When soft, scoop out each into mixing bowl. Add butter, salt, cream, and pepper. (Discard shells.) Mix lightly and transfer to flat baking dish. Dot heavily with more butter and sprinkle with cheese. Bake at 375° for 15 minutes. If made ahead and refrigerated, heat for 30 minutes. Yield: 8 servings.

Sue Case

GOURMET POTATOES

Great for a buffet

10 potatoes, cooked and
  cooled
2 cups shredded Cheddar
  cheese
¼ cup butter

1½ cups sour cream
½ cup onion, grated fine
1 teaspoon salt
¼ teaspoon pepper

Shred or grate cooked potatoes. Over very low heat, melt butter and cheese. Remove from heat and blend in sour cream and other ingredients. Fold in potatoes. Make the day before and refrigerate. An ice cream scoop can be used to measure out individual portions and place on baking sheet. Bake at 350° for 25 minutes. **HINT:** May be frozen; then bake 45 minutes after thawing. Yield: 10 servings.

Carol E. Austin

HERBED POTATO PUFF

Eye-catching way to serve potatoes

3 cups instant potatoes
1 pound small curd cottage
  cheese
1 cup sour cream
2 teaspoons celery salt
1 small clove garlic, minced

2 tablespoons minced chives
3 egg yolks, beaten
3 egg whites, stiffly beaten
½ cup chopped fresh parsley
3 tablespoons butter

Prepare potatoes following box instructions. Whip them into cottage cheese, sour cream, celery salt, garlic, chives and beaten egg yolks. Mix thoroughly. Fold in stiffly beaten egg whites and parsley. Turn into 2-quart shallow dish and dot with butter. Bake at 350° for 1 hour or until top is lightly browned. Yield: 6 to 8 servings.

Julie Squibb

POTATO CASSEROLE

1 (1 pound 8 ounce) box hash
  brown potato squares,
  thawed
1 (10½ ounce) can cream
  of chicken soup
¼ cup butter, melted

1 (8 ounce) package shredded
  Cheddar cheese
½ cup onion, chopped
1 pint sour cream
1 teaspoon salt
cornflake crumbs

Crumble potato squares and add remaining ingredients. Top with buttered cornflake crumbs. Bake in a 13x9x2-inch baking dish. Bake at 350° for 50 minutes. **HINT:** Recipe can be doubled. Yield: 8 to 10 servings.

Ruth Smith

SWEET POTATO PUDDING

Gary McPherson is in his second tour of duty as the top assistant coach of the West Virginia University basketball team.

1 (16 ounce) can sweet
  potatoes, mashed (2 cups)
½ cup melted butter
1 cup sugar
2 eggs
¼ teaspoon nutmeg
¼ teaspoon cinnamon

⅛ teaspoon cloves
1 teaspoon vanilla
1 cup evaporated milk
½ cup coconut
½ cup chopped nuts
  (walnuts, pecan, etc)

Blend potatoes, butter, sugar, and eggs. Add rest of ingredients. (A blender is very good for this or mixer.) Bake at 375° for 30 minutes or until set like a pie filling. **HINT:** You can use pumpkin and winter squash also in place of sweet potatoes. Yield: 6 servings.

Gary D. McPherson

Vegetables

John Brown's Fort, Harpers Ferry,
West Virginia

ROSIE'S VEGETABLES AND CHEESE BAKE

Easy and great for a crowd

1 pound mixed vegetables, diced and lightly steamed
2 large onions, chopped
4 tablespoons butter
pepper to taste
¼ pound tomatoes, sliced
sweet basil leaves

¼ pound sharp Cheddar cheese, shredded
3 eggs, beaten
2 tablespoons honey
1 cup milk
1 cup bread crumbs

Prepare vegetables; then dice and lightly steam until still crunchy. Peel and chop onions; sauté in 2 tablespoons butter until tender, adding pepper. Combine with mixed vegetables and stir well. Butter a deep quart casserole dish and begin layering: vegetables, cheese, and a few slices of tomato. Sprinkle tomatoes lightly with basil leaves. Repeat layers, topping with tomatoes and cheese. Heat milk, adding honey and eggs. Pour over casserole; top with thick layer of bread crumbs. Dot with plenty of butter. Bake at 350° for 30 minutes. **HINT:** If you are in a hurry, you can use canned or frozen vegetables, but it is fresher and there is more variety if you choose and steam your own. Freezes well and can be doubled. Yield: 4 to 6 servings.

Rosemarie Schieffer

VEGETABLE CASSEROLE

Super!

2 tablespoons butter
1 pound fresh mushrooms
2 onions, quartered
2 green peppers, cut in large pieces
2 large tomatoes, quartered

2 zucchini, sliced in large pieces
salt and pepper
garlic, parsley, and oregano to taste

Melt 1 tablespoon butter in 2-quart casserole. Place all vegetables in casserole; mix and dot with remaining butter. Add herbs. Bake covered at 350° for 45 minutes. Stir once or twice. **HINT:** Recipe can be doubled. Yield: 4 to 6 servings.

Karen DiOrio

MARINATED VEGETABLES

Easy and great for a crowd

VEGETABLES

1 (1 pound) can cut green beans, drained
1 (7 ounce) can pitted ripe olives, drained
1 (4½ ounce) jar sliced or whole mushrooms, drained
1 (4 ounce) jar diced pimento, drained

1 (15 ounce) can artichoke hearts, drained
1½ cups celery, cut diagonally
1 medium onion, sliced

DRESSING

¼ cup tarragon vinegar
1½ teaspoons MSG
1¼ teaspoons salt
1 teaspoon sugar
1 tablespoon fines herbes
¼ teaspoon TABASCO Brand Pepper Sauce

½ cup salad oil
¼ cup parsley
2 tablespoons capers, optional

Combine drained vegetables, celery, and onion. For dressing, measure vinegar into shaker-type jar. Add MSG, salt, and sugar; shake until dissolved. Add fines herbes, Tabasco and salad oil and shake until well blended. Pour this over vegetables and cover. Refrigerate several hours or overnight. Turn into a serving bowl and sprinkle with chopped parsley and capers. **HINT:** You may wish to delete any vegetable above and add one of your choice. Or, you may add one or two other vegetables. Yield: 15 servings.

Ange Lavy Joel

ZUCCHINI PARMESAN

6 small zucchini
1 cup sour cream

½ cup freshly grated Parmesan cheese

Slice zucchini lengthwise and parboil for 2 minutes, until barely tender. Arrange in rectangular baking dish, cut side up. Cover each zucchini with sour cream and sprinkle liberally with Parmesan cheese. Broil until golden brown. **HINT:** You may use well-drained plain yogurt for a low calorie version. Yield: 6 servings.

Charl Kappel

ZUCCHINI CASSEROLE

Kids will love its pizza taste!

1 medium zucchini, sliced
 ¼ inch thick
1 egg, beaten
¼ cup all-purpose flour
¼ cup Parmesan or Romano
 cheese, grated

1 onion, thinly sliced
1 small green pepper,
 chopped
2 cups spaghetti sauce
1 (8 ounce) package shredded
 mozzarella cheese

Dip zucchini slices into beaten egg, then into flour and grated cheese mixed together. Fry in skillet of hot grease on both sides. Drain on paper towel. In 1½-quart casserole layer fried zucchini, onion, green pepper, spaghetti sauce, and mozzarella cheese. Bake at 350° for 35 to 40 minutes. Yield: 4 servings.

Janet Kropp

ITALIAN ZUCCHINI SAUTÉ

2 tablespoons sweet cream
 butter
3 cups zucchini unpeeled,
 sliced ⅛ inch
¼ cup sliced green onion
½ teaspoon basil leaves
¼ teaspoon salt

1 medium tomato,
 cubed ½ inch
¼ cup shredded mozzarella
 cheese
¼ cup grated Parmesan
 cheese

In 10-inch skillet, melt butter over medium heat. Stir in zucchini, green onion, basil and salt. Cook, stirring occasionally, until zucchini is crisply tender (10 to 12 minutes). Stir in tomato; cook 1 minute. Sprinkle with cheeses. Cover; let stand 1 minute or until cheese is slightly melted. Yield: 6 (½ cup) servings.

Gladys Van Horne
Editor, Family Section
Wheeling News-Register

EGGPLANT CASSEROLE

1 large eggplant
6 strips bacon, diced
½ medium onion, diced
1 (16 ounce) can tomatoes

1 to 1½ cups sharp Cheddar
 cheese, shredded
¾ cup fine bread crumbs

Pare eggplant and slice into large cubes. In large saucepan, put diced eggplant in 2 inches or so water. Bring to boil and boil for 5 to 10 minutes, until eggplant is tender. Drain eggplant in colander. Place in bottom of 2-quart casserole. Fry bacon until almost brown. Add diced onion to bacon. When bacon is browned and onion is tender, pull pan from heat and add tomatoes and cheese. Stir until cheese melts. Pour this mixture over eggplant. Do not mix. Sprinkle bread crumbs on top. Bake uncovered 30 minutes at 350.° Yield: 4 to 6 servings.

Mary Lobert

EGGPLANT PARMESAN

One of the nation's leading female road racers, Patti Catalano won the women's crown in the Elby's Distance Race at Wheeling in 1980 and 1981, setting an American 20-K record for women in the process.

3 medium-sized eggplants
salt
water
4 eggs
flour for dusting
1 (15 ounce) container
  ricotta cheese
1 package frozen spinach or,
  preferably, 8 ounces fresh
  spinach

1 (3 ounce) block cream
  cheese
cottage cheese, small curd
2 pounds mozzarella cheese,
  shredded
1 large jar prepared
  spaghetti sauce, mild
  preferred
Parmesan cheese to taste

Peel and slice eggplant (very thin) and dip slices in salt. Rinse in cold water to remove salt and with it any bitter taste of eggplant. Beat 2 eggs thoroughly and dip slices of eggplant in batter and then lightly dust each slice with flour on both sides. Spray cookie sheets with vegetable coating and bake slices for about 15 minutes, turning once. They will be only lightly browned. Now mix ricotta cheese, spinach (which must be squeezed dry), cream cheese, and 2 eggs with a dash of salt. Blend in enough cottage cheese to hold mixture together. Spray a 13x9x2-inch baking pan or dish with vegetable coating. Brush some spaghetti sauce on bottom of pan. Layer with eggplant and put about a teaspoon of cheese and spinach mixture on each slice. Top with some sauce and mozzarella. Continue layers and end with sauce and mozzarella. Sprinkle Parmesan cheese over top. Bake 1 hour at 325.° Yield: 8 servings.

Patti Catalano

VEGETABLES

SUMMER SQUASH AT ITS BEST

Easy and great for a crowd

4 medium yellow summer
  squash
1½ (10¾ ounce) cans cream of
  chicken soup
1 medium chopped onion

1 cup sour cream
salt and pepper to taste
1 (8 ounce) package
  stuffing mix
dots of butter

Wash and trim ends of squash. Slice squash about ¼ inch thick. Cook in ½ to ¾ cup water, covered, for about 15 minutes. Simmer until squash is mushy. Drain in colander. Mix together soup, chopped onion, and sour cream. Sprinkle with salt and pepper to taste. Mix with squash. Sprinkle layer of stuffing mix over bottom of a 9x13-inch pan or a 3 to 4 quart casserole dish. Pour squash mixture on top. Sprinkle rest of stuffing over mixture. Dot with pats of butter. Bake at 350° for 1 hour uncovered. **HINT:** Can be done ahead and can also be doubled. Yield: 10 to 12 servings.

Susan Mansuetto

AUNT CLEO'S SQUASH

4 to 5 medium yellow
  summer squash or zucchini
1 small onion, chopped
½ cup chopped green
  peppers
1 (1 pound) can tomatoes

1 teaspoon Italian seasoning
dash of pepper
2 tablespoons butter or
  margarine
½ cup Cheddar cheese,
  shredded

Slice squash into circles. Sauté in butter with onions and green peppers for 10 minutes. Place in casserole dish. Add tomatoes, Italian seasoning, and pepper; mix well. Cover and bake at 350° for 30 minutes. Remove cover, sprinkle cheese on top; bake 10 minutes more, uncovered. Yield: 6 servings.

Donna Glass

CARROTS WITH ORANGE GLAZE

1½ pounds medium carrots
boiling water
½ teaspoon salt
¼ cup orange juice

1 tablespoon sugar
2 tablespoons butter
  or margarine
1 orange, sliced thin

Scrub carrots and cut off stems, but do not pare. Place in 10-inch skillet with tight-fitting lid. Add boiling water to measure 1 inch and salt. Bring back to boil. Reduce heat and simmer 10 minutes or until tender. Drain and cool 10 minutes. Peel skin off carrots with knife. In skillet, combine orange juice, sugar, butter and orange slices. Add carrots. Simmer gently, spooning glaze over carrots, for 5 or 10 minutes until tender. Yield: 6 servings.

Maria E. Sticco
Family Editor, Times Leader

COMPANY CARROT CASSEROLE

Superb with roast beef!

1½ pounds carrots, sliced
  (4½ cups)
½ cup mayonnaise or salad
  dressing
2 tablespoons chopped onion
2 tablespoons prepared
  horseradish

¼ teaspoon salt
dash of pepper
¼ cup crushed saltine
  crackers (7 crackers)
2 teaspoons melted
  margarine or butter

Cook sliced carrots in boiling, salted water until tender crisp. Place in shallow casserole. Mix mayonnaise, onion, horseradish, salt and pepper in small bowl. Spread over top of carrots. Add crushed saltines to melted butter. Sprinkle on top. Bake, uncovered, at 350° for 30 minutes. To prepare in microwave, cook carrots in 2 to 3 tablespoons water for 9 minutes on high or until tender crisp. Proceed with previous instructions. **HINT:** This recipe can easily be enlarged by simply adding more carrots. Yield: 4 to 6 servings.

Karen Recht

BAKED CARROT PUFF

2 pounds pared carrots,
  sliced
½ cup water
½ teaspoon salt
6 tablespoons butter
¾ cup graham cracker
  crumbs

2 eggs, separated
dash of ginger
¼ cup packed light brown
  sugar
¼ cup fine bread crumbs

Preheat oven to 375°. Combine carrots, water, and salt in heavy 3-quart pan. Bring to a boil; reduce heat to medium. Cook for 15 minutes or until carrots are tender. Drain liquid and mash carrots. Combine carrots, 4 tablespoons butter, graham cracker crumbs, and ginger. Blend until smooth. Beat in egg yolks. Cool. Beat egg whites until stiff peaks form. Combine remaining butter, brown sugar, and bread crumbs. Sprinkle over carrot mixture. Bake for 40 minutes. **HINT:** Recipe can be doubled. Yield: 8 servings.

Janie Altmeyer

MARINATED CARROTS

2 bunches carrots, peeled and chopped, or 2 (1 pound) cans sliced carrots
1 (10¾ ounce) can tomato soup
½ cup sugar
½ cup salad oil
½ cup vinegar
1 green pepper, diced
2 tablespoons dry onion flakes
salt and pepper to taste

Cook carrots in boiling water until barely tender. Mix rest of ingredients and pour over carrots while hot and refrigerate 24 hours. **HINT:** Remaining marinade makes a wonderful salad dressing! Must be prepared ahead and can be doubled. Yield: 6 servings.

Jerri Front

GREEN BEAN CASSEROLE

1 cup chopped onion
2 tablespoons butter
2 teaspoons sugar
2 tablespoons flour
dash of salt and pepper
2 cups milk
½ cup sour cream
2 (1 pound) cans green beans, drained well
1 cup shredded Swiss cheese
½ cup cornflake crumbs

Sauté onion with butter; stir in sugar, flour, salt and pepper. Slowly add milk, stirring until medium thick. Stir in sour cream. Add green beans. Layer ½ green bean mixture on bottom of casserole. Spread with ½ cup Swiss cheese. Repeat with green bean mixture and ½ cup cheese. Top with cornflake crumbs. Bake at 400° for 20 minutes or until cheese is melted and slightly brown. Yield: 6 servings.

Stacy Gilson

DELUXE GREEN BEANS

1 pound fresh green beans,
 cooked and drained, or 2
 (16 ounce) cans green beans
¼ cup chopped cashew nuts
¼ pound butter or margarine
½ pound mushrooms, sliced
3 tablespoons flour

¼ teaspoon pepper
¼ teaspoon salt
1½ cups milk
1 tablespoon minced onion
3 tablespoons Parmesan
 cheese

Cook nuts in butter over low heat until brown. Remove nuts. Add mushrooms to butter and cook 10 minutes. Blend in flour and seasonings. Add milk and cook until thick. Add onions, beans, and half of nuts; mix well. Pour into shallow casserole. Cover. Sprinkle top with remaining nuts and cheese. Bake at 350° for 20 minutes. **HINT:** Recipe can be done ahead and can be doubled. Yield: 6 servings.

Darlene Petri

ALMOND BEANS

Margaret Villers is a relative of Anna Jarvis of Grafton, West Virginia, who was the founder of Mother's Day.

1 (10 ounce) package frozen
 green beans, French style

½ cup slivered almonds
1 teaspoon lemon juice

Cook green beans as directed on package. When ready to serve, add slivered almonds which have been sautéed in butter until brown. Add lemon juice and serve immediately. **HINT:** Can be doubled easily. Yield: 4 servings.

Margaret Jarvis Villers

GREEN BEANS AND GREEN GRAPES

1 pound frozen French style
 green beans or 1 pound
 fresh green beans

1½ sticks butter
3 pinches of tarragon
½ pound green grapes

Cook beans until desired tenderness. Add butter and tarragon. Finally add fresh green grapes. Toss tarragon and grapes with beans and butter at last minute. Garnish with slivered almonds, if desired. **HINT:** Recipe can be doubled. Yield: 4 to 6 servings.

Debbie Marano

VEGETABLES

FIVE BEAN CASSEROLE

Easy and great for a crowd

2 (16 ounce) cans baked
  beans
1 (16 ounce) can kidney
  beans, drained
1 (16 ounce) can cut green
  beans, drained
1 (16 ounce) can wax beans,
  drained
1 (16 ounce) can lima beans,
  drained

1 (16 ounce) can tomato
  pieces, drained
½ cup ketchup
1 medium onion, diced
1 cup brown sugar
½ pound bacon, cut up and
  uncooked

Mix all ingredients together in large casserole dish. Bake at 300° for 2 hours, uncovered. **HINT:** Can be prepared ahead of time and can also be doubled. Yield: 12 servings.

Sue Harmon

SWEET AND SOUR BEANS

Great for a cookout

2 onions, finely chopped
8 slices bacon, fried and
  crumbled
1 cup brown sugar
1 teaspoon dry mustard
1 teaspoon salt
½ cup vinegar
2 (16 ounce) cans dried lima
  beans

1 (16 ounce) can green lima
  beans
1 (16 ounce) can dark red
  kidney beans
1 (16 ounce) can pork and
  beans

Fry bacon in skillet until crisp. Remove from pan and crumble. Place chopped onions in bacon grease and add sugar, mustard, salt, and vinegar. Cover and cook 20 minutes. Drain all beans except 1 can of pork and beans. Add beans to cooked mixture. Pour into a 3-quart casserole dish. Bake at 350° for 1 hour. Remove from oven and place crumbled bacon on top. Yield: 10 servings.

Carol Kinder

118

BEANS AU GRATIN

1 (10 ounce) box frozen cut
   green beans
1 (10 ounce) box frozen wax
   beans
1 (10 ounce) box frozen lima
   beans
4 tablespoons butter

2 tablespoons flour
1 teaspoon salt
dash of pepper
dash of Worcestershire sauce
1 cup half and half
½ cup grated Parmesan
   cheese

Cook beans separately according to package directions; drain. Mix lightly and put in shallow baking dish. Melt 2 tablespoons butter; stir in flour, salt, pepper and Worcestershire sauce. Add cream and cook until thickened, stirring. Pour over beans. Dot with butter and sprinkle with cheese. Bake in 375° oven for 15 minutes or until hot and browned. Yield: 6 servings.

Ann Bopp

HOBO BEANS

1 pound ground chuck
2 (16 ounce) cans pork
   and beans
1 (16 ounce) can butter limas
1 (16 ounce) can kidney beans
1 cup ketchup

½ cup water
1 package dried onion
   soup mix
2 tablespoons brown sugar
2 teaspoons dry mustard
2 teaspoons vinegar

Brown ground chuck and drain off fat. Add all other ingredients. Bake at 400° for 30 to 35 minutes. Yield: 12 servings.

Pauline Taylor

CORN PUDDING

1½ cups milk
2 eggs
2 tablespoons flour

½ teaspoon sugar
2 cups frozen corn

Beat eggs and milk slightly with fork. Add flour and sugar and beat until well blended. Stir in corn. Pour into buttered 2-quart casserole and place casserole in pan of water. Bake at 350° for 1 hour. Yield: 4 servings.

Diana T. Ihlenfeld

ARTICHOKES WITH BLENDER HOLLANDAISE SAUCE

6 fresh artichokes

Rinse artichokes in cold water. Break off any discolored leaves. Place artichokes upright in 1½ inches of boiling water. Cook covered 30 to 45 minutes or until leaves pull off easily. Drain and serve with hollandaise sauce. Yield: 6 servings.

HOLLANDAISE SAUCE

4 egg yolks
½ teaspoon salt
½ pound butter

¼ teaspoon Dijon mustard
3 tablespoons lemon juice

Place egg yolks, salt, and mustard in blender. Melt butter. Add lemon juice to eggs in blender; cover and turn it to low speed for 5 seconds. Take off top and pour in butter in a steady stream. Turn off blender the moment sauce thickens. Yield: Approximately 1 pint.

Lou Crawford

SPINACH CASSEROLE

Great for a crowd

1½ cups carrots, sliced
½ medium onion, chopped
1 (10 ounce) package frozen
  chopped spinach
2 tablespoons butter
2 tablespoons flour
¼ teaspoon salt

⅛ teaspoon pepper
1 cup milk
¾ cup Cheddar cheese,
  shredded
packaged herb-seasoned
  stuffing crumbs (fine)

Cook carrots with onion until tender. Drain; set aside. Cook spinach according to package directions. Drain and set aside. Melt butter over low heat. Blend in flour, seasonings. Cook over low heat, stirring until mixture is smooth and bubbly. Remove from heat. Stir in milk. Bring to boil, stirring constantly until thickened. Boil 1 minute. Add cheese. In 1½-quart casserole layer carrots, spinach, and white sauce. Sprinkle with packaged herb-seasoned stuffing crumbs mixed with melted butter. Bake at 350° until bubbly. **HINT:** Freezes well. Can be doubled. Yield: 4 to 6 servings.

Sally Holmes

STUFFED TOMATOES

8 large tomatoes
⅓ cup chopped bacon
2 tablespoons chopped onions
¼ cup chopped celery
¼ cup chopped green pepper
½ cup toasted bread cubes

1 (10¾ ounce) can cream of mushroom soup
1 teaspoon salt
1 teaspoon pepper
1 cup shredded Cheddar cheese

Cut tops off tomatoes. Scoop out tomatoes and reserve. Brown bacon until crisp; drain and save drippings. Sauté onion, celery and green pepper in drippings. Combine all ingredients and 2 tablespoons of drippings. Stuff tomatoes. Sprinkle cheese over each tomato. Place in greased 12x8x2-inch glass baking pan. Bake in oven 350° for 30 minutes. Yield: 6 to 8 servings.

Sherry Hennen

FANCY PEAS

1 (10 ounce) package frozen peas, cooked and drained
1 (10¾ ounce) can cream of mushroom soup
¼ cup milk
¼ cup margarine
⅓ cup diced celery

⅓ cup chopped onion
⅓ diced green pepper
1 small can water chestnuts, sliced
¼ cup chopped pimento
½ cup Cheddar cheese crackers, crumbled

Combine soup and milk. Sauté celery, onion, and green pepper in margarine until soft. Combine with soup. Stir in peas and water chestnuts. Add pimento; mix thoroughly. Pour into buttered 1½-quart casserole. Refrigerate overnight. Preheat oven to 350°. Cover top of casserole with crumbs. Bake, uncovered, at 350° for 25 minutes. **HINT:** Recipe can be done ahead and can be doubled. Yield: 6 to 8 servings.

Jean Carson

SPRUCED SPROUTS

3 (10 ounce) packages brussel sprouts
¼ pound butter
¼ cup white wine

3 tablespoons dark mustard
½ teaspoon sage
1 cup heavy cream
slivered almonds

121

Cook defrosted sprouts in wine and butter. Stir in mustard, sage and cream. Cook until thickened. Sprinkle almonds over top and serve. **HINT:** Recipe can be doubled. Yield: 12 servings.

Dee Dee McCuskey

CREAMED CAULIFLOWER CASSEROLE

Good and easy!

1 medium head cauliflower	¾ teaspoon salt
3 tablespoons butter or margarine	⅛ teaspoon pepper
	1 package stuffing mix
¼ cup flour	1 cup water
2 cups milk	½ cup butter, melted

Cook cauliflower 15 to 20 minutes and break into flowerets. Place in 2-quart casserole. Melt 3 tablespoons butter; stir in flour and cook, stirring well. Blend in milk. Bring to boil and simmer until thickened. Add salt and pepper. Pour over cauliflower. Combine last 3 ingredients. Spoon on top of mixture. Bake at 350° for 30 to 40 minutes. Yield: 6 servings.

Mary Eleanor Colvin

BROCCOLI SUPREME

Wonderful and very easy!

2 (10 ounce) packages frozen chopped broccoli	2 teaspoons chopped onion
	½ teaspoon salt
1 (10¾ ounce) can cream of mushroom soup	dash of pepper
	1 egg, well beaten
½ cup sharp Cheddar cheese, shredded	½ cup cracker crumbs or bread crumbs
½ cup mayonnaise	

Cook broccoli as directed on package. Drain well. In 1½-quart casserole, place all other ingredients and mix well. Add broccoli and mix well again. Sprinkle crumbs on top and bake uncovered at 400° for 20 minutes. Yield: 6 servings.

DeAnna Joel Taylor

FRENCH FRIED ONION RINGS

Marvelous! Very light!

1½ cups all purpose flour	3 very large Bermuda onions
1½ cups beer, active or flat, cold or warm	3 to 4 cups shortening

Combine flour and beer in large bowl and allow batter to sit at room temperature for no less than 3 hours. Twenty minutes before batter is ready, preheat oven to 200.° Place brown paper bags or layers of paper towels on jellyroll pan. Carefully peel papery skins from onions so that you do not cut into outside onion layers. Cut onions into ¼ inch thick slices. Separate slices into rings and set aside. On top of stove, melt enough shortening in a 10-inch skillet to come 2 inches up sides of pan. Heat to 375.° With metal tongs, dip a few onion rings into batter. Carefully place in hot fat. Fry rings, turning once or twice until they are an even, delicate golden brown. Transfer to jellyroll pan. To keep warm, place on middle shelf of preheated oven until all onion rings have been fried. **HINT:** To freeze, fry rings and drain on brown paper at room temperature. Arrange on jellyroll pan and freeze. When frozen, pack in plastic bags and return to freezer. To reheat, arrange on jellyroll pan and place in a preheated 400° oven for 4 to 6 minutes. Yield: 4 servings.

Elizabeth M. Day

FRENCH ONION CASSEROLE

4 medium onions, sliced	1½ cups seasoned croutons
3 tablespoons butter	2 tablespoons butter, melted
2 tablespoons flour	½ cup (2 ounces) Swiss cheese, shredded
dash of pepper	
¾ cup beef bouillon	3 tablespoons grated Parmesan cheese
¼ cup dry sherry	

Cook onions in butter until tender. Add flour, pepper, bouillon, and sherry. Cook and stir until thickened. Put into greased casserole. Toss croutons with remaining butter, spoon on top and sprinkle with cheeses. Place under broiler just until cheese melts. Yield: 6 servings.

Jeanne Hicks

MUSHROOMS BAKED IN CREAM

1 pound mushrooms having
   1 to 2 inch caps
¼ cup butter
1 tablespoon minced onion
⅓ cup (about one slice) fine,
   dry bread crumbs
½ teaspoon salt

¼ teaspoon paprika
⅛ teaspoon pepper
3 to 5 slices bacon
1 cup cream
½ teaspoon Worcestershire
   sauce

Clean mushrooms and remove stems from caps. Set caps aside. Chop stems finely. Heat butter in skillet. Add chopped mushroom stems and onion. Cook slowly for about 5 minutes, gently stirring. Add and toss gently next 4 ingredients. Pile mixture lightly into mushroom caps. Place caps in baking dish. Cut bacon into small pieces to top mushroom caps. Pour remaining 2 ingredients around mushrooms. Bake at 400° for 15 to 20 minutes or until bacon is cooked. Yield: 6 to 8 servings.

Nancy M. Nuzum

ASPARAGUS CASSEROLE

2 (15 ounce) cans asparagus
1 (10 ounce) can cream
   of mushroom soup
½ cup liquid drained
   from asparagus
¼ teaspoon pepper

1 cup shredded American
   cheese
1 cup bread crumbs
4 tablespoons butter
½ cup blanched almonds

Place asparagus in oblong casserole dish. Mix together mushroom soup, liquid drained from asparagus, and pepper. Pour over asparagus. Sprinkle with shredded cheese. Melt butter, then mix with bread crumbs and sprinkle over cheese. Dot with almonds. Bake 45 minutes in 300° oven. Yield: 6 servings.

Mary Lobert

Breads

Old Stone Church, Lewisburg, West Virginia

GREAT FRENCH BREAD

This great bread is easy—even for a beginning baker!

2 cups lukewarm water	1 tablespoon cornmeal
1 package dry yeast	melted butter
1 tablespoon sugar	
2 teaspoons salt	
4 cups bread flour (all-purpose may be substituted)	

In a large bowl, combine water, yeast, sugar, and salt. Stir until dissolved; then add flour. Stir to mix well. Turn dough onto a floured surface. Butter a large bowl and place dough in it to rise. Cover with a damp towel and put in a warm place to rise until double, about 1 hour. Grease a baking sheet and sprinkle with cornmeal. On floured surface, divide dough in half and shape each half into an oblong loaf, without kneading. Place on baking sheet and allow to rise until almost doubled, about 45 minutes. Preheat oven to 425°. Brush loaves with a little melted butter and bake for 10 minutes. Then turn oven temperature down to 375° and bake for 20 minutes. Brush loaves again with melted butter, after baking. Yield: 2 loaves.

Sharon Byrd

SPONGE METHOD FRENCH BREAD

Easy and terrific!

BASIC SPONGE

2 packages dry yeast	¼ cup honey
3 cups warm water	3 cups unbleached flour

Combine yeast with warm water. Stir in honey and flour. Beat until you have a thick, smooth batter. Allow this sponge to rise in a warm place for 1 hour.

¼ cup corn oil	4 to 5 cups unbleached flour
1 tablespoon salt	water

Mix oil and salt. Then gradually stir in enough flour so that mixture leaves sides of bowl. Turn onto floured surface. Knead, adding flour as necessary, until dough is smooth and elastic, about 10 minutes. Place in a greased bowl. Let rise in a warm place for 50 minutes. Punch down dough. Allow to rise 40 minutes. Form into 4 cylindrical loaves. Bake in greased traditional french bread pans for best results. Make diagonal slashes along tops of loaves. Brush with water. Preheat oven to 425°. Let bread rest while oven is heating. Bake for 10 minutes. Brush with water again. Reduce heat to 375°. Bake until crisp and golden brown, about 30 minutes.

Charl Kappel

FEATHER ROLLS

Light as a feather!

2 packages active dry yeast	⅓ cup sugar
½ cup warm water	¼ cup shortening
(105° to 110°)	2 eggs, well beaten
1 tablespoon sugar	4 cups flour
1 cup milk	¼ cup butter, melted
2 teaspoons salt	

Dissolve yeast in warm water; add 1 tablespoon sugar and set aside. Scald milk; add salt, ⅓ cup sugar, and shortening. Cool to lukewarm. Combine milk mixture and yeast together. Add eggs and flour. Beat with mixer until smooth. (This may be mixed in a food processor.) Dough will be sticky. Cover and refrigerate overnight. Divide dough in half. Place half dough on a well-floured board and roll ¼ inch thick. Spread with melted butter. Roll like a jelly roll. Cut into twelve 1-inch pieces. Repeat process with remaining dough. Place in greased muffin pans. Let rise in a warm place until doubled, about 1½ hours. You may wish to preheat your oven to warm and turn to off position placing rolls in oven to rise. Bake 10 minutes at 400.° Yield: 24 rolls.

Vaughn Miller

MOM'S DINNER ROLLS

2 packages active dry yeast	2 teaspoons salt
½ cup warm water	4½ to 5 cups all-purpose
½ cup sugar	flour
½ cup shortening	3 eggs
½ cup milk	

Soften yeast in ½ cup warm water. In a saucepan, combine sugar, shortening, milk and salt. Heat, stirring constantly until sugar dissolves. Place in a large bowl and cool to lukewarm. Stir in 1½ cups flour and beat well. Add softened yeast and eggs; beat thoroughly until smooth. Stir in enough of remaining flour to make a stiff dough. Turn out on a lightly floured surface and knead until smooth and elastic (5 to 8 minutes). Shape into a large ball. Place in a lightly greased bowl, turning once. Cover and let rise in a warm place until doubled in size (about 1 to 1½ hours). Punch dough down and turn out on a lightly floured surface. Cover and let rest for 10 minutes. Shape dough into rolls (crescents or any shape that you desire). Place on lightly greased baking sheets or pans. Cover and let rise in a warm place until doubled, 30 to 45 minutes. Bake at 400° until done, 10 to 12 minutes. Yield: 3 to 4 dozen.

Mary Retta Lavy

FILLED FRENCH ROLLS

Easy and very good! Great for entertaining.

8 French rolls
½ cup softened margarine
½ cup grated Parmesan
  cheese
2 tablespoons salad oil
½ cup parsley, fresh and
  finely chopped

1 clove garlic, finely chopped
  (or equivalent garlic
  powder)
½ teaspoon sweet basil
salt to taste

With roll on its side, cut at ½-inch intervals, not cutting all the way through. Make filling by blending remaining ingredients. Spread filling between each slice. Wrap each roll individually in foil. Bake at 375° for 20 minutes. Rolls may be frozen before baking. Add 10 minutes longer from frozen state. **HINT:** Can do ahead. Yield: 8 servings.

Edi Altmeyer

WHOLE WHEAT BREAD (COOL RISE)

5½ cups all-purpose
  flour
2 cups whole wheat flour
3 tablespoons sugar
4 teaspoons salt

2 packages dry yeast
2 cups milk
¾ cup water
¼ cup margarine

Combine flours and set aside. In a large mixer bowl, mix 2½ cups of the flours, sugar, salt, and yeast. Combine milk, water and margarine in saucepan and heat to 120° to 130°. Add to dry ingredients and beat with electric mixer for 2 minutes at medium speed. Add 1 cup flour and continue beating at high speed for 2 minutes. By hand, stir in additional flour to make a stiff dough. Knead on floured surface until elastic, about 8 minutes. Allow to rest on floured surface covered with a piece of plastic wrap and a towel for 20 minutes. Divide dough in half or fourths. Form into loaves and fit in either two 9x5-inch greased pans or four 7x3-inch greased pans. Cover with plastic wrap and refrigerate for 2 to 8 hours. When ready to bake, remove from refrigerator and allow to stand at room temperature for 10 minutes, while preheating oven to 400°. Bake large pans for 45 minutes or more and small pans for 30 minutes or until done. Test by tapping with a finger to get a hollow sound. Cool on rack. When cool, remove loaves from pans. **HINT:** Freezes well. Wrap tightly in foil to freeze. Yield: 2 large loaves or 4 small loaves.

Nada Heyl

OLD FASHIONED HONEY WHEAT BREAD

Nutritious and delicious!

1½ cups water
1 cup small curd cottage
  cheese
½ cup honey
¼ cup butter or margarine
5½ to 6 cups all-purpose
  flour

1 cup whole wheat flour
2 tablespoons sugar
3 teaspoons salt
2 packages active dry
  yeast
1 egg

In a medium saucepan, heat water, cottage cheese, honey and butter to very warm (120° to 130°). In large bowl, combine warm liquid, 2 cups all-purpose flour, and remaining ingredients; beat 2 minutes at medium speed with a mixer. By hand, stir in enough remaining flour to make a stiff dough. On a well-floured surface, knead dough until smooth and elastic, about 2 minutes. Place in greased bowl. Cover; let rise in warm place until light and doubled in size, 45 to 60 minutes. Grease two 9x5-inch loaf pans. Punch down dough; divide and shape into 2 loaves. Place in greased pans. Cover and let rise until doubled, 45 to 60 minutes. Preheat oven to 350° and bake loaves for 40 to 50 minutes. Loaves should sound hollow when lightly tapped. Remove from pans immediately to cool. **HINT:** Freezes well. Yield: 2 loaves.

Dottie Stobbs

MULTI-GRAIN BREAD

2 packages active dry yeast
1 tablespoon sugar
½ cup warm water (110°)
½ cup rye flour
½ cup whole wheat flour
8 cups all-purpose flour

1 tablespoon salt
1¼ cups whole milk
1 cup water
⅔ cup prepared Ralston
  cereal
1 tablespoon melted butter

In a 5-quart mixing bowl, combine yeast, sugar and ½ cup warm water. Let stand 5 minutes until bubbles appear on surface. In a 4-quart bowl, combine rye, whole wheat, and all-purpose flours with salt and blend well. Set aside. Add milk, 1 cup water and prepared Ralston to yeast mixture, stirring to blend. Gradually add flour mixture, 1 cup at a time, stirring between each addition. Turn onto a floured board and knead well for 10 to 15 minutes, until smooth and elastic. Form dough into a ball and place in an oiled 5-quart bowl, turning dough to coat all sides. Cover and let rise in a warm place for 1 hour. When it has risen to almost double its bulk, punch down and place on a floured board. Let rest, covered, for 10 minutes. Cut into 2 equal pieces and form each piece into a loaf to fit a 9x5x3-inch bread pan. Cover and allow dough to rise again for 1 hour. Brush loaves with melted butter and slash loaves 3 times with a sharp knife. Bake in a preheated 400° oven for 1 hour, or until loaves sound hollow when tapped on top and bottom. Let cool on a wire rack 1 hour before slicing. Yield: 2 loaves.

Susie Godish

HOT SANDWICH BUNS

This is a favorite at Doc and Chickie Williams' house.

3 cups warm water
½ large cake yeast
2 teaspoons salt
1 cup sugar

½ cup lard or
  solid shortening
flour

Mix water and yeast. Then add salt, sugar, and shortening. Add enough flour to make a stiff dough. Mix well and knead until elastic. The more you knead the lighter the bun. Let rise once and punch down. Let rise again. Form into small round balls. Place close together on greased baking sheet but not touching. Press gently with fingertips. Let rise until double; brush with butter. Bake at 375° for 20 to 25 minutes. Yield: 36.

Chickie Williams

POPOVERS

4 eggs	1 cup flour
1 cup milk	1 teaspoon sugar
1 tablespoon melted butter	1 teaspoon salt

Beat eggs until light and fluffy. Add milk and butter, mixing well. Combine dry ingredients and add to egg mixture, beating until smooth. (Alternate method: Put all ingredients in blender or food processor and blend 1 minute, stopping to scrape sides once.) Pour batter into 6 greased custard cups, dividing evenly. Place cups on baking sheet with edges and put in preheated 400° oven for 25 minutes. Reduce oven temperature to 350° and continue baking for an additional 25 minutes. Turn off oven and allow popovers to stand in oven 5 to 10 minutes. Serve hot with butter and jam. These can be used for main dishes by removing the top third. Fill with hot creamed chicken, seafood, cold chicken salad, or shrimp salad and put top on slightly open to reveal filling. Yield: 6 servings.

Jenny Seibert

ONION BREAD

1 cup milk, scalded	2 tablespoons sugar
1 cup water	1 tablespoon salt
¼ cup hot water	6 cups unbleached flour
1 package active dry yeast	½ cup chives
2 tablespoons butter	¼ cup poppy or sesame seeds

Preheat oven to 425°. In large bowl, dissolve yeast in hot water and let stand for 10 minutes. In smaller bowl, combine scalded milk, 1 cup water, butter, sugar, and salt. Mix and add to larger bowl. Add 1 cup of flour, chives, and poppy seeds. Continue adding flour, about 1½ cups at a time, until mixture is stiff enough to come away from sides of bowl (about 2½ more cups). Turn dough out on floured board or counter and work in at least 2 more cups of flour. Form dough into a ball and place in greased bowl. Grease top of dough ball; cover and let stand in a warm place until doubled (about 1 to 1½ hours). Punch the dough down, split, and form into 2 loaves. Place loaves in greased 9x5-inch pans. Bake for 15 minutes at 425°. Reduce heat to 350° and bake for 25 to 30 minutes. **HINT:** This bread is not as intimidating as most breads can be. It keeps its freshness a long time and is particularly good as toast. The onion flavor is very light, a good companion to soups or stews. **HINT:** Recipe can be doubled: Yield: 2 loaves.

Kathleen Gibbs

BREADS

POTATO BREAD

Excellent bread for sandwiches!

2 cups warm water
2 packages dry yeast
½ cup sugar
1 tablespoon salt
1 cup warm mashed potatoes

½ cup soft butter
2 eggs
7½ cups of unsifted
  all-purpose flour

Dissolve yeast in water; add sugar, salt, potatoes, butter, and eggs. Add 3½ cups of flour and beat 2 minutes with a mixer. Add remaining flour and knead. Melt 3 tablespoons butter and grease bread. Place in bowl and put in refrigerator for 2 hours. Take out and work down. Refrigerate overnight. Remove, work down, and knead. Divide dough in half and shape into 2 balls. Place in two 9-inch cake pans. Make 3 slashes across top; let rise in a warm place. Bake at 325° for 35 to 40 minutes. **HINT:** If desired, divide dough in half and make 1 loaf of bread and 24 rolls. Freezes well. Yield: 30 to 40 servings.

Iva White

PEPPERONI BREAD

1 (13¾ ounce) package hot
  roll mix
½ pound pepperoni, thinly
  sliced

½ teaspoon oregano
½ teaspoon garlic powder
2 cups shredded mozzarella
  cheese

Prepare hot roll mix as directed on package, letting it rise once. Knead on well-floured surface until smooth, adding a little all-purpose flour if sticky. Divide dough in half. Roll each half out oblong about ¼ inch thick, and about 16 inches long and 8 inches wide. Place pepperoni on each half. Sprinkle oregano and garlic powder over pepperoni. Then sprinkle the cheese evenly on top. Roll the short ends (8 inch end) up, jelly roll style. Tuck under the ends and pinch seams by moistening. Place far apart on a lightly greased cookie sheet. Let rise again for 30 minutes. Bake in 350° oven for 20 minutes. Slice and serve warm. **HINT:** A rising tip, place plastic wrap over bowl of dough and put in a cold oven with a pan of hot water on the lowest rack underneath the dough. Recipe can be done ahead and can be doubled. Freezes well. Yield: 2 loaves.

Janet Kropp

YORKSHIRE PUDDING

Delicious with roast beef

1 cup flour
½ teaspoon salt
1 cup milk

2 eggs
½ cup butter

Combine flour and salt in small bowl. In another bowl, combine milk and eggs, mixing well. Add flour and salt mixture to milk and eggs; stir well. Melt butter in a 9x9-inch pan. Pour in batter. Bake at 400° for 30 minutes. Yield: 6 to 9 servings.

Lin Companion

BUTTERMILK BISCUITS

These are good and good for you!

2 cups whole wheat flour
¼ cup wheat germ
2 teaspoons baking powder
½ teaspoon baking soda

½ teaspoon salt
5 tablespoons butter, cold
1¼ cups buttermilk

Preheat oven to 400°. In a bowl, combine dry ingredients. Add butter and work into flour with fork until mixture is crumbly. Mix in buttermilk. Dough should be soft, but hold together. (Alternate method: Put dry ingredients in work bowl of food processor with steel blade. Add butter and combine with 10 pulses on/off. Add buttermilk and pulse 3 to 4 times until combined well.) Turn out onto floured board and pat to 1-inch thickness. Cut with 2-inch biscuit cutter. Place on ungreased baking sheet. Bake 10 to 15 minutes until biscuits begin to brown. Serve hot. **HINT:** These are light and fluffy even though made with whole wheat flour. Yield: 10 biscuits.

Joan Corson

BRAN MUFFINS

6 cups bran cereal
2 cups boiling water
1 cup margarine
3 cups sugar
4 eggs, beaten

1 quart buttermilk
5 cups flour
5 teaspoons baking soda
2 teaspoons salt

In a large bowl, pour boiling water over 1 cup of bran and add margarine. In a separate large bowl, mix rest of bran with sugar, eggs and buttermilk. Sift flour, soda, and salt together. Combine all of the ingredients. Bake as needed at 400° for 20 minutes in muffin tins. Batter will keep for 6 weeks in refrigerator. Yield: 4 dozen.

Deborah Sauder

GRAHAM CRACKER MUFFINS

Easy and great for a crowd

1 cup sugar	large pinch salt
1 cup graham cracker	1½ cups raisins
crumbs	1½ cups chopped nuts
1 teaspoon baking powder	3 eggs, beaten

Lightly mix together sugar, graham cracker crumbs, baking powder, salt, raisins, and nuts. Add beaten eggs. Put in greased mini muffin pans. Bake at 350° for 15 to 20 minutes. **HINT:** Freezes well. Yield: 2 dozen.

Jo Kepner

ORANGE MUFFINS

A special treat

1 cup margarine, softened	3 cups all-purpose flour
1 cup sugar	grated rind of 1 orange
2 eggs	¼ cup orange juice
1 teaspoon baking soda	1 teaspoon lemon extract
¾ cup buttermilk	

Cream margarine and sugar until light and fluffy. Add eggs, 1 at a time, beating well after each addition. Combine soda and buttermilk, stirring well. Add to creamed mixture alternately with flour. Stir in orange rind, orange juice, and lemon extract, mixing well. Fill greased, miniature muffin pans ¾ full. Bake at 400° for 10 to 12 minutes or until lightly browned. Remove muffins from muffin tins. Dip top and sides of warm muffins in orange sauce. Place on wire rack to drain.

ORANGE SAUCE

¾ cup orange juice   1½ cups sugar

Combine orange juice and sugar in small saucepan. Bring to a boil, stirring until sugar dissolves. Cool. **HINT:** Freezes well. Yield: 7 dozen.

Marianne Hazlett

GRANDMA ROLF'S BUTTERMILK WAFFLES

2 eggs   2 cups flour
2 cups buttermilk   4 tablespoons melted butter
1 teaspoon baking soda   dash of salt
⅔ teaspoon baking powder

Beat eggs. Add buttermilk. Add baking soda and baking powder; combine well. Add other ingredients. Warm waffle iron and oil surface. When ready, pour in and cook until brown and crispy. Serve immediately with butter and syrup. **HINT:** Easy. Yield: 4 servings.

Dee Dee McCuskey

DUTCH BOY PANCAKES

1 tablespoon butter   ½ cup flour
½ cup milk   dash of nutmeg
2 eggs   powdered sugar

Melt butter in a glass or ceramic 9-inch pie plate. Mix milk, eggs, flour, and nutmeg until blended. Pour batter in pie plate and bake 12 to 15 minutes at 400° until cake rises high. Remove from oven and sprinkle with powdered sugar. **HINT:** Easy. Yield: 2 to 4 servings.

Karen DiOrio

DOUGHNUT BALLS

2 cups sifted flour
⅓ cup sugar
1 tablespoon baking powder
1 teaspoon salt

1 teaspoon nutmeg
¼ cup vegetable oil
¾ cup milk
1 egg, well beaten

Sift together flour, sugar, baking powder, salt, and nutmeg. Then add vegetable oil, milk, and beaten egg. Stir with a fork until thoroughly mixed. Drop by teaspoonsful into deep fryer with oil heated to 375°. Fry until golden brown, about 3 minutes. Drain on absorbent paper. Roll warm puffs in cinnamon-sugar or glaze puffs by dipping into a thin powdered sugar icing. **HINT:** Fry only 5 puffs at a time. If too many puffs are cooked at a time, the fat cools and puffs will become grease soaked. Yield: 2½ dozen puffs.

Etta Rice

BUTTER BREAD

Excellent for a breakfast! Really yummy!

1 package yellow cake mix
  (without pudding)
1 (3 ounce) package vanilla
  instant pudding
4 eggs
¾ cup oil

¾ cup water
1 teaspoon vanilla
1 teaspoon butter extract
¼ cup brown sugar
1 teaspoon cinnamon

GLAZE

½ cup powdered sugar
1 tablespoon milk

1 teaspoon vanilla
1 teaspoon butter extract

Combine cake mix, pudding, oil, water, eggs, vanilla, and butter extract in mixing bowl and beat at medium speed for 8 minutes. Pour batter in two greased 9x5x3-inch loaf pans. Combine brown sugar and cinnamon. Swirl ½ of the mixture in each loaf pan. Bake at 350° for 45 to 55 minutes. Cool 5 minutes before removing from pans. Spread glaze on top of loaves while warm. **HINT:** Can do ahead, freezes well. Yield: two loaves.

Sharon Byrd

SOUR CREAM COFFEE CAKE

½ cup chopped walnuts
2 teaspoons cinnamon
½ cup sugar
½ cup margarine
1 cup sugar
2 eggs

1 teaspoon vanilla
2 cups flour
1 teaspoon baking powder
½ teaspoon salt
1 teaspoon baking soda
1 cup sour cream

Mix walnuts, cinnamon and ½ cup sugar in a small bowl. Set aside. Grease well a 9-inch tube pan. Set aside. Heat oven to 375.° Cream margarine in a large mixing bowl and gradually add 1 cup of sugar. Add eggs 1 at a time and then vanilla, beating until well blended. Sift flour with baking powder, salt, and baking soda. Add this mixture alternately with sour cream to creamed mixture. Spread ½ of batter in greased tube pan. Top with ½ of cinnamon mixture. Top this with remaining batter and then remaining cinnamon mixture. Bake 40 minutes at 375.° Remove cake from oven and let stand in pan on wire rack 30 minutes. Remove outer rim of pan and let cool. Then loosen from tube and remove. **HINT:** Easy and freezes well. Yield: 12 servings.

Jeanne Hicks

GOLDEN CAKE BREAD

*This bread is the first bread I ever made, taught to me by my grandmother.
It is a sweet bread—great for beginners. No kneading!*

1 package dry yeast
¼ cup warm water
1 cup hot scalded milk
½ cup butter
½ cup sugar

2 eggs, beaten
  (reserve 1 tablespoon)
2 teaspoons vanilla
1 teaspoon salt
4 to 4½ cups sifted flour

Soften yeast in ¼ cup warm water. Combine milk, butter, and sugar in large mixing bowl. Cool to lukewarm. Stir in eggs, vanilla, salt, and yeast mixture. Gradually add flour, beating well after each addition. Cover; let rise in warm place until light and doubled in size, about 1 hour. Punch down and let rise again until doubled in size, about 45 minutes. Turn dough into two well-greased 9x5x3-inch pans. Let rise about 45 minutes. Brush with reserved egg. Bake at 350° for 25 to 30 minutes. **HINT:** Easy and freezes well. Yield: 2 loaves.

Lin Companion

BREADS

PARTY ORANGE-PECAN BREAD

¼ cup butter, softened
¾ cup sugar
2 eggs, beaten
2 teaspoons grated
  orange rind
2 cups flour

2½ teaspoons baking powder
1 teaspoon salt
¾ cup orange juice
½ cup chopped pecans

In large mixing bowl, cream butter. Gradually add sugar, mixing well. Add grated orange rind and beaten eggs; mix well. Combine flour, baking powder, and salt in separate medium-size bowl. Add small amounts of this to creamed mixture alternately with orange juice, beginning and ending with flour mixture. Mix well following each addition. Stir in chopped pecans. Pour batter into greased 8x4-inch loaf pan. Bake at 350° for 50 to 55 minutes until tests done. Cool loaf in pan 15 minutes. Remove and cool completely.

GLAZE

2½ teaspoons orange juice   ½ cup sifted powdered sugar

Combine orange juice and powdered sugar to make glaze. Drizzle over loaf. Wrap and store overnight before serving. **HINT:** Freezes well. Yield: 1 loaf

Joyce M. Kalkreuth

OVERNIGHT PECAN BREAKFAST ROLLS

So easy and so good!

butter
1½ cups chopped pecans
1 package frozen dinner rolls
  (12 to a package)

1 (3½ ounce) box butterscotch
  pudding (not instant)
6 tablespoons butter
⅔ cup brown sugar

Heavily butter a 10-inch bundt or tube pan; sprinkle with ½ cup pecans. Arrange rolls on top of pecans; sprinkle pudding over rolls. Melt butter; add brown sugar. Sprinkle over rolls. Top with rest of pecans and place in cold oven overnight. In morning, remove from oven, preheat to 375° and bake for 20 to 25 minutes. Let cool for 1 minute. Then invert on serving platter. Yield: 1 dozen.

Patti Kota

GREEK ALMOND BREAD

Very good!

¾ cup vegetable oil
1 cup sugar
3 eggs
1 teaspoon almond extract

1 teaspoon baking powder
3 cups flour
1 cup finely chopped
  almonds

Mix oil, sugar, and eggs until creamy yellow. Add remaining ingredients. Refrigerate dough for at least 1 hour. Grease cookie sheets and mold dough into 3 long rolls, 1 per cookie sheet. Bake at 350° for 30 minutes. Remove from oven and slice on an angle; then bake slices for 3 to 5 minutes. Store in an airtight container. Yield: 3 rolls.

Betty Kademenos

BANANA NUT BREAD

½ cup butter or margarine
2½ cups sugar
3 eggs
3 ripe bananas
3 cups flour

1 teaspoon baking soda
1 cup milk
½ teaspoon salt
2 teaspoons baking powder
½ cup chopped nuts

Beat butter and sugar. Add eggs, ripe bananas, and flour. Dissolve baking soda in milk; add to mixture. Beat in rest of ingredients. Pour into a greased and floured 10-inch tube or bundt pan or two 9x5-inch loaf pans. Bake at 350° for 1 hour or until tests done. Yield: 16 to 18 servings.

Marlene Yahn

CRANBERRY NUT BREAD

Moist and delicious! Colorful for the holidays!

1 cup sugar	2 teaspoons grated orange
2 cups flour	rind
1½ teaspoons baking powder	1 egg, well beaten
½ teaspoon baking soda	½ cup chopped nuts
1 teaspoon salt	1 cup fresh cranberries,
¼ cup shortening	coarsely chopped
¾ cup orange juice	

Sift together flour, sugar, baking powder, soda, and salt. Cut in shortening until mixture resembles coarse cornmeal. Combine orange juice and grated rind with well beaten egg. Pour into dry ingredients and mix just enough to moisten. Fold in chopped nuts and coarsely chopped cranberries. Spoon into a greased 9x5x3-inch pan. Spread corners and sides a little higher than center. Bake in a 350° oven for about 1 hour or until crust is golden brown and toothpick inserted comes out clean. Remove from pan and cool. Store overnight for easy slicing. **HINT:** Freezes well. Yield: 1 loaf.

Patti Sparachane

BLUEBERRY-NUT BREAD

Delicious!

3 cups flour	½ cup milk
2 teaspoons baking powder	1½ teaspoons lemon juice
1 teaspoon baking soda	1 cup crushed pineapple,
½ teaspoon salt	drained
⅔ cup corn oil	2 cups blueberries
1⅓ cups sugar	1 cup nuts, chopped
4 eggs	

Sift together flour, baking powder, soda, and salt. In large bowl, combine oil, sugar, eggs, milk, lemon juice, and pineapple. Mix thoroughly. Add dry ingredients; beat until blended. Fold in blueberries and nuts. Pour dough into two greased and floured 9x5x3-inch loaf pans. Bake at 350° for 40 to 45 minutes or until tests done. Remove from pans at once and cool on rack. **HINT:** Can be spooned into muffin pans and baked 15 to 20 minutes. Can do ahead and freezes well. Yield: 2 loaves.

Julie Seibert

APRICOT NIBBLE BREAD

2 (3 ounce) packages cream
  cheese, softened
⅓ cup sugar
1 tablespoon all-purpose
  flour
1 egg

1 slightly beaten egg
½ cup orange juice
½ cup water
1 (17 ounce) package
  apricot-nut quick
  bread mix

Combine cream cheese, sugar, and flour; beat in the first egg. Set mixture aside. Combine the slightly beaten egg, orange juice and water. Add quick bread mix, stirring until moistened. Turn two-thirds of apricot batter into greased and floured 9x5x3-inch loaf pan. Pour cream cheese mixture over top; spoon on remaining apricot batter. Bake in a 350° oven for 1 hour and 10 minutes. Cool 10 minutes; remove from pan. Cool. Wrap in foil; refrigerate. **HINT:** Can be frozen. Yield: 1 loaf.

Ann R. Bopp

LEMON BREAD

Great for a special brunch!

½ cup shortening
1 cup sugar
2 eggs, lightly beaten
1¼ cups flour

2 teaspoons baking powder
¼ teaspoon salt
½ cup milk
½ cup chopped walnuts

GLAZE
1 lemon, rind grated,
  then juiced

¾ cup sugar

Grease a 9x5-inch loaf pan. Preheat oven to 350.°In large bowl, cream shortening and sugar. Add eggs, which have been beaten. Sift together flour, baking powder and salt. Add sifted ingredients alternately with milk. Add walnuts and lemon rind. Reserve lemon juice combined with ¾ cup sugar for glaze after baking. Do not over beat bread. Put batter in loaf pan and bake in 350° oven for approximately 1 hour or until loaf tests done. Remove from oven when done, but leave in pan. Using a toothpick or skewer, poke about 25 holes over top of loaf and spoon lemon juice and sugar mixture slowly over loaf. Allow time for liquid to be absorbed. Let loaf remain in pan 20 minutes before turning out to cool completely. **HINT:** Easy and freezes well. Yield: 1 loaf.

Cookbook Committee

STRAWBERRY BREAD

2 (10 ounce) packages frozen strawberries, thawed
4 eggs
1¼ cups vegetable oil
3 cups all-purpose flour
1 teaspoon baking soda
1 teaspoon salt
3 teaspoons cinnamon
2 cups sugar
1¼ cups chopped pecans

In large bowl, mix together strawberries, eggs, and oil. Sift dry ingredients into strawberry mixture. Stir to blend thoroughly. Stir in chopped pecans. Line waxed paper on bottoms of two greased 7⅞x3⅞x2½-inch loaf pans. Pour batter into pans. Preheat oven to 350° and bake for 1 hour or until a toothpick comes out clean. Let cool slightly in pan. Remove from pan, peel off the waxed paper, and cool on a rack. **HINT:** Easy and freezes well. Can also be doubled. Yield: 12 servings.

Joyce McFarland

HOLIDAY PUMPKIN BREAD

2 cups sugar
2 eggs
1 cup canned pumpkin
½ cup oil
2½ cups flour
1½ teaspoons baking soda
1½ teaspoons pumpkin pie spice
1 teaspoon cinnamon
½ teaspoon salt
½ orange, grated (use peel, fruit and juice—disregard large pieces of membrane)
1 apple, peeled, cored and grated
¾ cup golden raisins
1 cup chopped walnuts

In large bowl, beat together sugar, eggs, and pumpkin until blended. Beat in oil. Beat in remaining ingredients until blended. Pour batter into four 3x5-inch greased loaf pans and bake at 350° for 45 to 50 minutes or until tester comes out clean. Cool for 10 minutes. Remove breads from pans and continue cooling on a rack. Place breads back into pans for storing. **HINT:** Bread freezes beautifully! Wrap in a double thickness of plastic wrap and then foil. Remove wrappers when defrosting. Yield: 4 mini-loaves.

Ange Lavy Joel

Desserts

Woodburn Hall, West Virginia University,
Morgantown, West Virginia

CHEESECAKE
(SERVED BY LINDY'S FAMOUS NEW YORK RESTAURANT)

Pastry is a little tricky to roll, but the finished result is wonderful!

PASTRY

2 cups sifted flour
1 cup sugar
2 teaspoons grated lemon
 peel

2 egg yolks
½ cup butter, melted
½ teaspoon vanilla

Prepare pastry by combining flour, sugar, and lemon rind in mixing bowl. Egg yolks, butter, and vanilla are placed in a center well, and mixture is worked with fingers until blended. It may be necessary to add a small amount of water to hold mixture together. Dough is chilled, then rolled out to ⅛ inch thickness. A circle of dough that fits bottom of a 10-inch springform pan is cut out and baked on bottom of springform pan only. Bake at 325° for 10 to 15 minutes or until brown. Remove pan from oven and let cool. Attach sides of springform and lock. Make sure you let bottom cool so that crust will not crack when attaching sides. After securing springform, line sides of pan with remaining pastry.

FILLING

2½ pounds cream cheese
1¾ cups sugar
5 whole eggs
2 egg yolks
¼ cup cream

3 tablespoons flour
¼ teaspoon vanilla
1½ teaspoons lemon rind
1½ teaspoons orange rind

The filling is made by creaming cheese with sugar, adding whole eggs and extra yolks, one at a time, and then beating thoroughly. After cream, flour, vanilla, and lemon and orange rinds are beaten in, mixture is poured into pastry-lined pan. Pan is placed in oven preheated to 500.° After 15 minutes of baking, heat is reduced to 300° and baking is continued until cake has set (about 1½ hours). The cake should be cooled when cut. Yield: 12 servings.

Dorothy Shymansky

MINI CHEESECAKES

2 (8 ounce) packages cream
 cheese, softened
¾ cup sugar

2 eggs
16 "Sunshine" vanilla
 wafers

Preheat oven to 350°. In a mixing bowl, beat together cream cheese, sugar, and eggs until smooth. Fill muffin tins with paper liners. In each paper liner place one (1) "Sunshine" vanilla wafer. Pour filling over vanilla wafer, filling paper liner ¾'s full. Bake at 350° for 15 minutes. Remove from oven and allow muffin tins to stand on a cooling rack for 45 minutes. Cover, and refrigerate or freeze, as desired. **HINT:** "Sunshine" vanilla wafers must be used for this recipe because other brands become too soggy. **HINT:** Recipe must be done ahead of time and can also be doubled. Freezes well. Yield: 16 mini cheesecakes.

Kim Truax

ITALIAN CHEESECAKE

John D. Rockefeller, IV was elected to two four-year terms as West Virginia's governor in 1976 and 1980.

PASTRY

1¼ cups sifted flour
¼ cup sugar
½ teaspoon salt
½ teaspoon grated lemon
  peel

½ cup butter
1 egg yolk
2 tablespoons Amaretto di
  Saronno (liqueur)

Mix first 4 ingredients, then cut in butter until mixture resembles coarse meal. Mix in remaining ingredients and blend well. Press pastry in bottom and up sides of a 9-inch springform pan. Bake at 350° for 15 minutes until dry, but not browned.

FILLING

2 (15 ounce) containers ricotta
  or cottage cheese
4 eggs
½ cup sugar
¼ cup flour
¼ cup Amaretto di Saronno
  (liqueur)

2 tablespoons golden raisins
1 tablespoon candied orange
  peel, finely chopped
1 tablespoon candied lemon
  peel, finely chopped

Blend first 4 ingredients in bowl, then stir in remaining ingredients. Pour filling into crust in pan and bake at 325° for 1 hour, or until cake tests done. Remove cake and cool on rack. Yield: 6 servings.

Jay Rockefeller

CHEESECAKE WITH AMARETTO

Distinct amaretto flavor

CRUST

1½ cups graham cracker
    crumbs
2 tablespoons sugar

1 teaspoon ground cinnamon
6 tablespoons butter, melted

Combine graham cracker crumbs, sugar, cinnamon and butter. Mix well. Press mixture firmly into bottom and ½ inch up sides of 10-inch springform pan.

FILLING

3 (8 ounce) packages cream
    cheese, softened
1 cup sugar
4 eggs
⅓ cup amaretto
1 (8 ounce) carton
    commercial sour cream

1 tablespoon and 1 teaspoon
    sugar
1 tablespoon amaretto
¼ cup toasted slivered
    almonds
1 square chocolate, shaved

Beat cream cheese with electric mixer until light and fluffy. Gradually add 1 cup sugar. Add eggs, one at a time, beating well after each addition. Stir in ⅓ cup amaretto; pour into prepared pan. Bake at 375° for 45 to 50 minutes or until set. Combine sour cream, 1 tablespoon and 1 teaspoon sugar and 1 tablespoon amaretto. Stir well and spoon over cheesecake. Bake at 450° for 7 minutes. Let cool to room temperature; refrigerate 24 to 28 hours before eating. Garnish with almonds and shaved chocolate. **HINT:** Must be done ahead of time. Freezes well. Yield: 10 to 12 servings.

Joyce Kalkreuth

CHOCOLATE CHEESECAKE

Tasty milk chocolate flavor!

1 pound ricotta cheese
½ pound sour cream
1 pound cream cheese
1½ cups sugar
½ cup butter, melted
3 jumbo eggs
3 tablespoons flour

3 tablespoons cornstarch
4½ teaspoons vanilla extract
4½ teaspoons fresh lemon
    juice
1 cup chocolate chips, melted
    and cooled

Place all ingredients, except chocolate chips, in order given in large mixing bowl. Beat with electric mixer; start on low speed, move to medium and finish with about 10 minutes on high speed. Batter should be smooth and liquid. Stir in melted and cooled chips. Grease and lightly flour a round baking pan, 10 inches in diameter and 3 inches high. Pour batter into pan and bake 1 hour in preheated 350° oven. Leave cake in oven with door closed for additional hour after heat is turned off. Cool on rack and refrigerate for storage. **HINT:** Recipe can be done ahead. Yield: 20 servings.

Patricia DeFrancis

TEXAS SHEET CAKE

Chocolate lovers will want this recipe!

BATTER

1 cup margarine
1 cup water
4 tablespoons cocoa,
  heaping
2 cups flour

2 cups sugar
½ teaspoon salt
2 eggs
½ pint sour cream
1 teaspoon baking soda

In large saucepan, bring margarine, water and cocoa to boil. Remove from heat and add flour, sugar and salt. Beat in eggs, sour cream and soda. Pour into large greased cookie sheet with sides. Bake at 375° for 20 to 22 minutes. Prepare icing and ice as soon as cake comes out of the oven.

ICING

½ cup margarine
6 tablespoons milk
4 tablespoons cocoa,
  level

1 cup chopped nuts,
  your choice
1 teaspoon vanilla
1 box powdered sugar

Bring to boil margarine, milk and cocoa. Remove from heat and add nuts, vanilla, and powdered sugar. Ice cake immediately. **HINT:** This can be done ahead of time. Yield: 20 servings.

Dr. Henry Marockie

CAKES

MISSISSIPPI MUD CAKE

Great for a crowd.

BOTTOM LAYER

1 cup margarine
½ cup cocoa
4 eggs
dash of salt
2 cups sugar

1½ cups chopped pecans
1½ cups all-purpose flour
4 cups miniature
  marshmallows

Melt margarine; add cocoa, well-beaten eggs, flour, sugar, and salt. Mix well and add nuts. Place in a greased and floured 13x9x2-inch baking pan. Bake at 350° for 35 minutes. While cake is still hot, pour miniature marshmallows on top.

ICING

2 cups powdered sugar
⅓ cup cocoa
½ cup milk

¼ cup margarine, melted
½ teaspoon vanilla

Beat together powdered sugar, cocoa, milk, margarine, and vanilla. Pour on top of marshmallows while cake is still hot. **HINT:** Recipe can be done ahead. Yield: 18 to 20 servings.

Linda C. Morrison

CHOCOLATE SYRUP CAKE

You can almost taste this when you read the directions.

½ cup butter or margarine
1 cup sugar
4 eggs
1¼ cups sifted all-purpose
  flour

¾ teaspoon baking soda
1 (16 ounce) can chocolate
  syrup
1 teaspoon vanilla extract
1 cup walnuts, chopped

Cream butter and sugar in mixing bowl until fluffy. Add eggs, one at a time. Sift together flour and baking soda. Add flour mixture alternately with chocolate syrup. Add vanilla extract. Mix well. Pour into a 13x9x2-inch greased and floured baking pan. Sprinkle top with walnuts. Bake at 350° for 40 to 45 minutes. Let cool. Yield: 16 Servings.

Sue Ann Messerly

HO HO CAKE

Serves a crowd and kids really like it!

1 devil's food cake mix	1 cup sugar
5 tablespoons flour	½ cup margarine
1¼ cups milk	½ cup shortening

Bake cake mix in a jelly roll pan according to box directions. Cool. Cook flour and milk until thick and then cool. Cream sugar, margarine and shortening and combine with flour mixture. Spread on cake layer. Refrigerate for ½ hour.

ICING

¼ pound margarine	2½ tablespoons hot water
1 egg	1½ cups powdered sugar
1 teaspoon vanilla	
3 (1 ounce) packages	
pre-melted chocolate	

Melt margarine and cool slightly. Add remaining ingredients. Spread gently over first topping. Refrigerate. Yield: 12 servings.

Diana Davis

TURTLE CAKE

A unique taste that satisfies both chocolate and caramel admirers

1 German chocolate cake mix
  or devil's food cake mix

Mix cake according to directions on box. Pour ½ of batter into greased and floured 9x13x2-inch pan. Bake at 350° for 15 minutes. Let cool.

1 (14 ounce) package light	1 (6 ounce) package
colored caramels	chocolate morsels
1 stick margarine or butter	1 cup chopped walnuts
1 (13 ounce) can sweetened	
condensed milk	

CAKES

In a double boiler, melt caramels, margarine and sweetened condensed milk until thick and creamy. When cake is cool, pour caramel mixture over cake. Sprinkle chocolate morsels and chopped walnuts on top of caramel mixture. Pour remaining cake mixture on top. Bake at 350° for 20 minutes. After cake cools, may top with powdered sugar or whipped cream. Yield: 24 to 26 servings.

Vicky Pascu-Godwin

LEMON SHEET CAKE

Easy and great for a crowd

1 unprepared box lemon
  cake mix
4 eggs, two beaten ahead of
  time
¼ pound melted butter or
  margarine

1 (16 ounce) box powdered
  sugar
1 teaspoon vanilla
1 (8 ounce) package cream
  cheese

Grease and flour jelly roll pan. Mix together cake mix, two unbeaten eggs and melted butter. Spread mixture in jelly roll pan with greased rubber spatula. Cover pan. In mixing bowl, combine sugar, beaten eggs, vanilla and cream cheese. Beat until smooth. Pour this mixture over layer in jelly roll pan. Bake at 350° for 20 to 25 minutes or until sides are golden and center is firm. Yield: 15 to 20 servings.

Genny McIntyre

POUND CAKE

Guests will give a lot of compliments to this.

1 pound butter, softened
1 pound sugar
1 pound eggs (approximately
  8 large eggs)

1 pound cake flour
1 teaspoon baking powder
1 teaspoon vanilla
1 teaspoon almond extract

Cream butter; add sugar gradually to butter and beat until light and fluffy. Add eggs, one at a time, beating 1 minute after each egg. Gradually add cake flour sifted with baking powder. Fold in vanilla and almond extract. Bake in a 10-inch greased and floured angel food cake pan for 1 hour and 15 minutes at 350°. Yield: 16 servings.

Mrs. S. G. Nazzaro

CRUMB CAKE

Tastes great with a glass of cold milk!

CAKE

2¼ cups flour
2 cups brown sugar
½ teaspoon baking powder
1 teaspoon nutmeg
1 teaspoon salt, scant

¼ cup shortening
1 egg
1 teaspoon baking soda
1 cup sour milk (1 cup milk
 and 1 tablespoon vinegar)

Combine flour, brown sugar, powder, nutmeg, salt and shortening with a pastry blender. To this, add egg, soda and sour milk; mix well with a spoon. Pour in a 9x13x2-inch greased and floured pan and cover with topping.

TOPPING

½ cup flour
½ cup brown sugar

1 tablespoon butter
cinnamon

Mix all ingredients except cinnamon with a pastry blender. Sprinkle on batter. Sprinkle over this evenly with cinnamon. Bake at 350° for 35 minutes. Cool, cut and serve from pan. **HINT:** Must be done ahead of time. Yield: 12 to 15 servings.

Debbie Kahle

FRESH PEACH CAKE

*Sharon Rockefeller, West Virginia's First Lady from 1977
to the present, chairs the board of directors of the
Corporation for Public Broadcasting*

½ cup margarine
1½ cups brown sugar, firmly
 packed
1 egg
2 cups flour
1 teaspoon baking soda

dash of salt
1 cup buttermilk
4 peaches, peeled and
 diced
½ cup sugar
1 teaspoon cinnamon

Cream margarine and brown sugar until light. Add egg. Sift together flour, soda, and salt and add alternately with buttermilk. Stir in peaches. Pour into greased 9x13-inch pan. Sprinkle mixture of sugar and cinnamon on top. Bake at 350° for 30 to 35 minutes. Yield: 10 to 12 servings.

Sharon Rockefeller

CAKES

RED VELVET CAKE

½ cup solid shortening
1½ cups sugar
2 eggs
2 tablespoons cocoa
2 ounces red food coloring
1 teaspoon salt

1 teaspoon vanilla
1 cup buttermilk
2½ cups sifted cake flour
1 teaspoon baking soda
1 tablespoon vinegar

Cream shortening and sugar well. Add eggs and beat well. Mix cocoa
and coloring in small bowl and then add to shortening. Combine salt,
vanilla, and buttermilk; add to above mixture with sifted flour and beat
well. Add soda to vinegar and then fold into batter. Pour batter into
3 greased 8-inch cake pans. Bake at 350° for 25 to 30 minutes.

ICING

1 cup milk
5 tablespoons flour
1 cup sugar

1 cup margarine or
butter, salt-free
1 teaspoon vanilla

Cook milk and flour until it forms a stiff paste, stirring constantly. Cool,
then chill in refrigerator. Cream sugar and butter well; add cold paste,
a little at a time. Beat until like whipped cream and then add vanilla.
Ice cake and store in refrigerator. **HINT:** Use salt-free butter for white
icing. Yield: 12 servings.

DeAnna Joel Taylor

SCOTCH CAKE

A very moist cake

BATTER

2 cups flour
2 cups granulated sugar
½ cup margarine
½ cup shortening
4 tablespoons cocoa

1 cup water
1 teaspoon baking soda
1 teaspoon cinnamon
2 eggs
1 cup buttermilk

Combine flour and sugar. In saucepan, combine margarine, shortening, cocoa, and water. Heat until melted and blended. Pour into flour
and sugar mixture; combine well. Add soda, cinnamon, eggs and buttermilk. Mix well. Bake in 11x16x2-inch greased and floured pan for
30 minutes in 400° oven.

ICING

½ cup margarine
4 tablespoons cocoa
6 tablespoons milk
1 (16 ounce) box powdered
  sugar

1 teaspoon vanilla
1 cup chopped nuts, optional

Five minutes before cake has finished baking, prepare icing. Heat margarine, cocoa and milk until blended. Remove from heat and stir in powdered sugar and vanilla. Add nuts, if desired. Spread over hot cake. Cool before cutting. Yield: 10 servings.

Margaret Ann Barry

NANNY'S APPLESAUCE CAKE

Great for Christmas!

2½ cups applesauce
¾ cup vegetable shortening
3 teaspoons baking soda
1½ cups sugar
3 cups flour
dash of salt
¾ cup cherry preserves

1 cup chopped dates
1½ cups pecans
¾ cup raisins
¾ teaspoon cinnamon
¾ teaspoon nutmeg
¾ teaspoon cloves
1 cup mixed fruit, optional

In saucepan, add applesauce, shortening, soda, and sugar. Heat and cool. Put in a large mixing bowl and add flour and salt. Add cherry preserves. Lightly flour dates, nuts, and raisins and add to mixture. Fold in cinnamon, nutmeg, and cloves. The pan should be greased, floured, and lined with waxed paper. Bake at 300° for 2 hours and 30 minutes. **HINT:** Do not double. Yield: 2 loaves or 1 tube pan.

Mrs. Edgel Grose

WHITE ICING

Light and fluffy!

1½ cups powdered sugar
6 tablespoons butter
¼ cup shortening

1 egg white
½ teaspoon vanilla

Cream sugar, butter and shortening. Slowly add unbeaten egg white and vanilla. Beat well. Yield: Frosting for a double-layered cake.

Cynthia D. Kennard

PUMPKIN CAKE ROLL

You won't believe the delectable taste! Guests will rave!

3 eggs
1 cup granulated sugar
⅔ cup canned pumpkin
1 teaspoon lemon juice
¾ cup all-purpose flour
1 teaspoon baking powder

2 teaspoons cinnamon
½ teaspoon ginger
½ teaspoon nutmeg
½ teaspoon salt
1 cup chopped walnuts

Beat eggs at high speed 5 minutes; gradually beat in sugar. Stir in pumpkin and lemon juice. Stir dry ingredients together; fold into pumpkin mixture. Grease and cover with sheet of waxed paper or foil a 15x10-inch pan and spread batter evenly. Top batter with nuts. Bake at 375° for 15 minutes. Turn out on tea towel sprinkled with powdered sugar. Starting at narrow end roll towel and cake together while warm. Let cool. Unroll and spread filling over cake. Reroll and chill.

FILLING

1 cup powdered sugar
1 (8 ounce) package
  cream cheese, softened

4 tablespoons margarine
½ teaspoon vanilla

Combine sugar, cream cheese, margarine and vanilla. Beat until smooth.
HINT: Can be iced with whipped cream. Yield: 8 to 10 servings.

Diane Montani

CARROT CAKE AND NUT ICING

2 cups flour
1 teaspoon cinnamon
1 teaspoon baking powder
¼ teaspoon salt
1 teaspoon baking soda
1¾ cups salad oil

2¼ cups sugar
5 eggs
2 cups finely grated raw
  carrots
1 cup coarsely chopped nuts

Sift together first 5 ingredients. Mix oil, sugar, and eggs. Blend in slowly dry ingredients. Then add carrots and nuts. Place in a greased 13x9x2-inch pan. Bake at 325° for 50 to 60 minutes.

ICING

8 ounces cream cheese,
  room temperature
½ cup butter or margarine

1 pound package powdered
  sugar
1 teaspoon vanilla

Mix thoroughly and spread on cooled cake. Sprinkle with finely chopped nuts. **HINT:** Raisins or seedless grapes may also be added. Yield: 14 to 16 servings.

Mrs. Daniel B. Crowder

CARROT CAKE

A special cake! Really good!

4 eggs
1½ cups sugar
1½ cups oil
2 cups flour
2 teaspoons baking powder

2 teaspoons baking soda
2 teaspoons cinnamon
2 teaspoons salt
2 cups shredded carrots
1 cup chopped nuts

Combine eggs, sugar, oil, flour, baking powder, baking soda, cinnamon, salt, carrots and chopped nuts. Mix well and pour into 13x9x2-inch baking pan. Bake at 350° for 40 to 45 minutes.

ICING

4 ounces cream cheese,
  softened
½ pound powdered sugar

1 teaspoon vanilla
½ teaspoon salt

Combine all ingredients. Mix well and ice cooled cake. **HINT:** Cake batter and icing may be mixed in food processor. Yield: 12 to 15 servings.

Ruth Smith

BOILED RAISIN CAKE

This was my grandmother's recipe

1 pound seedless raisins
½ cup shortening
1½ cups sugar
2 eggs, beaten
2 cups all-purpose flour
1 teaspoon baking soda

1 teaspoon nutmeg
2 teaspoons cinnamon
1½ teaspoons salt
1 cup raisin water
1 cup nuts

CAKES

Wash raisins and cover well with water. Simmer for 20 minutes. Drain raisins and save 1 cup liquid. Cream shortening and sugar; add well-beaten eggs and blend thoroughly. Sift together flour, soda, spices and salt. Starting with dry ingredients, add alternately with raisin liquid to creamed mixture. Fold in raisins and nuts. Grease and flour well a 10-inch tube pan. Bake at 325° for 1½ hours. Test after 1 hour with toothpick. Frost with caramel icing or serve plain. Hard sauce is good, too. Yield: 12 to 14 servings.

Thelma M. Henry

BÛCHE DE NOËL

CAKE

3 eggs
1 cup sugar
⅓ cup water
1 teaspoon vanilla
¾ cup all-purpose flour
1 teaspoon baking powder

¼ teaspoon salt
1 cup whipping cream
2 tablespoons sugar
1½ teaspoons powdered
  instant coffee

Heat oven to 375°. Line jelly roll pan, 15½x10½x1-inch, with aluminum foil or waxed paper, greased. Beat eggs in small mixer bowl on high speed until very thick and lemon colored, about 5 minutes. Pour eggs into larger mixer bowl; gradually beat in 1 cup sugar. Beat in water and vanilla on low speed. Gradually add flour, baking powder, and salt, beating until batter is smooth. Pour into pan, spreading batter to corners. Bake until wooden pick inserted in center comes out clean, 12 to 15 minutes. Loosen cake from edges of pan; immediately invert on towel generously sprinkled with powdered sugar. Remove foil; trim stiff edges of cake, if necessary. While hot, roll cake and towel from narrow end. Cool on wire rack at least 30 minutes. Make butter cream frosting.

156

BUTTER CREAM FROSTING

3 egg whites, room
  temperature
dash of salt
dash of cream of tartar
1⅓ cups sugar
⅓ cup water
½ pound unsalted butter,
  room temperature, cut into
  small pieces

1 tablespoon vanilla extract
8 (1 ounce) squares semi-
  sweet chocolate, melted
  in top of double boiler
2 tablespoons rum or strong
  coffee

In a large mixing bowl with electric mixer, beat egg whites until frothy. Add salt and cream of tartar and beat until stiff. Meanwhile, dissolve sugar and water in a medium saucepan. Turn up heat and cook without stirring, until sugar reaches the soft-ball stage, 236° to 238° on a candy thermometer. Mixing constantly, slowly pour sugar syrup into whites. Do not be concerned with the syrup that splatters onto the sides of the bowl. Continue beating until mixture feels cool to the touch, approximately 10 minutes. When cool, beat in butter a small piece at a time. Add vanilla. Remove ¾ cup butter cream to a small bowl. Beat chocolate and rum or coffee into remaining butter cream. Unroll cool cake. Spread cake with half the chocolate butter cream. Reroll as tightly as possible. Roll cake onto heavy foil. Wrap cake in foil and refrigerate or freeze until well chilled, about 1 hour. It is easier to frost when it is very cold. Leave remaining chocolate and plain butter cream at room temperature. Place chilled cake on a serving platter lined with strips of waxed paper. Refrigerate plain butter cream for 15 minutes, while frosting and decorating cake. Cut a small diagonal piece off each end of cake. Place these pieces on top of log to make stumps. Frost entire cake, except ends of logs and stumps, with chocolate butter cream. Run tines of fork along the frosting to resemble bark. Spread a layer of plain cream on ends of logs and stumps. Place butter cream in pastry bag fitted with small writing tip. Pipe in circles on ends of logs and stumps to resemble age rings. Blur slightly with toothpicks. Refrigerate until firm or may be refrigerated overnight. Carefully remove strips of waxed paper. Bring to room temperature 1 hour before serving. Yield: 12 servings.

Janie Altmeyer

OLD-FASHIONED APPLE PIE

Very high pie! Will need a spill catcher underneath.

½ cup raisins
½ cup nuts
1 cup brandy
3 to 5 cups sliced apples
½ cup oats

1 cup dark brown sugar
1 cup white sugar
dash of lemon juice
1 tablespoon cinnamon
¾ teaspoon nutmeg

Presoak raisins and nuts in brandy for 3 hours. Make one 10-inch piecrust. Place apples in pie shell. Sprinkle oats, sugars, lemon juice, cinnamon, and nutmeg on apples. Drain raisins and nuts when plump. Sprinkle over pie ingredients. Place only amount of ingredients that will comfortably fit in pie shell. The rest can be placed in a casserole and baked separately.

CRUMB TOPPING

⅓ cup sugar
¾ cup flour

6 tablespoons butter

Cut ingredients into butter. Sprinkle over pie. Bake at 400° until brown (about 1 hour) or until pie bubbles out of the crust. Turn on broiler for 2 minutes to brown top of pie. Yield: 8 servings.

Dee Dee McCuskey

APPLE CRUMB PIE

This is an apple lover's dream.

6 McIntosh apples
1 cup sugar
1 teaspoon cinnamon

⅓ cup butter
¾ cup flour
pastry for 9-inch shell

Pare apples and cut into thick slices. Mix half sugar with cinnamon and sprinkle over apples. Put into unbaked pastry shell. Blend flour, remaining half cup of sugar, and butter; work into small crumbs. Sprinkle crumbs over apples. Bake in hot oven, 425°, for 10 minutes and then reduce heat to 350° and bake for 35 minutes more. Yield: 6 to 8 servings.

Bob Dix
Publisher, The Times-Leader

APPLE CRISP

Easy and great for a crowd

5 to 6 peeled and sliced
  apples
1 cup sifted flour
¾ teaspoon salt
1 egg
½ to 1 cup sugar, depending
  on tartness of apples

1 teaspoon baking powder
⅓ cup melted and cooled
  shortening
½ teaspoon cinnamon

Place in greased 6x10-inch baking dish peeled and sliced apples. Mix together with fork flour, salt, egg, sugar and baking powder until mixture is crumbly. Then sprinkle crumbly mixture over apples. Pour melted and cooled shortening over ingredients in baking dish. Sprinkle with cinnamon. Bake in 350° oven for 30 to 40 minutes until apples are cooked. Yield: 6 to 8 servings.

Helen Gompers Beltz

BRANDY ALEXANDER PIE

CRUST

2 cups crushed vanilla
  wafers

¼ cup margarine

Mix and press into a 9-inch pie pan. Bake for 10 minutes at 375.°(A regular piecrust may also be used.)

FILLING

36 large marshmallows
½ cup milk
¼ cup crème de cocoa

¼ cup brandy or cognac
½ pint whipping cream

Place marshmallows and milk in top of double boiler. Stir with wooden spoon until marshmallows are well coated. Place pan over hot water and stir frequently until marshmallows are completely melted. Remove from heat and add creme de cocoa and brandy. Refrigerate for 50 minutes. Remove and mix well with portable mixer. Fold in ½ pint whipping cream, whipped. Put in pie shell, decorate with chocolate curls, and refrigerate until serving. **HINT:** Must be done ahead of time. Yield: 6 servings.

Mrs. R. L. Meek

PIES

MILLIONAIRE PIE

Very rich!

1 can sweetened condensed
  milk
¼ cup lemon juice
1 can crushed pineapple,
  drained
1 can diced peaches, drained

1 large container prepared
  whipped topping
1 dozen cherries
1 (9 inch) graham cracker
  crust

Mix above ingredients except for cherries. Pour into graham cracker crust. Place cherries on top of the filling. Chill for 8 hours. Yield: 8 servings.

Beth Ann Dague

BLUEBERRY PEACH COBBLER

Finished product looks like you slaved all day in the kitchen—but you didn't!

1 package blueberry
  muffin mix
½ cup sugar
1½ teaspoons cinnamon
4 tablespoons butter or
  margarine

½ cup chopped pecans
2 cans peach pie filling
1 teaspoon almond extract

Preheat oven to 350.° Wash blueberries; set aside. Combine dry muffin mix, ¼ cup sugar and ½ teaspoon cinnamon. Cut in butter, then stir in nuts. In a 13x9x2-inch pan, combine pie filling, ¼ cup sugar, 1 teaspoon cinnamon, almond extract and drained blueberries. Spoon crumb topping over peach mixture. Bake for 35 to 40 minutes until topping is brown. Serve warm. Delicious with ice cream. Yield: 12 to 14 servings.

Edi Altmeyer

RASPBERRY PASTEL PIE

Other frozen fruits can be successfully substituted.

2 (10 ounce) packages frozen
  raspberries
water
1 (6 ounce) package
  raspberry gelatin

1 quart vanilla ice cream
2 (8 inch) graham cracker
  crusts

160

Drain berries. Add water to juice to make 2½ cups of liquid; heat to boiling. Dissolve gelatin in hot liquid. Add ice cream by spoonfuls, stirring until melted. Chill until thick, not set. Fold in berries. Pour into two 8-inch pie shells. Chill until firm, at least 4 hours. Yield: 12 servings.

Jane Fleming

LEMON CHIFFON PIE

Melts in your mouth!

MERINGUE PIE SHELL

3 egg whites
⅛ teaspoon cream of tartar
pinch of salt
¾ cup sifted sugar

¾ cup finely chopped
  walnuts or pecans
1 teaspoon vanilla

Beat egg whites with rotary beater until foamy. Add cream of tartar and salt; beat until they stand in soft peaks. Gradually add sugar and beat until very stiff. Fold in chopped nuts and vanilla. Turn meringue into buttered 9-inch pie plate and make a nestlike shell, building up sides ½ inch above edge of the plate. Bake in slow oven (300°) for 50 to 55 minutes and cool meringue after it is removed.

FILLING

1½ teaspoons plain gelatin
⅓ cup cold water
4 egg yolks
⅓ cup granulated sugar
1 tablespoon grated lemon
rind

¼ cup lemon juice
4 egg whites
¼ teaspoon salt
½ cup granulated sugar

Add gelatin to cold water and set aside. Put yolks in double boiler; stir in ⅓ cup sugar, lemon rind, and juice. Cook over hot water for 5 minutes or until thick, stirring all the time. Stir in gelatin until thoroughly melted. Remove from heat. Beat egg whites and salt until they stand in stiff peaks when beater is raised. Add slowly, ½ cup sugar while beating stiff. Fold, gently, into hot mixture. Turn into pie shell. Put into ice box to cool **HINT:** Can be done ahead of time. Yield: 6 to 8 servings.

Sue Farnsworth

LEMON MERINGUE PIE

This is very good and lemony!

FILLING

1 cup sugar	4 egg yolks
juice of 3 lemons	2 egg whites
rind of 1 lemon, grated	1 tablespoon cornstarch
¼ cup butter	1 (9 inch) pie shell, baked

In top of double boiler, combine sugar, lemon juice, lemon rind and butter. Add egg yolks, egg whites, and cornstarch. Mix well. Cook over simmering water, until thickened. Fill baked pie shell.

MERINGUE

2 egg whites	¼ cup sugar

Beat egg whites until foamy. Gradually add sugar, beating until stiff peaks form. Spread over filling to the crust rim. Bake in a 300° oven until lightly browned, about 15 minutes. Yield: 6 to 8 servings.

Mrs. Louis D. Corson

FROZEN LIME PIE

E. Gordon Gee became West Virginia University's 19th president in 1981, after serving as dean of the WVU College of Law.

1 cup graham cracker crumbs	1½ cups sweetened condensed milk
¼ cup butter, melted	1 cup lime juice
1 teaspoon sugar	1 lime rind, grated
2 eggs, separated	sliced extra limes for garnish
few drops green food coloring	

Mix together crumbs, butter, and sugar. Turn into 8-inch pie plate. Press against bottom and sides of pan to make an even shell. Chill while making filling. Using wooden spoon, beat egg yolks with the sweetened condensed milk. Do not use electric mixer. Gradually stir in juice and rind. Beat egg whites until stiff and dry; fold into lime mixture. Add food coloring. Pour into pie shell and freeze until firm. Allow to stand at room temperature 10 to 15 minutes before serving. Yield: 6 to 8 servings.

E. Gordon Gee

PEANUT BUTTER PIE

Especially good for a warm weather dessert

1 (8 ounce) package cream
  cheese, softened
¾ cup crunchy peanut butter
1 cup powdered sugar
½ cup milk

1 (9 ounce) carton non-dairy
  topping, thawed
1 (9 inch) graham cracker
  crust
¼ cup chopped peanuts

Whip cream cheese until fluffy. Beat in peanut butter and powdered sugar. Slowly add milk, blending thoroughly. Fold topping into mixture. Pour into piecrust and sprinkle with chopped peanuts. Freeze until firm. Remove from freezer 20 minutes before serving. **HINT:** Must be done ahead of time. This recipe is easy and can be doubled. Yield: 6 to 8 servings.

Ann Welty

PECAN PIE

3 eggs, beaten
1 cup sugar
6 tablespoons butter or
  margarine, melted
½ cup dark corn syrup

1 teaspoon vanilla
1 cup pecans, pieces
  or halves
1 (9 inch) pie shell,
  unbaked

Beat eggs thoroughly with sugar, corn syrup and melted butter or margarine. Add pecans and vanilla. Pour into unbaked pie shell. Bake at 350° for 45 minutes to 1 hour, or until knife inserted halfway between outside and center comes out clean. **HINT:** Large whole pecans look nicer. Yield: 8 servings.

Elizabeth M. Day

CHEESE CUSTARD PIE

1 (8 ounce) package of
  cream cheese, softened
⅔ cup sugar
2 tablespoons flour
2 eggs

1¼ cups milk
1 tablespoon vanilla
1 (9 inch) pie shell,
  unbaked

In large mixing bowl, blend together cream cheese, sugar, flour and eggs. Add milk and vanilla to above ingredients and blend well. (Mixture will be slightly lumpy.) Pour into unbaked pie shell. Bake at 350° for 35 minutes. Let cool completely before serving. Yield: 6 to 8 servings.

Holly Joseph

PASTRY FOR PIE SHELL
This will work every time!

SINGLE CRUST

1½ cups flour
½ teaspoon salt
½ cup shortening

4 to 5 tablespoons cold water

DOUBLE CRUST

2 cups flour
1 teaspoon salt
⅔ cup shortening

5 to 7 tablespoons cold water

Sift flour and salt. Cut in shortening until pieces are size of peas. Sprinkle water, one tablespoon at a time, tossing flour mixture with fork after each addition. Knead 10 or 12 times to form dough. Do not handle dough excessively or it will be tough. Flatten on floured surface and roll out with floured rolling pin. Divide double crust before rolling out. To bake, preheat oven to 450°. Prick entire crust. Bake 12 minutes. **HINT:** It is best to use ice cold water.

Laura Carter

NO WEEP MERINGUE
Really does work!

½ cup water
¼ cup sugar
1 tablespoon cornstarch

dash of salt
3 egg whites

Combine all ingredients except egg whites and cook over low heat until mixture turns white. Cool. Beat 3 egg whites until very stiff and add cooled mixture. Spread over pie and bake at 350° until brown, 12 to 15 minutes.

Sharon Byrd

MERINGUE ICE CREAM PIE

Delicious on a warm summer evening!

3 eggs whites	1 (9 inch) baked pie shell
¼ teaspoon cream of tartar	1 quart ice cream
¾ cup sugar	Sauce which compliments
3 tablespoons cocoa	ice cream

Preheat oven to 325°. Beat egg whites until frothy and add cream of tartar; beat until soft peaks form. Gradually add sugar and beat until stiff. Sift cocoa over meringue and fold in carefully. Spread evenly over baked pie shell taking care to seal over the fluted edges. Bake 25 minutes. Cool thoroughly. Fill with scoops of ice cream. Freeze. Drizzle with sauce just before serving. Ice cream and sauce suggestions: Cherry ice cream or mint ice cream with marshmallow sauce or coffee ice cream with chocolate sauce. Yield: 6 servings.

Laura Carter

YUMMY ICE CREAM PIE

Good dessert in either summer or winter!

¼ cup brown sugar	½ cup margarine, melted
1 cup flour	⅔ cup chocolate sauce
½ teaspoon salt	(can be purchased)
½ cup finely chopped nuts	1 pint any flavor
(peanuts, walnuts,	ice cream, softened
almonds can be used)	

Put brown sugar, flour, salt, and nuts in blender. Grind. Pour in melted margarine. Spread on cookie sheet and bake 10 to 15 minutes at 400.° Take off cookie sheet and place into bowl; stir while hot, crumble. (Will be crunchy.) Press ¾'s of mixture into a 9 inch pie plate. Drizzle ½ of chocolate sauce over. Freeze bottom crust. Fill with softened ice cream and sprinkle remaining crumbs on top. Add rest of sauce; freeze overnight. Take out of freezer 10 minutes before serving. **HINT:** Other sauces are good, too. Yield: 8 servings.

Ann Gleason

BARS AND BROWNIES

O'HENRY BARS

1 cup sugar
1 cup white corn syrup
1½ cups peanut butter
6 cups Kellogg's®
  Special K®cereal

6 ounces semi-sweet
  chocolate chips
6 ounces butterscotch chips

Mix sugar and syrup; bring to a boil. Stir peanut butter into hot mixture. Pour this mixture over cereal. Mix well. Press into a greased 9x13x2-inch pan. Melt chocolate chips and butterscotch chips over low heat. Spread on top. Yield: 4 to 5 dozen.

Sharon Byrd

LINDA'S CHOCOLATE CHIP BARS

Fantastic!

1 cup solid shortening
½ cup brown sugar
½ cup white sugar
3 egg yolks
1 tablespoon cold water
2 cups flour

1 teaspoon baking powder
¼ teaspoon soda
¼ teaspoon salt
6 ounces chocolate chips
3 egg whites
1 cup brown sugar

Cream together shortening, ½ cup brown sugar, white sugar, egg yolks and water. Add dry ingredients except for chocolate chips. Mix well. Grease a 9x13x2-inch pan and press dough down to make a crust. Pour chocolate chips over dough. Beat egg whites to a soft peak and then add 1 cup brown sugar, beating until stiff. Spread egg white mixture over chocolate chips. Bake at 350° for 30 minutes or until golden brown. Yield: 4 dozen.

Dottie Stobbs

CHEWY OATMEAL BARS

1 cup all purpose flour
¾ teaspoon baking soda
½ teaspoon salt
1 teaspoon cinnamon
¾ cup vegetable shortening

1⅓ cups brown sugar, packed
2 eggs
1 teaspoon vanilla extract
2 cups uncooked oatmeal,
  old fashioned

In small mixing bowl, blend flour, soda, salt, and cinnamon together and set aside. In large bowl, cream shortening, sugar, vanilla, and eggs until smooth. Add flour mixture. Blend together; add oatmeal. Spread into 9x13x2-inch baking pan and bake for 15 to 20 minutes at 350.° Yield: 4 dozen.

Dea Kennen

VAMINO BARS

Anise Catlett is the wife of Gale Catlett,
West Virginia University's head basketball coach since 1978.

½ cup butter or margarine
¼ cup sugar
5 tablespoons cocoa
1 teaspoon vanilla

1 egg
1½ cups graham cracker
  crumbs
½ cup nuts, chopped

Combine first 5 ingredients and bring to a boil over low heat, stirring constantly for 2 minutes. Then add graham cracker crumbs and nuts. Spread this mixture in a 13x9x2-inch pan. Pat down and cool.

TOPPING
½ cup margarine
6 tablespoons milk
4 tablespoons instant
  vanilla pudding

4 cups powdered sugar
3 tablespoons margarine
3 (1 ounce) squares
  semi-sweet chocolate

Combine margarine, milk, pudding and powdered sugar. Spread this mixture over bottom layer. Melt chocolate and margarine. Spread on top. Refrigerate. Cut in squares to serve. Yield: 4 dozen.

Anise Catlett

SODA CRACKER BARS

Easy recipe for children to make

soda crackers
1 (12 ounce) package
  chocolate chips

1 cup margarine
1 cup brown sugar

BARS AND BROWNIES

Line 9x13x2-inch pan with foil. Add layer of soda crackers on bottom of pan. In saucepan, melt margarine; add brown sugar. Bring to a boil and simmer 3 to 5 minutes. Pour over soda crackers. Bake 5 to 7 minutes at 400.° Remove from oven and let sit 1 minute. Scatter chips over mixture and spread as soon as they melt. Put in refrigerator until hard; break into small pieces. Yield: 3 dozen.

Julie Seibert

BUTTERSCOTCH BROWNIES

2 cups light brown sugar
½ cup (¼ pound) melted
   butter or margarine
2 eggs

1 teaspoon vanilla
1 cup flour
1 cup pecans

Stir together sugar and melted butter. Stir in eggs, vanilla and flour. Add pecans. Pour into buttered 9-inch square pan. Bake at 350° for 35 minutes. Yield: 1½ dozen.

Ella Jane Howard

BEST GOOEY BROWNIES

Rich cookie

1 (12 ounce) package semi-
   sweet chocolate chips
1 can sweetened condensed
   milk
2 tablespoons butter
1 cup butter, melted
2¼ cups packed brown
   sugar (1 box)

2 eggs
2 cups flour
1 teaspoon salt
1 teaspoon vanilla
¾ cup pecans or walnuts,
   chopped

Melt first 3 ingredients, stirring slowly. Stir sugar into melted butter and add to chocolate mixture. Beat in eggs and add remaining ingredients. Pour mixture into a greased 13x9x2-inch pan and bake at 350° for 30 to 35 mintues. Best if still gooey in center. Cut warm. **HINT:** Will freeze nicely. Also divine if cut in larger squares, while warm, and served with ice cream as a dessert.

Stephanie Bloch

CHOCOLATE MINT BROWNIES

1 (22½ ounce) box brownie
  mix, with or without nuts

1½ teaspoons peppermint
  extract

Follow directions on brownie mix, added peppermint extract. Bake in greased and floured 15x10x1-inch jelly roll pan for 25 minutes at 350.° Cool.

ICING

¼ cup butter or margarine,
  softened
3 cups powdered sugar
2 to 4 tablespoons milk

dash of salt
1 teaspoon peppermint
  extract

Cream butter, half of sugar, and other ingredients in a large mixing bowl. Gradually add remaining sugar. Frost cooled brownies. Yield: 4 dozen.

VARIATION

Melt 1 ounce unsweetened chocolate and 2 teaspoons butter and drizzle over icing.

Joanne Winters

BEST EVER BROWNIES

These are super!

2 cups granulated sugar
1 cup salad oil
1 teaspoon vanilla
1¾ cups all-purpose
  flour
½ teaspoon salt

½ cup cocoa
5 eggs
6 ounces semi-sweet
  chocolate chips
1 cup chopped nuts, optional

Put all ingredients except chips in large bowl. Mix well with spoon. Pour into greased 9x13x2-inch baking pan. Sprinkle chips on top and bake at 350° for 25 to 30 minutes or until toothpick inserted in center comes out clean. Yield: 4 to 5 dozen.

Donna M. Glass

COOKIES

BLOND BROWNIES

2¾ cups cake flour	3 eggs
1 teaspoon salt	1 teaspoon vanilla
2½ teaspoons baking powder	1 cup chopped pecans
1 (16 ounce) box brown sugar	1 (12 ounce) package
½ cup and 5 tablespoons	chocolate chips
butter	

In saucepan, melt brown sugar and butter. Let cool. In large mixing bowl, add cake flour, salt and baking powder. Add brown sugar and butter mixture. Add eggs, one at a time, vanilla, chopped pecans, and chocolate chips. Put in a 9x13x2-inch greased pan. Bake at 300° for 35 to 45 minutes. Yield: 4 dozen.

Mary Jo Thompson

SHORTBREAD HEARTS

These cookies are simple, but delicate and melt in your mouth.
Good accompaniment to fresh fruit, ice creams, or mousses!

¾ cup butter (unsalted	2 cups flour
preferred)	1 egg yolk beaten with
⅔ cup sugar	1 teaspoon water
2 egg yolks	

Place steel blade in food processor bowl. Add butter and sugar and process until creamy. Add 2 egg yolks and mix for 30 seconds. Add half of flour and process until smooth. Add remaining flour and process to blend. Wrap dough in a piece of plastic wrap and refrigerate until dough is well chilled. When ready to bake, remove ½ dough, leaving rest in refrigerator until needed. Roll out on well-floured board to thickness of ⅛ inch. Cut with cookie cutters. I like to use a 2-inch heart cutter. Place on greased cookie sheet. Chill cut cookies until all dough has been rolled and cut. Preheat oven to 350°, brush top of each cookie with some of egg yolk-water mixture and sprinkle with a little sugar (can use colored sugar for added sparkle). Bake 8 to 10 minutes until just barely golden. Cool on rack. **HINT:** Easy and freezes well. Yield: 50 cookies.

Joan Stamp

MISS STEWART'S FROSTED ORANGE COOKIES

Easy and great for a crowd.

COOKIE

1 cup shortening
1½ cups sugar
2 eggs
grated rind of one large
 orange
½ cup strained orange juice
 from an orange

4 cups sifted flour
⅛ teaspoon salt
1 teaspoon baking soda
1 teaspoon baking powder
1 cup sour milk (1 cup
 milk and 1 tablespoon
 vinegar)

Cream shortening and sugar together. Add eggs, grated orange rind, and orange juice. Add flour, salt, soda and baking powder alternately with sour milk. Drop from teaspoon on greased cookie sheet. Bake for 10 minutes in a 375° oven. Allow cookies to cool before frosting.

FROSTING

1 pound box powdered
 sugar

¼ cup butter or margarine
juice of one orange

Mix powdered sugar, butter and orange juice. **HINT:** May be sprinkled with green sugar crystals for Christmas. This recipe can be done ahead of time and can also be doubled. Yield: 100 cookies.

Gertrude Beltz

BEST PEANUT BUTTER COOKIES

A real winner with both kids and adults

1 cup shortening
1 cup white sugar
1 cup brown sugar
2 well-beaten eggs
1 teaspoon vanilla

3 cups flour
½ teaspoon salt
1½ teaspoons baking soda
1 cup peanut butter (crunchy
 or smooth)

Cream sugars and shortening until fluffy. Add eggs and vanilla and beat. Sift flour with salt and soda into bowl with creamed ingredients. Mix well. Add peanut butter; mix again, then knead until smooth. Roll into ¾- to 1-inch balls. Place 1 inch apart on greased cookie sheets. Flatten with fork, crisscross. Bake at 400° for 5 to 10 minutes. Yield: 3 to 4 dozen.

Laura Carter

CHEESECAKE COOKIES

1 cup flour
⅓ cup butter, softened
⅓ cup firmly packed
   brown sugar
½ cup chopped nuts
1 (8 ounce) package
   cream cheese

¼ cup sugar
1 egg
2 tablespoons milk
2 tablespoons lemon juice
½ teaspoon vanilla

In large bowl, combine flour, butter, and brown sugar. Blend until particles are fine. Stir in nuts. Reserve 1 cup for topping. Press remaining mixture in ungreased 8-inch square pan. Bake at 350° for 12 to 15 minutes until lightly brown. In same mixing bowl, combine remaining ingredients. Blend well. Spread on crust. Sprinkle with reserve crumbs. Bake at 350° for 25 to 30 minutes. Cool and cut into squares. **HINT:** Recipe can be doubled.

Carol Aaron

CHOCOLATE NUT DROPS

You will have trouble stopping after just one of these!

½ cup shortening
¾ teaspoon salt
1 teaspoon vanilla
⅔ cup brown sugar,
   firmly packed
1 egg, well beaten

2 ounces chocolate, melted
1¾ cups sifted flour
½ teaspoon baking soda
½ cup milk
½ cup nut meats, chopped

Combine shortening, salt and vanilla. Add brown sugar gradually and cream well. Add beaten egg and mix thoroughly. Add chocolate and blend. Sift flour and baking soda together and add to creamed mixture alternately with milk, mixing well. Add nuts and blend. Drop from tablespoon onto greased baking sheet. Bake in 350° oven for 10 to 15 minutes. Yield: 2½ dozen nut drops.

Adelaide H. Kuntz

GRAHAM CRACKER CRISPS

1 (16 ounce) box honey
   graham crackers
½ cup butter

½ cup margarine
½ cup granulated sugar
½ cup nuts, chopped

Line two 15x10x1-inch jelly roll pans with foil. Break crackers in fourths. Bring butter, margarine and sugar to boil and boil for 3 minutes. Pour over crackers, sprinkle with chopped nuts, and bake at 350° for 10 minutes. Remove from pan and cool on rack. **HINT:** For best results, must use half butter and half margarine. Yield: 7 to 8 dozen.

Ruth Mozley

MOCHA TORTE

Excellent for a dinner party

4 teaspoons instant coffee
1 tablespoon boiling water
4 eggs, separated
½ cup sugar
1½ to 2 cups frozen whipped
  topping

3 tablespoons coffee liqueur
1 graham cracker crust
  recipe

Dissolve instant coffee into boiling water. Set aside. Separate 4 eggs. Beat egg whites until stiff. Add sugar gradually. Beat until glossy. Fold in coffee mixture and set aside. Beat egg yolks until thick and light in color. Set aside. Add coffee liqueur to whipped topping. Fold 3 mixtures together. Pour into an 8-inch springform pan that has been lined with the graham cracker crust recipe. Cover and freeze overnight. Before using, decorate with almond slivers or shaved chocolate. Store leftover in freezer.

CRUST
1¼ cups graham cracker
  crumbs
¼ cup sugar

¼ cup butter, softened

Blend cracker crumbs, sugar, and butter with fork. Firmly press mixture to bottom and sides of 8-inch springform pan. Chill 30 minutes before adding mocha torte. Yield: 10 servings.

Barbara Strauss

COLD RASPBERRY SOUFFLÉ

A real pleaser!

1 envelope unflavored gelatin
2 tablespoons cold water
1 (10½ ounce) package
  frozen raspberries,
  thawed

¾ cup sugar
1 cup egg whites
  (approximately 7 to 8 eggs)
1 cup heavy cream

Tear off piece of waxed paper long enough to surround 1-quart soufflé dish. Fold in half lengthwise and spray with vegetable oil spray or lightly oil. Put oiled side inward around dish allowing 2 inches to extend above rim. In medium saucepan, soften gelatin in water. Purée and strain raspberries, discarding seeds. Add puréed berries to gelatin with sugar, and heat, stirring until gelatin and sugar are dissolved. Transfer to large bowl and chill until cool but not gelled. Beat egg whites until stiff and fold into berries. Then whip cream and fold into berry mixture. Carefully spoon into soufflé dish. Mixture should rise above rim. Chill overnight or freeze until several hours before serving. Remove collar, when ready to serve, and accompany with sauce.

SAUCE

1 (10½ ounce) package frozen
  raspberries, thawed
¼ cup sugar

2 tablespoons framboise
  (a raspberry liqueur)

Purée and strain berries; discard seeds. Combine with sugar and framboise. Yield: 8 to 10 servings.

Joan C. Stamp

LEMON SOUFFLÉ

6 eggs, separated
½ cup granulated sugar
1½ tablespoons gelatin
juice of 2 lemons

grated rind of ½ lemon
1 cup heavy cream,
  stiffly whipped

TOPPING

1 cup heavy cream,
  stiffly whipped

1 cup fresh strawberries

Beat egg yolks with sugar until thick and light in color. Soften gelatin in lemon juice. Dissolve by placing over pan of boiling water. When gelatin is dissolved, add it to egg mixture along with grated lemon rind. Set mixture over bowl of cracked ice until it begins to thicken. Fold in whipped cream. Beat egg whites until stiff and fold into lemon mixture. Pour into a 1½-quart soufflé dish and chill for 2 hours or until set. Decorate top with freshly whipped cream just before serving. Garnish with fresh strawberries. **HINT:** This recipe must be done ahead of time. Yield: 6 to 8 servings.

Marianne Hazlett

CHOCOLATE CROWN MOUSSE

Great for a crowd

20 lady fingers	1½ cups brown sugar
½ cup dry sherry	¼ teaspoon salt
1 (12 ounce) package chocolate chips	4 eggs, separated
2 (8 ounce) packages cream cheese	2 teaspoons vanilla
	2 cups heavy cream, whipped

Split lady fingers lengthwise and place cut side down on a cookie sheet in 375° oven for 5 minutes. Cool about 10 minutes and brush cut side with sherry. Place about 24 pieces around sides of 10-inch springform pan. Arrange remaining pieces on bottom of pan. Melt chocolate over hot water; let cool about 10 minutes. Blend softened cheese and half the sugar. Beat in egg yolks, one at a time. Stir in cooled chocolate. Beat egg whites with salt until stiff but not dry. Beat in vanilla and remaining sugar until stiff and satiny. Fold egg whites and whipped cream into chocolate mixture and pour into pan of lady fingers. Chill overnight or at least 5 hours. **HINT:** This recipe must be done ahead of time and it also freezes well. Yield: 20 servings.

Janie Altmeyer

CHILLED DESSERTS

CHOCOLATE MOUSSE

2 egg yolks
dash of salt
2 cups whipping cream
6 ounces semi-sweet
  chocolate chips
1 (1 ounce) square
  unsweetened chocolate

1 (8 ounce) container
  whipped topping
chocolate shavings for
  garnish

In small mixing bowl, combine egg yolks and salt, and beat until light yellow. In large mixing bowl, beat whipping cream until fluffy. In double boiler, melt together both chocolates. Combine egg yolks with whipping cream. Fold in chocolate mixture and gently stir until whipping cream is absorbed. Transfer to 1-quart serving bowl and refrigerate for at least 4 hours. Before serving, garnish with whipped topping and chocolate shavings. **HINT:** Easy and can be done ahead of time. Yield: 8 to 10 servings.

Sally Bodkin

RUSSIAN CREAM

Easy and great for a crowd.

1 envelope gelatin
½ cup cold water
½ cup sugar
1 cup light cream

1 cup sour cream
1 teaspoon vanilla
1 (10 ounce) package
  frozen strawberries

In large bowl, soften gelatin in cold water for 5 minutes. Meanwhile, mix sugar and light cream in small saucepan and heat until lukewarm. Pour cream mixture over gelatin and stir until dissolved. Cool in refrigerator, about 1 hour, until it begins to thicken. Add sour cream and vanilla; beat at low speed until smooth. Pour into mold or custard cups which have been rinsed in cold water. Chill. Serve with thawed frozen or cooked strawberries on top. **HINT:** Recipe must be done ahead and can be doubled.

Marilyn Whitt

OREO ICE CREAM DESSERT

Don Nehlen, head coach of the West Virginia University
football squad during the 1980s, is a proven motivator
of players with a reputation as a winner.

½ gallon vanilla ice cream
1 (8 to 9 ounce) container
frozen whipped topping,
thawed

1 large package Oreo®
cookies, crushed

Soften ice cream and mix with whipped topping. Add Oreo cookies to this mixture after they have been crushed, filling and all. Place mixture in tube pan and freeze. Unmold to serve. Yield: 10 servings.

Don Nehlen

BUSTER BAR DESSERT

Fantastic! Rich and excellent!

1 (15 ounce) package Oreo®
Chocolate Sandwich
Cookies
½ cup melted butter
1 (13 ounce) can evaporated
milk
½ cup butter, solid
⅔ cup chocolate semi-sweet
morsels

2 cups powdered sugar
1½ cups spanish peanuts
½ gallon vanilla ice cream
1 (9 ounce) container frozen
whipped topping

Crush Oreos and mix with melted butter. Pat all but ¾ cup into a 9x13x2-inch pan and freeze 1 hour. Soften ice cream. Spread on crust and freeze. In a saucepan, combine milk, butter, chocolate chips and powdered sugar. Boil 8 minutes and stir while cooking. Cool to lukewarm. Spread peanuts over ice cream. Pour cooled chocolate mixture over peanuts and freeze again. Spread whipped topping over sauce. Sprinkle with reserved crumbs. Freeze. Remove from freezer 15 minutes before serving. Cut in small serving pieces. Yield: 14 to 16 servings.

Dottie Stobbs

ITALIAN TORTONI

Great ending to an Italian dinner!

1 cup dry crushed coconut
  macaroons
2 cups whipping cream,
  well chilled
½ cup powdered sugar

pinch of salt
¼ cup rum
1½ teaspoons vanilla
¼ cup sliced almonds,
  toasted

Combine macaroons, 1 cup cream, sugar, and salt in medium bowl and blend well with spoon. Cover and refrigerate 30 to 45 minutes until macaroons are soft. Whip remaining cup of cream until soft peaks form. Fold in macaroon mixture with rum and vanilla. Spoon into small dessert dishes or wine glasses. Sprinkle with almonds, cover, and freeze for about 2 hours before serving. **HINT:** This recipe must be done ahead of time. Also, this is a very rich dessert and a small serving is satisfying! Yield: 8 to 10 servings.

Ange Lavy Joel

ECLAIR DESSERT

BOTTOM LAYER

2 (3½ ounce) packages
  instant vanilla pudding

1 box graham crackers
8 ounces whipped topping

Line 13x9x2-inch pan with crackers. Prepare pudding using 3 cups milk instead of 4 cups. Fold in whipped topping. Pour half of the mixture over crackers. Repeat the cracker layer and pour other half of pudding mixture onto second layer of crackers. Layer top with crackers.

TOPPING

3 tablespoons margarine,
  softened
2 teaspoons light corn syrup
3 tablespoons milk
1 teaspoon vanilla

2 packages liquid semi-sweet
  chocolate (or 2 ounces
  semi-sweet chocolate
  squares)
1½ cups powdered sugar

Mix topping and frost. Chill. Yield: 8 to 10 servings.

Jill Ruckman

STRAWBERRY DELIGHT

1 cup all-purpose flour
½ cup pecan pieces
½ cup melted butter
  or margarine
½ cup firmly packed
  brown sugar
1 (10 ounce) package frozen
  strawberries, thawed

1 cup sugar
2 teaspoons fresh lemon juice
2 egg whites
1 cup whipping cream,
  whipped
sliced fresh strawberries,
  optional

Combine flour, pecans, butter and brown sugar in an 8-inch square baking pan; stir well. Bake at 350° for 20 minutes, stirring occasionally; cool. Combine strawberries, sugar, lemon juice and egg whites in large mixing bowl and beat at high speed 10 to 12 minutes or until stiff peaks form. Fold in whipped cream. Press ⅔ of crumb mixture into 9-inch springform pan. Spoon in strawberry mixture. Sprinkle remaining crumbs on top. Freeze until firm. Garnish with fresh strawberries, if desired. Yield: 8 to 10 servings.

Sally Goodspeed Riley

STRAWBERRIES JESSICA

Classy ending to a meal!

½ cup coffee cream
½ cup sour cream
juice of ½ lemon
⅓ cup powdered or
  granulated sugar

10 to 20 strawberries cut in
  half (depending on size)
few drops vodka

Mix coffee cream, sour cream, lemon juice, and sugar. Fold in strawberries (save a few for top of sherbet glass). Fill glasses. Sprinkle few drops vodka. **HINT:** Looks elegant in tall, thin continental wine glasses. This recipe can be doubled. Yield: 4 to 6 servings.

Gladys Van Horne
Family Section Editor
Wheeling News-Register

CHILLED DESSERTS

DREAM PUDDING DESSERT

½ cup margarine, softened
1¼ cups flour
1½ cups ground nuts
1 (13½ ounce) carton whipped
  topping
1 (8 ounce) package cream
  cheese, softened

1 cup powdered sugar
2 (3 ounce) packages, any
  flavor, instant pudding
3 cups milk

Mix margarine, flour and ½ cup ground nuts. Pat into bottom of
9x11-inch baking dish. Bake 20 minutes at 375°. Cool completely. Mix
half of whipped topping with cream cheese and powdered sugar. Mix
well. Pour over bottom layer when cool. Mix pudding with milk. Pour
over creamed cheese mixture. Spread other half of whipped topping over
top. Sprinkle with nuts. Refrigerate for 2 hours or overnight. Yield: 12
to 14 servings.

Carrie Brandt

VELVET PUDDING

The meringue is easy and good!

1 quart whole milk
4 egg yolks
1 whole egg
3 tablespoons flour,
  well sifted

½ cup sugar
1½ teaspoons vanilla
4 egg whites
few grains salt
8 tablespoons sugar

In a large mixing bowl, to 1 quart whole milk, add the 4 egg yolks and
1 whole egg. Mix flour with ½ cup sugar. Blend flour/sugar mixture
with milk and eggs and cook, stirring, in double boiler until consistency of thick custard. Add 1 teaspoon vanilla and pour in a 9x5-inch
glass pan. In separate bowl, place 4 egg whites. Add salt. Beat until
quite stiff; then add 8 tablespoons sugar gradually, beating all the time.
Add ½ teaspoon vanilla. Add meringue by large spoonfuls. Bake at 350°
until meringue peaks brown. Yield: 8 servings.

Sue S. Farnsworth

Nationality
and
Heritage

Stonewall Jackson's Birthplace,
Clarksburg, West Virginia

MOUSSAKA (GREECE)

3 eggplants
2 pounds ground lamb
  or ground beef
¼ cup butter
¼ teaspoon salt
¼ teaspoon pepper
2 onions, chopped
1 garlic clove, minced
¼ teaspoon cinnamon

¼ teaspoon nutmeg
½ teaspoon fines herbes
2 tablespoons parsley
1 (8 ounce) can tomato sauce
½ cup red wine
olive oil
grated Parmesan cheese
2 cups bechamel sauce

Peel and cut eggplant lengthwise into ½-inch slices; sprinkle with salt, and set aside on paper towels to absorb moisture. To prepare meat sauce, sauté ground meat in butter with salt and pepper, onions, and garlic, crumbling meat with a fork. When meat is evenly browned, add cinnamon, nutmeg, fines herbes, parsley, and tomato sauce; stir and mix well. Add wine and simmer for 20 minutes. Wipe salted eggplant; lightly oil a skillet with pastry brush and quick fry the eggplant over very high heat; lay on paper towels to drain. (By following this method carefully, your eggplant will not absorb too much oil.) In greased 9x13x2-inch baking pan, place layer of eggplant, top with meat mixture, sprinkle with grated cheese, and cover with remaining eggplant. Sprinkle with grated cheese and cover with bechamel sauce. Top moussaka lavishly with grated cheese and bake at 350° for 1 hour. Allow to cool and then cut into 3-inch squares.

BECHAMEL SAUCE

¼ cup butter
3 tablespoons flour
2 cups milk, warmed

dash of salt and
  white pepper
3 egg yolks, optional

Melt butter in a pan; add flour and stir until smooth. Lower heat and gradually add hot milk, stirring constantly until it thickens. Season with salt and pepper. For a very rich sauce, add 3 egg yolks to sauce after it is cooked. Yield: 12 servings.

Laura Pappas

BAKED STUFFED LEBANESE KIBBI (LEBANON)

1 cup bulgur wheat	1 teaspoon pepper
1 pound ground round	½ teaspoon crushed mint
steak or lamb	¼ teaspoon cinnamon
1 small onion, grated	stuffing
1 teaspoon salt	

Prepare bulgur wheat. Pour into bowl; add just enough cold water to cover wheat; set bowl in refrigerator until ready to use (about 15 minutes) until wheat doubles in size. Mix meat, onion, salt, pepper, mint, and cinnamon. Remove wheat from refrigerator; press between palms to squeeze out excess moisture, and mix with meat mixture, kneading well. Divide into 2 equal portions, and smooth first half into a layer on bottom of greased 13x9x2- inch glass baking pan. Spread stuffing evenly over pan. Smooth remaining meat mixture over all. With knife (dipped often in cold water), cut diagonal lines to make diamond shaped wedges, cutting all the way to bottom and around edges. Dot with butter and bake in preheated 350° oven for 30 minutes.

STUFFING

½ pound ground beef	¼ teaspoon pepper
1 onion, chopped	½ teaspoon salt
3 tablespoons pine nuts	

Brown ground beef and onion. Drain fat and mix in pine nuts, pepper and salt. Yield: 8 servings.

Cynthia Reasbeck

SAUSAGE JAMBALAYA (NEW ORLEANS, LOUISIANA)

Part of each Mardi Gras celebration

1 pound smoked sausage
1 cup cooked and diced
   chicken or turkey
1 (10 ounce) can condensed
   cream of mushroom soup
1 medium onion, chopped

1½ stalks celery, chopped
¼ green pepper, chopped
2 tablespoons Worcestershire
   sauce
1 cup uncooked rice

Cut sausage into 1-inch pieces. Mix with chicken, soup, onion, celery, green pepper, Worcestershire sauce, and rice. Place in a 3-quart greased casserole. Bake, uncovered, at 350° for 1 hour or until all liquid is absorbed. Yield: 4 servings.

Kitty J. Doepken
Food Editor
Wheeling News Register

CHICKEN WITH CASHEW NUTS (TAIWAN)

2 pounds chicken breast
   meat
1 tablespoon soy sauce
1½ tablespoons cornstarch
5 cups peanut oil
2 tablespoons peanut oil

1 teaspoon ginger, chopped
seasoning sauce
½ cup roasted cashew nuts
8 pieces dry red pepper,
   optional

SEASONING SAUCE

2 tablespoons soy sauce
1 tablespoon wine
½ tablespoon brown vinegar
1 tablespoon sugar

1 teaspoon cornstarch
½ teaspoon salt
1 teaspoon sesame oil

Debone chicken, cut into 1-inch cubes; add 1 tablespoon soy sauce and 1½ tablespoons cornstarch. Stir evenly in one direction and soak for ½ hour. Set aside. Wipe clean and remove tips and seeds of dry red pepper. Cut into 1-inch long pieces. Set aside. Fry soaked chicken in 5 cups boiling peanut oil for half a minute. Remove chicken and drain oil from frying pan. Heat 2 tablespoons oil to fry dry red pepper until it turns black. Add ginger and chicken; stir quickly. Next add seasoning sauce; stir until thickened and heated thoroughly. Remove from heat. Add cashew nuts. Mix well just before serving. Yield: 4 servings.

Mrs. Yueh-Chin Carson

PIROHY (SLOVAK-AMERICAN-POLISH)

DOUGH

1 cup flour
1 egg

¼ teaspoon salt
4 tablespoons cold water

Mix all above ingredients to make medium soft dough. A little more flour may be needed. Knead well until smooth. Roll out on a floured surface until very thin. Cut into 2-inch squares. Place 1 teaspoon filling on each square. Fold into triangles. Pinch edges well. Drop into salted, boiling water until pirohy comes to top. Cook for 5 minutes. Strain and rinse with cold water. Place in a serving dish and pour melted butter over. Pirohy may also be fried in butter in a skillet after following directions for boiling.

CHEESE FILLING

½ cup extra dry
   cottage cheese
1 egg yolk

1 teaspoon butter
pinch of salt

Mix thoroughly.

POTATO FILLING

1 large potato,
   cooked and mashed

1 cup shredded sharp or
   longhorn cheese

Mix thoroughly while potato is hot. Yield: 2 dozen.

Judy Stechly

KOOGLE
(ISRAEL-PINEAPPLE CHEESE NOODLE PUDDING)

1 pound medium noodles	1 cup milk
1 pint sour cream	1 teaspoon salt
1 pound cottage cheese	3 teaspoons vanilla
7 eggs, beaten	1 (8¼ ounce) can crushed
1½ cups sugar	pineapple, drained
½ cup butter	cinnamon sugar

Cook noodles in boiling water according to package directions. Fold together noodles, sour cream, cottage cheese, eggs, sugar, butter, milk, salt, vanilla, and pineapple. Keep covered in refrigerator overnight. Next day, grease one 13x9x2-inch pan with butter. Spread noodle mixture evenly in pan and top with cinnamon sugar. Bake at 325° for 1½ hours. Yield: 12 servings.

Irene Romano

SPINACH PETA (GREECE)

5 (10 ounce) boxes frozen chopped spinach	1 medium onion, grated
	5 eggs, beaten
1 (15 ounce) small curd cottage cheese	1 teaspoon cracked pepper
	1 pound butter, melted
¾ cup Parmesan cheese	1 pound filo leaves
½ pound feta cheese	

Squeeze chopped spinach until all moisture has been removed. Combine with next 6 ingredients. Divide filo leaves. Layer filo leaves with melted butter until ½ leaves and butter are used. Place in 11x15-inch pan. Pour in spinach mixture and repeat process with filo leaves and butter, reserving enough butter to brush over top after cutting through with sharp knife to make squares. Bake at 350° for 50 minutes. Yield: 20 servings.

Betty Kademenos

CREAM OF VEGETABLE SOUP (ITALY)

My version of a soup we enjoyed in Rome at Tre Scalini

1 small onion, chopped
2½ tablespoons olive oil
½ tomato, peeled and
  chopped
1 quart boiling water
2 to 3 potatoes, diced
1 garlic clove, minced

4 small to medium zucchini,
  chopped
1½ stalks celery, diced
salt and pepper
¼ cup cream or milk
½ (10 ounce) package frozen
  peas, optional

Sauté onion in oil until golden brown. Add tomato and cook until soft. Add 1 quart boiling water, potatoes, and garlic. Cook on high flame 10 minutes. Add zucchini, celery, peas, and salt and pepper to taste. Cook 15 to 30 minutes or until vegetables are soft. Put through a food mill twice. Add milk or cream, ¼ cup or more, to your liking. Bring almost to a boil and serve. Yield: 6 servings.

Irene Romano

BORSH (UKRAINE-BEET SOUP)

4 medium beets, cut in thin
  strips
1 large onion, chopped
¼ medium-sized cabbage,
  shredded
2 carrots, chopped fine
3 stalks celery, diced
3 tablespoons parsley,
  chopped

1½ tablespoons salt
2 cups tomato juice
¼ cup butter
1 cup whipping cream,
  unwhipped
⅛ teaspoon sour salt,
  optional

Boil beets in 4 quarts of water over medium heat for ½ hour. Add onion, cabbage, carrots, celery, parsley, and salt. Boil for ½ hour more. Add tomato juice. Bring to a boil and boil for about 2 minutes. Add butter and remove from heat. If desired, sour salt may be added. Lastly, add whipping cream. Heat but do not boil. Serve hot. Yield: 6 servings.

Hali Exley

WEDDING SOUP (ITALY)

Delicious and nutritious!

2 quarts chicken broth
2 carrots, sliced thin
1 pound escarole, cooked
   and drained

25 small meatballs (about ¼
   teaspoon meat), cooked
⅛ pound spaghetti noodles,
   broken in very small pieces

Boil broth; add carrots, escarole, and meatballs. Boil 10 minutes, until carrots are tender. Add spaghetti noodles and cook 5 to 10 minutes longer. Serve with Parmesan cheese. **HINT:** Easy and freezes well. Yield: 4 to 6 servings.

Fran Schmitt

ITALIAN WEDDING SOUP (ITALY)

1 whole chicken
4 celery stalks
1 medium-size onion
1 pound hamburger
5 (10 ounce) packages frozen
   spinach

10 chicken bouillon cubes
6 ounces grated Romano
   cheese
12 eggs, whipped

Place chicken, celery, and onion in a very large pot. Add water to cover and boil until chicken falls off bones. While this is cooking, brown hamburger, separating into small chunks and cook spinach according to package directions. Remove chicken, celery, and onion from pot. Clean all meat from chicken, breaking into bite-size pieces. Replace chicken pieces into pot of broth along with browned hamburger and drained spinach. Add enough water to double broth. Bring to boil. Add bouillon cubes and Romano cheese. Whip eggs in separate bowl. Pour eggs in soup and as they touch the soup whip very fast. When serving, sprinkle with Romano cheese. **HINT:** Recipe freezes well and can be doubled. Yield: 20 servings.

Patti Sparachane

POTATO TOMATO OMELET (PERSIA)

A nice summer dish served with thin Persian bread and yogurt

4 tablespoons margarine	½ teaspoon salt
1 large onion, finely chopped	¼ teaspoon pepper
2 tablespoons lemon juice	4 eggs
1 large potato	¼ teaspoon salt
2 large tomatoes, sliced	¼ teaspoon cinnamon

In a 10- or 12-inch skillet, melt margarine and sauté onions until golden. Remove onions from skillet and add lemon juice to onions; let stand. Peel and slice potatoes ¼ inch thick and rinse them in cold water. Fry potatoes in same skillet in which onions were sautéed. Fry until golden brown. Arrange tomato slices over potatoes and add onions. Add salt and pepper. Cover and simmer for 10 minutes on low. Beat eggs with salt and cinnamon. Pour over potato mixture. Cover and let cook on low another 10 minutes. Cut into portions and serve. Yield: 4 to 6 servings.

Marylon Rahbar

"VINAIGRETTE" BEET-POTATO SALAD (RUSSIA)

2 to 3 beets, boiled and cut into julienne strips	1 onion, minced
1 carrot, boiled and cut into small pieces	8 potatoes, boiled and diced
½ to 1 fresh apple, peeled and diced	1 dill pickle, diced
1 cup cooked pinto beans	salt to taste
½ (16 ounce) bag sauerkraut	1 teaspoon sugar or more, to taste
	oil

Mix all ingredients together with enough oil to bind but not so much that it will be runny. **HINT:** "Bags" of sauerkraut may be found in the meat section of supermarkets. Yield: 6 to 8 servings.

Irene Romano

NATIONALITY AND HERITAGE

TUCSON TACOS (TUCSON, ARIZONA)

½ pound ground chuck
¼ teaspoon salt
⅛ teaspoon pepper
¼ teaspoon cumin
¼ teaspoon ground oregano
1 package corn tortillas
shredded lettuce

finely chopped tomatoes
shredded Cheddar cheese
chopped black olives
sour cream
guacamole
your favorite taco sauce

Spread meat into a thin circle. Season with salt, pepper, cumin, and oregano and pound in with back of fork. Spread small amount of meat mixture on half of each tortilla, pressing down firmly. Fry in 1 inch hot oil. (Lay tortilla in flat, let soften for a few seconds, then fold over.) Drain on paper towels. Place remaining ingredients in separate bowls and let guests choose any or all toppings. Note: Fry longer time for crisp tacos, shorter for soft—you have to watch them and adjust to your taste.

GUACAMOLE

1 or 2 ripe avocados   1 to 2 tablespoons taco sauce

Mash avocados and mix in taco sauce. Yield: 4 servings.

Jo Lamb

SHOYU CHICKEN (HAWAII)

1 frying chicken
2 tablespoons powdered
  ginger
2 tablespoons dry mustard
2 tablespoons brown sugar

2 tablespoons grated
  orange peel
½ cup soy sauce
1½ cups water

Cut chicken into serving size pieces. Place in large pot (dutch oven size). Sprinkle chicken with ginger, mustard, sugar, and organge peel. Pour soy sauce and water over chicken. Cover pot. Simmer over medium heat for approximately 1 hour, until chicken is cooked and liquid has partially evaporated and glazed chicken. Good with seasoned or saffron rice. Yield: 4 to 6 servings.

Elsie Worls Domingo

VEAL IN MARINARA SAUCE (ITALY)

2 garlic cloves, halved
2 tablespoons olive oil
1 (1 pound) can tomatoes
½ teaspoon basil
½ teaspoon oregano
½ teaspoon minced parsley
½ teaspoon sugar
⅛ teaspoon pepper
2 pounds boneless veal
steaks, ½ inch thick
½ cup flour

1 teaspoon paprika
⅛ teaspoon pepper
3 tablespoons oil
3 tablespoons butter
1 pound mushrooms, sliced
1 large green pepper, sliced
1 garlic clove, sliced
½ cup marsala wine
1 cup chicken stock or
chicken broth

In stainless steel or enameled saucepan, sauté 2 garlic cloves in olive oil over moderately high heat until golden; remove and discard cloves. Add tomatoes, which have been pureed in a blender or food processor, basil, oregano, parsley, sugar, and ⅛ teaspoon pepper. Simmer mixture, stirring occasionally, for 30 minutes and season marinara sauce with salt. Trim veal steaks; pound between sheets of waxed paper to ¼ inch thick. Cut veal into 1-inch squares. Combine flour, salt, paprika, and ⅛ teaspoon pepper; add veal and coat it with mixutre. In flameproof casserole, brown veal, several at a time, in oil over high heat and transfer to a bowl. Add butter to casserole; sauté mushrooms, green pepper, and 1 garlic clove over moderately high heat, stirring, for 3 minutes or until they are softened. Add marsala and cook mixture for 1 minute. Add chicken stock, veal, and marinara sauce. Simmer mixture for 20 minutes or until veal is tender; add salt and pepper to taste. Garnish with additional minced parsely. Yield: 6 servings.

Anna Mae Koehler

WEINER SHNITZEL
(VEAL CUTLET VIENNESE)

2 pounds veal cutlet, cut
in large pieces
2 eggs, beaten
½ cup flour, seasoned with
garlic salt and lemon
pepper

1½ cups fine bread crumbs
1 cup butter or margarine

Chill meat. Dip meat into beaten egg and mixture of seasoned flour and bread crumbs. Let breading dry for 30 minutes. Heat butter in heavy frying pan. Sauté cutlets slowly in butter over medium heat until golden brown. Serve with lemon wedges or slices. **HINT:** Easy and can be doubled. Yield: 4 servings.

Phil Day, Executive Director, Wheeling Area Chamber of Commerce

SWEDISH CHRISTMAS WREATH COOKIES
(SWEDEN—"BAKELS")

6 cups flour, before sifting
3 heaping teaspoons baking
  powder
1 pound butter

4 tablespoons lard
3 cups whipping cream,
  unwhipped
1 cup sugar

Sift flour and baking powder together. Add butter and lard, blending as you would for a piecrust. In separate bowl, add sugar to whipping cream. Add cream mixture to flour mixture. Continue mixing as for a piecrust. Roll out ½ inch thick on a floured board. Cut with doughnut center. Place on cookie sheet which has been greased and floured. Bake 10 minutes at 350°. Do not let them brown. Ice with any white icing and sprinkle with red, green, or blue colored granulated sugar. Yield: 5 dozen.

Mrs. George Stimac

ITALIAN EASTER BREAD

It is a traditional part of Easter and can be decorated by putting colored Easter eggs in a twisted·loaf. Great with coffee.

2 packages dried yeast
1 cup shortening
1 dozen eggs
1½ cups sugar
pinch of salt
½ teaspoon cloves

¼ teaspoon black pepper
½ teaspoon cinnamon
2 tablespoons anise seed
¼ cup of vegetable oil to
  knead
10 cups flour

Dissolve yeast in ½ cup of lukewarm water. Melt shortening. Let cool. Beat eggs well. Combine eggs, sugar, shortening, yeast, and spices in a large bowl. Gradually add flour and mix well. Knead dough with oil, adding oil gradually as needed. Knead until silky. Let rise 2 to 3 hours in a warm place. Punch down and rise until double again. Punch down and form into shapes. Rise again. Bake at 350° for 30 to 35 minutes. **HINT:** Traditionally, some loaves are made twisted by dividing a portion or ¼ of total in half; roll into long ropes and twist together. Easter eggs can be put in between twisted sections. Yield: 4 loaves.

Mrs. Frank Compagnone

CHOCOLATE FIATONE (ITALY-CHEESECAKE)

FILLING

2 pounds ricotta cheese
1 cup seedless raisins
1 cup sugar
3 eggs

8 ounces German sweet
  chocolate, grated
1 teaspoon cinnamon

Mix filling ingredients together and set aside.

CRUST

⅓ cup butter
⅓ cup sugar
½ teaspoon lemon rind
½ teaspoon lemon extract

1 egg, beaten
1½ cups sifted flour
¼ teaspoon salt
¾ teaspoon baking powder

Cream together butter, sugar, lemon rind, lemon extract, and egg. In separate bowl, stir together flour, salt, and baking powder. Stir flour mixture into creamed mixture. Divide dough into ¾ for crust and ¼ for lattice top. Roll out crust. Fit into an 8-inch glass pie pan. Spread ricotta filling into crust. Make a lattice top from the ¼ remaining dough. Place on top. Bake at 350° for 1 hour. **HINT:** Make at least 1 day ahead. Must refrigerate cake. Can be made up to 3 days ahead. Will keep 2 weeks. Yield: 8 servings.

Maria Donatelli

KOURAMBEDES (GREECE-COOKIES)

1 pound unsalted butter,
  softened
¾ cup powdered sugar
½ heaping teaspoon baking
  powder

4½ cups sifted cake or pastry
  flour
1 (1 pound) box powdered
  sugar

Cream butter with an electric mixer. Add ¾ cup powdered sugar and beat well for 10 to 15 minutes. Add baking powder. Stir in flour. Transfer to large bowl and knead. More flour is sometimes needed so dough will roll easily. To shape, there are several methods. The dough may be rolled into long logs and cut diagonally. These shapes may then be formed into crescents, "s" shapes, or wedding bell domes. Bake in a preheated 350° oven for 15 to 20 minutes. Cookies should be white in color and set but not brown. When cool, roll cookies in powdered sugar, at least 2 times. **HINT:** Unsalted butter is a must for this recipe. Yield: 4½ dozen.

Edith Menedis

JULEKAKE (NORWAY)

*Julekake, Norwegian Christmas cake, is
delicious with a cup of coffee any time of year.*

2 packages active dry yeast	½ cup sugar
½ cup warm water	1 teaspoon salt
1 cup milk, scalded	1 teaspoon ground cardamon
¼ cup butter	¾ cup diced citron or
1 egg, beaten (reserve 1	mixed candied peel
tablespoon for brushing	¾ cup raisins
on loaves)	5 cups all-purpose flour

Dissolve yeast in warm water. Mix scalded milk, butter, and egg in bowl. When lukewarm, add yeast. Add sugar, salt, cardamon, and 2 cups flour and beat well. Stir in fruit and remaining flour, reserving some for kneading. Turn out onto a lightly-floured surface and knead until smooth and elastic, about 8 to 10 minutes. Shape into a ball and place in a greased bowl. Cover and let rise in a warm place until doubled, about 1 hour. Punch dough down and divide into 2 parts. Form 2 round loaves and place in greased 8-inch cake pans or on cookie sheets. Cover and let rise until nearly doubled, about 45 minutes. Preheat oven to 350°. Brush loaves with beaten egg. Bake for 30 to 35 minutes. **HINT:** Stale Julekake makes toast and excellent bread pudding. Yield: 2 loaves.

Melody Favish

AMERICAN AS APFELKUCHEN (GERMANY)

Delicious served warm with vanilla ice cream

vegetable cooking spray
½ cup butter, softened
1 package yellow cake mix
    (plain or with pudding
    added)
½ cup flaked coconut
1 (20 ounce) can (1 cup
    drained) pie-sliced apples
    or 2½ cups baking apples,
    peeled and sliced

½ cup sugar
1 teaspoon cinnamon
1 cup sour cream
2 egg yolks, lightly beaten or
    1 whole egg, lightly beaten
⅓ cup chopped walnuts or
    pecans, optional

Preheat oven to 350°. Spray 9x13x2-inch oblong baking pan with vegetable spray. With pastry blender, cut butter into dry cake mix until crumbly. Add coconut; toss to distribute. Spread mixture in baking pan, smoothing lightly (do not pack down) and building up slightly at edges. Bake 10 minutes. Arrange apples on warm crust. (1 can covers surface closely.) If using nuts, sprinkle nuts over apples. Mix sugar and cinnamon and sprinkle over apples. Blend sour cream and egg. Drizzle over apples. (This mixture does not cover surface completely.) Bake 25 minutes or until edges are light brown. Do not overbake. **HINT:** To soften butter, cut into pats and place flat on a plate. Allow to set for 5 to 10 minutes (while assembling ingredients). Must be refrigerated if kept longer than one day. Yield: 12 servings.

Susan Conner

DESERE HOLU (PERSIA-PEACH DESSERT)

⅔ cup water
⅓ cup sugar
5 to 6 medium firm peaches,
    peeled and sliced or 1
    (16 ounce) can peach halves
    in light syrup

1 teaspoon rose water or
    ½ teaspoon cardamon

NATIONALITY AND HERITAGE

Pour water in a medium saucepan. Add sugar and bring to boil. Add peaches and simmer in syrup for 10 to 15 minutes. Cool. Add rose water or cardamon. Serve over vanilla ice cream. If using canned peaches, simmer peaches in their own syrup until soft. Cool and add rose water or sprinkle with cardamon and a favorite liqueur. Yield: 6 to 8 servings.

Marylon Rahbar

SLOVENIAN KIFLES (YUGOSLAVIA-NUT HORNS)

My mother-in-law's old family recipe

DOUGH

2 cups flour
1 cake compressed yeast
½ cup margarine
2 egg yolks

½ cup sour cream
3 tablespoons melted margarine
¼ cup powdered sugar

Put flour in 4-quart mixing bowl. Crumble yeast over flour. Cut in ½ cup margarine with pastry blender until mixture is crumbly. Add egg yolks and sour cream, mixing well. Form into a ball and knead on floured board 5 to 10 minutes, until smooth. Divide dough into 3 equal parts. Wrap in waxed paper and chill 1 hour. Roll each portion of dough into a 10-inch circle. Cut circle into 12 wedges. Spread each wedge with a well-rounded teaspoonful of walnut filling. Roll from wide end to point. Place on greased baking sheets. Brush with melted margarine. Bake at 350° for 20 minutes or until golden brown. Dust with powdered sugar. **HINT:** Dough keeps in the refrigerator up to 1 week.

WALNUT FILLING

1 cup finely chopped walnuts
½ cup sugar

1 teaspoon vanilla
2 egg whites, stiffly beaten

Combine walnuts, sugar and vanilla. Fold in egg whites. Spread on cookies. Yield: 3 dozen.

Susie Godish

UKRANIAN COFFEE-NUT TORTE (UKRAINE)

For coffee lovers

LAYERS:

10 egg yolks
1 cup plus 2 tablespoons
   sugar
1 teaspoon instant coffee

2 tablespoons grated
   unsweetened chocolate
10 egg whites
2 cups ground walnuts

Preheat oven to 325°. Beat egg yolks with sugar until thick and lemon colored. Stir in coffee and chocolate. Set aside. Beat egg whites in medium bowl until soft peaks form; gradually add nuts, beating to stiff peaks. Fold whites into yolk mixture. Line four 9-inch or 10-inch round pans with baking paper. Spoon batter equally into four pans. Bake at 325° for 20 to 30 minutes.

COFFEE FILLING

2 tablespoons instant coffee
2 tablespoons boiling water
1 cup unsalted butter,
   softened

3 cups sifted powdered sugar
1 tablespoon corn syrup

Dissolve instant coffee in boiling water; set aside and cool to lukewarm. Beat butter until creamy. Add sugar and beat until fluffy. Add coffee slowly; beat in. Stir in corn syrup.

ICING

⅔ cups shortening
2 cups sifted powdered sugar
2 heaping tablespoons dry
   cocoa

water

Cream shortening. Stir in sugar and beat until fluffy. Set aside. Add a little water to cocoa, stirring to make a thick paste. Stir into shortening mixture. To assemble, stack layers with filling spread in between and frost with icing. Refrigerate for several hours. Yield: 12 to 14 servings.

Hali Exley

SALLY LUNN BREAD

This recipe is from the King's Arms Tavern in Williamsburg, Virginia

1 cup milk	⅓ cup sugar
½ cup shortening	2 teaspoons salt
¼ cup water	2 packages active dry yeast
4 cups sifted flour, divided	3 eggs

Preheat oven to 350° for 10 minutes before Sally Lunn is ready to be baked. Grease a 10-inch tube pan or a bundt pan. Heat milk, shortening, and ¼ cup water until very warm, about 120°. Shortening does not need to melt. Blend 1⅓ cups flour, sugar, salt, and dry yeast in large mixing bowl. Blend warm liquids into flour mixture. Beat with electric mixer at medium speed about 2 minutes, scraping sides of bowl occasionally. Gradually add ⅔ cup of remaining flour and eggs. Beat at high speed for 2 minutes. Add remaining flour and mix well. Batter will be thick, but not stiff. Cover and let rise in a warm, draft-free place (about 85°) until double in bulk, about 1 hour and 15 minutes. Punch dough down with spatula and turn into prepared pan. Cover and let rise in a warm, draft-free place until increased in bulk from ⅓ to ½, about 30 minutes. Bake for 40 to 50 minutes at 350°. Run knife around center and outer edges of bread and turn onto plate to cool. **HINT:** Freezes well. Yield: 1 loaf.

Lin Companion

NEW ORLEANS PIE (AMERICA)

41 vanilla wafers
3 tablespoons light brown
  sugar
1 teaspoon grated orange
  rind
3 tablespoons butter, melted
1 (3⅝ ounce) package vanilla
  pudding and pie filling

1½ cups milk
2 egg yolks, beaten
1 cup sour cream
½ cup chopped pecans
¼ cup light brown sugar
1 tablespoon butter, softened

To make crust, crush 25 vanilla wafers with 3 tablespoons brown sugar, orange rind, and melted butter. Press into greased 9-inch pie plate. Arrange remaining cookies around edge of pie plate, upright. Bake crust for 8 minutes in a 375° oven. Cool. Prepare pudding and pie filling according to package directions using milk and adding egg yolks. Cool. Pour into shell and cover with waxed paper. Chill. Remove paper and spread with sour cream. Combine pecans, ¼ cup brown sugar, cinnamon, and softened butter. Sprinkle on top. Cover with foil and keep refrigerated. **HINT:** Must be done ahead of time. Yield: 8 servings.

Mrs. Edith Kropp

HUNGARIAN GOULASH (HUNGARY)

2 pounds beef chuck or
  bottom round, cut into
  1-inch cubes
¼ cup shortening
1 cup sliced onions
1 small garlic clove, minced
¾ cup ketchup
1 tablespoon brown sugar
2 tablespoons Worcestershire
  sauce

2 teaspoons paprika
2 teaspoons salt
½ teaspoon dry mustard
1½ cups cold water
2 tablespoons flour
¼ cup cold water
8 ounces cooked noodles
parsely

In large skillet, brown beef in shortening. Add onions and garlic. Cook until tender. Mix ketchup, brown sugar, Worcestershire sauce, paprika, salt, and dry mustard. Add to beef, stirring to mix. Add 1½ cups cold water. Cover and simmer for 2 to 2½ hours. In small bowl or shaker, blend flour and ¼ cup water. Add to beef and heat to boiling, stirring constantly. Boil for 1 minute. Pour over hot noodles. Garnish with parsley. Yield: 4 to 6 servings.

Debbie Gallagher

MRS. CHILLES' GREEK TURKEY STUFFING (GREECE)

1 bunch parsley leaves
3 large onions, chopped
1 pound milk bulk sausage
giblets and liver from turkey
¾ pound butter
1 (16 ounce) can whole
   tomatoes, drained

¼ pound pine nuts
2 pounds chestnuts, boiled
   and finely chopped
½ pound walnuts, chopped
salt and pepper to taste
½ teaspoon cinnamon

Boil parsley leaves with onions; drain when tender. Fry sausage and drain. Boil liver and giblets, chop fine, and save broth. In a large skillet, melt butter and fry onions and parsley. Add liver, giblets, and sausage. Add tomatoes and all nuts, salt, pepper, and cinnamon. If too dry, add broth from giblets to moisten. If too much dressing is left after stuffing turkey, you may bake the remainder in a casserole at 325° for 1 hour. When removing dressing from turkey, combine with dressing in casserole. **HINT:** Best to cook chestnuts the day before; they are easier to peel when hot. Yield: 8 servings.

Betty Kademenos

Special Parties

The Greenbrier, White Sulphur Springs,
West Virginia

ELEGANT DINNER FOR SIX

Artichokes
with Hollandaise Sauce

Lobster Wrapped in Phyllo

Green Beans with Grapes

Riz Pilaf a la Valencienne

Caesar Salad

Great French Bread

Mocha Torte

COCKTAIL BUFFET

Crab Quiche Squares

Scallion Flowers

Chili Con Queso

Lacy Mushroom Caps

Marinated Shrimp

Clam Rolls

Cheese Puffs

Cheese Ball

Spinach Dip

Swedish Meatballs

Crab Meatballs

Cheesecake Cookies

Chocolate Mint Brownies

TAIL GATE PARTY

Super Taco

Asparagus Dip

Hot Sausage Rolls

Pepperoni Rolls

Marinated Mushrooms

Shredded Beef Sandwiches

Best Gooey Brownies

Mini Cheesecakes

FESTIVE BACKYARD DINNER

Summer Slush

Fresh Vegetable Dip

Gazpacho Soup

Marinated Flank Steak

Cold Spaghetti Salad

Sweet and Sour Beans

Onion Bread

Russian Cream

CHRISTMAS DINNER

Wassail Punch

Potato Soup

Crown Pork Roast

Fruit Stuffing

Carrot Puff

Curried Fruit

Potato Casserole

Blueberry Bread

Bûche de Noël

Potpourri

Grist Mill, Babcock State Park,
West Virginia

PEANUT GRANOLA

Kids love this and it is so nutritional!
(About 160 calories per ¼ cup)

1 cup raisins
¾ cup peanut butter
⅔ cup honey
1 tablespoon cinnamon
⅛ teaspoon cloves
1 tablespoon vanilla

4 cups rolled oats
½ cup wheat germ
½ cup chopped dates
1 cup sunflower seeds or
  nuts, unsalted (I use
  ½ cup each)

Put raisins in a bowl and cover with warm water; allow to stand until plumped, then drain and set aside. In a small saucepan, combine peanut butter, honey, cinnamon and cloves. Stir over low heat until just warmed through. Cool and stir in vanilla. In a large bowl, combine oats and peanut butter mixture. Stir to coat evenly. Spread in large roasting pan. Bake at 300° for 35 minutes, stirring occasionally. Turn off oven. Stir in raisins, wheat germ, dates, sunflower seeds and/or nuts. Let granola stand in oven for 1½ hours to dry. Stir every 30 minutes. Store covered in refrigerator. **HINT:** Easy and can be doubled. Yield: 8 cups.

Cookbook Committee

LYNN'S GRANOLA

Delicious with milk for morning cereal.

3 cups regular rolled oats
¼ cup shredded coconut
¼ cup wheat germ
¼ cup sesame seeds
¼ cup slivered almonds
¼ cup raisins

¼ cup dates, cut up
1 tablespoon butter or
  margarine
¼ cup honey
¼ cup brown sugar
1 teaspoon vanilla

Mix together oats, coconut, wheat germ, sesame seeds, almonds, raisins and dates. Melt butter; add honey, brown sugar, and vanilla. Add this to rolled oats mixture and mix well. Spread on lightly greased cookie sheet. Bake at 350° for about 15 minutes, stirring every 5 minutes. Store in airtight container. Yield: 6 to 8 cups.

Sally Holmes

CARAMEL CORN

Easy and great for a crowd

1 cup butter	½ teaspoon baking soda
2 cups brown sugar	1 teaspoon vanilla
½ cup light corn syrup	6 quarts popped corn
1 teaspoon salt	

Melt butter in saucepan. Add sugar, corn syrup and salt. Bring to a boil, stirring constantly. When mixture reaches a boil, stop stirring and allow to boil 5 minutes. Remove from heat and stir in baking soda and vanilla. Pour caramel over popcorn slowly, stirring to coat evenly. Spread into two large pans. Bake at 250° for 1 hour, stirring every 15 minutes. Remove from oven. **HINT:** Can be stored, after cooling, in covered container—if there is any left! Can also be doubled. Yield: 6 quarts.

Cookbook Committee

SWEET AND SPICY NUTS

Great for the Christmas season!

3 cups mixed nuts	1 teaspoon ground cinnamon
1 egg white	½ teaspoon ground allspice
1 tablespoon orange juice	½ teaspoon ground ginger
⅔ cup sugar	

Place nuts in a large bowl; set aside. In a small bowl, beat egg white and orange juice with a fork until frothy. Add sugar, cinnamon, allspice and ginger until well blended. Pour over nuts, stirring to coat well. Spread nuts on a greased 15x10x1-inch jelly roll pan. Bake at 275° for 45 to 50 minutes or until light brown and crisp. Stir every 15 minutes. Cool. Store in an airtight container in a cool place. **HINT:** Easy and can be doubled. Yield: 4 cups.

Donna Niess

HARD TAC CANDY

My grandmother made this candy.
My kids found this great fun to make.

1 cup granulated sugar	½ teaspoon flavoring oil
½ cup water	2 to 6 drops food coloring
⅓ cup light corn syrup	powdered sugar

Cook sugar, water, and corn syrup, stirring occasionally, until the syrup reaches 300°. Remove from heat and immediately add flavoring oil and food coloring. Stir to mix, and pour on buttered dinner plate. As mixture begins to harden, cut into pieces with scissors and put in powdered sugar. Make sure each piece is coated with sugar. Shake off excess sugar and store in tightly covered container. **HINT:** This recipe can be doubled. Yield: 1½ cups.

Donna M. Glass

CHRISTMAS SUGAR MINTS

5 cups sugar	1 teaspoon peppermint
2 cups water	flavoring
4 cups powdered sugar	pinch of cream of tartar

Combine sugar, water, and cream of tartar in large pan. Put over medium-high heat and bring to boiling and continue cooking to 230° on candy thermometer or just below soft-ball stage. While boiling, brush side of pan with pastry brush dipped in water to wipe away and build up of sugar crystals. Remove immediately from heat and add powdered sugar and flavoring. Stir with hand whip until creamy (about 2 to 3 minutes). Drop from teaspoon to waxed paper. Keep unused syrup quite hot but not boiling. Total time for candy—10 minutes. Store in airtight container. Yield: 2 to 3 dozen.

Virginia Conley

DARK PRALINES

2 cups sugar
1 cup buttermilk
1 teaspoon baking soda

2 cups pecan halves
2 tablespoons butter or
margarine

Combine first 3 ingredients in large heavy saucepan; bring to boil, and boil 5 minutes. Stir in pecans and butter; cook over medium heat, stirring occasionally, until mixture reaches soft-ball stage. Remove from heat; beat with wooden spoon 2 to 3 minutes or until mixture is creamy and begins to thicken. Working rapidly, drop mixture by rounded tablespoon onto waxed paper. Let cool. **HINT:** Easy to do. Yield: 3 dozen.

Marie Driehorst

FROZEN STRAWBERRY JAM

6 cups mashed strawberries,
approximately 2 quarts
6 cups sugar

1 cup cold water
1 box Sure-Jell®
Fruit Pectin

Mash strawberries and add sugar, stirring until sugar is dissolved. Add water to sure jell and boil for 1 minute. Add this mixture to berries and let stand for 1 hour. Pack in freezer containers and freeze. Yield: 5 to 6 pints.

Sharon Byrd

SEA FOAM

3 cups pure cane light
brown sugar
¼ teaspoon salt

¾ cup water
2 egg whites
1 teaspoon vanilla

In medium saucepan, dissolve sugar and salt in water. Cook over medium heat without stirring to 255° or hard ball. Beat egg whites until stiff in medium mixing bowl. Remove sugar and salt mixture from heat, and pour gradually over beaten egg whites, beating constantly. Add vanilla. Continue beating until mixture cools and will hold its shape. Drop by tablespoonsful onto waxed paper. Allow to cool ½ to 1 hour. **HINT:** Be sure to use only pure cane sugar. Yield: 35 to 40 pieces.

Mary Kahle

HOMEMADE VANILLA ICE CREAM

4 eggs
1½ cups granulated sugar
1½ pints heavy whipping
  cream
1 (14 ounce) can condensed
  milk

1 tablespoon vanilla
⅛ teaspoon salt
milk to fill
rock salt and ice

VARIATIONS

1 (16 ounce) can chocolate
  syrup
1½ pints crushed
  strawberries

1 (20 ounce) can crushed
  pineapple

In large mixing bowl, beat eggs well; add sugar, and beat until sugar is dissolved. Add whipping cream; mix well. Add condensed milk, vanilla, and salt. Beat well. Add milk to fill to top of mixing bowl. Pour entire contents of mixing bowl into 6-quart ice cream can. Fill can with milk until it is 2 to 3 inches from the top of 6-quart can. For variations, add chocolate syrup, berries, or pineapple in mixing bowl before pouring into ice cream can. Mix well. Use lots of rock salt on ice while packing ice cream can. Yield: 24 servings.

Cathy Depew

FORGOTTEN CANDY

Easy for kids!

2 egg whites
⅔ cup granulated sugar
1 (6 ounce) package semi-
  sweet chocolate chips
  (add a little more chips
  if omitting nuts)

1 cup chopped nuts, optional

Preheat oven to 350°. Beat egg whites until soft peaks form, adding sugar gradually until very, very stiff and glossy. Fold in chocolate chips and nuts and drop by teaspoonsful onto foil-lined cookie sheet. Place in oven, shut door, turn off oven, and leave in oven until it cools or overnight. **HINT:** Can place close together on cookie sheet. Must be done ahead of time and can also be doubled. Yield: 40 pieces.

Patricia Downie

WASSAIL PUNCH

Easy and great for a crowd

48 ounces cranberry juice	16 whole cloves
48 ounces apple juice	1⅓ cups sugar
48 ounces hot tea	1 cup lemon juice
24 ounces orange juice	1 orange, sliced
4 pieces stick cinnamon	1 lemon, sliced

Combine all ingredients (except orange and lemon slices) in large pan and bring to a boil, stirring often. To serve, carefully pour punch into large punch bowl. Float orange and lemon slices on top. Yield: 30 servings.

Cheryl Cox

WASHINGTON PUNCH

1 cup sugar	2 cups sliced pineapple
2 cups diced pineapple	ice ring with cherries
1 bottle Moselle wine	frozen in it
2 bottles Rhine wine	1 quart champagne
1 bottle Claret wine	

Sprinkle sugar over diced pineapple. Add half a bottle of Moselle wine and let stand at room temperature for 24 hours. Strain. Add sliced pineapple, Rhine wine, Claret, and remaining Moselle. Pour over ice in a punch bowl and add champagne just before serving. **HINT:** Recipe must be done ahead and can be doubled. Yield: 12 servings.

Laura Carter

POTPOURRI

SUMMER SLUSH

7 cups water
1½ cups sugar
1 (6 ounce) can frozen
orange juice
1 (12 ounce) can frozen
lemonade

2 cups strong tea
2 cups whiskey (bourbon)
or rum

Boil water and sugar until dissolved; cool. Thaw orange juice and lemonade. Mix all other ingredients together and freeze 24 hours before serving. Scoop into sherbets or goblets and pour 7-Up or Sprite over the top. Yield: 12 servings.

Janet Kropp

BANANAS FLAMBÉ

6 bananas, sliced
½ cup margarine
½ cup brown sugar
¼ cup orange juice

½ cup light rum
vanilla ice cream
(amount optional to
individual)

In chafing dish, melt margarine. Stir in brown sugar; stir to dissolve. Add orange juice. Cook until mixture bubbles. Add bananas; stir to coat. Cook until warm. Then sprinkle rum over bananas. When hot, ignite rum. Let flame die down. Serve over vanilla ice cream. Yield: 8 servings.

Teresa Brown

CURRIED FRUIT

1 (16 ounce) can sliced
peaches
1 (20 ounce) can pineapple
chunks
1 (16 ounce) can pear halves

6 maraschino cherries
¾ cup brown sugar, packed
¾ teaspoon curry powder
⅓ cup butter

Drain fruit *very well*. Arrange in a 1½-quart casserole. Melt butter. Remove from heat; add sugar and curry powder. Stir until dissolved. Pour over fruit. Bake at 325° for 1 hour uncovered. Serve warm. **HINT:** Recipe can be doubled.

Judi Hendrickson

PISTACHIO PUDDING DESSERT

The answer for St. Patrick's Day dessert!

1 (20 ounce) can crushed
    pineapple, undrained
1 (4 serving size) box
    pistachio-flavored
    instant pudding

1 (8 ounce) container dairy
    whipped topping
1½ cups small marshmallows
¼ cup shredded coconut
¼ cup walnuts, chopped

In large mixing bowl, mix all ingredients well. Pour mixture into 13x8-inch baking dish. Refrigerate 3 to 4 hours or until firm. **HINT:** This recipe must be done ahead of time. It is easy and can be doubled. Yield: 10 to 12 servings.

Linda Comins

SERVICEBERRY PIE (OR JUNEBERRY PIE)

*The name "serviceberry" came about because
circuit-riding preachers would make their rounds,
holding church "services," in the mountain communities
about the time of the flowering of these beautiful trees.*

5 cups serviceberries
⅔ cup sugar
¼ cup flour

½ teaspoon cinnamon
3 tablespoons butter

Line 10-inch pie pan with your favorite piecrust. Fill with serviceberries. Mix sugar, flour and cinnamon and sprinkle evenly over serviceberries. Dot with butter. Bake 45 to 50 minutes at 425°. Yield: 6 to 8 servings.

*Bill Beatty, Naturalist
Brooks Nature Center
Oglebay Institute*

SPAGHETTI SAUCE

For canning or freezing

½ cup vegetable oil
6 large onions, chopped
4 green peppers, chopped
3 (18 ounce) cans tomato
  paste
4 (18 ounce) cans water
2 (29 ounce) cans tomato
  puree
35 medium-size fresh
  tomatoes, peeled and
  chopped in small pieces

¼ cup oregano
⅓ cup sugar
3 tablespoons salt
½ teaspoon pepper
2 tablespoons garlic powder
½ teaspoon basil
5 bay leaves

Cover bottom of a 14-quart kettle with oil. Sauté onion and pepper in oil until transparent. Stir in tomato paste, blending into oil. Stir in water, tomato puree and chopped tomatoes with any juice they have produced. Simmer 1 hour, covered, on low heat, stirring occasionally. Add oregano, sugar, salt, pepper, garlic powder, basil and bay leaves. Simmer another hour, covered, on low heat, stirring occasionally. While hot, pour into sterilized jars and process the boiling water bath or steam pressure canner method. **HINT:** This sauce can also be used for pizza, lasagna, and hot sausage. Yield: 12 quart jars or 24 pint jars.

Susie Godish

ZUCCHINI BREAD AND BUTTER PICKLES

6 quarts sliced zucchini
6 medium onions, sliced
1 sweet red pepper, cut in
  strips
¾ cup salt

5 cups sugar
3 cups vinegar
1 tablespoon mustard seeds
1½ teaspoons turmeric
1½ teaspoons celery seed

Cover first 4 ingredients with ice water for 3 hours. Drain well. Boil remaining ingredients together 3 minutes; then add drained zucchini. Let come to a good rolling boil. Seal in sterilized jars. Yield: 6 to 8 pints.

Susan Hazlett

CORN RELISH

12 ears of corn, scrape
  kernels
1 sweet green pepper
1 sweet red pepper
1 onion
2 celery stalks
1½ cups sugar

1½ cups vinegar
1 tablespoon salt
1½ teaspoons dry mustard
¼ teaspoon turmeric
½ teaspoon celery seed

Chop vegetables and combine with corn kernels. To vegetables, add all remaining ingredients. Slowly bring mixture to boil. Boil 30 minutes. Pour into hot sterilized jars and seal. Yield: 3 pints.

Olive W. Bigelow

SARA'S PRESERVED DILL PICKLES

16 small cucumbers,
  scrubbed and
  sliced thin

2 heads fresh dill
½ teaspoon mustard seed

Slice scrubbed cucumbers thin. Fill 6 hot jars, layering slices diagonally until full. Place fresh dill on top and add mustard seed.

BRINE

1½ cups cider vinegar
1½ cups water

1½ tablespoons pickling
  or kosher salt

Mix vinegar, water, and salt together. Fill the 6 pint jars of cucumbers with prepared brine to within ½ inch from top. Adjust lids. Water-bath and process 20 minutes. Six weeks on the shelf allows dill to penetrate. Yield: 6 pints.

Ruth Foose

GREEN TOMATO RELISH

½ peck green tomatoes
  (4 quarts)
12 green peppers
12 large onions
1 quart vinegar
2 sticks cinnamon

2 tablespoons whole
  cloves
2 tablespoons salt
2 tablespoons mustard
  seed
2 pounds sugar

Grind onions, tomatoes, and peppers. Boil for 15 minutes. Drain. Put cinnamon and cloves in cheesecloth bag and add to vinegar and sugar. Boil 5 minutes. Add salt, mustard seed, and vegetable mixture and again bring to boil. Seal in sterile jars. Yield: 5 pints.

Olive W. Bigelow

PICKLED MUSHROOMS

A great gift from the kitchen

⅓ cup dry white wine
⅓ cup white wine vinegar
⅓ cup salad oil
¼ cup chopped onion
2 tablespoons snipped
  parsley
1 small clove garlic
1 bay leaf

1 teaspoon salt
¼ teaspoon dried thyme,
  crushed
dash of ground pepper
3 (6 ounce) cans mushroom
  crowns, drained (about 3
  cups) (fresh mushrooms
  may be substituted)

In saucepan, combine all ingredients except mushrooms. Bring to a boil. Add mushrooms and return to boiling. Simmer, uncovered, 8 to 10 minutes. Ladle into hot scalded jars, or cool and store in covered container in refrigerator until ready to serve. Yield: 3 half-pints.

Ann Bopp

PEKING DUCK

1 (4 or 5 pound) duck
6 cups water
½ cup orange blossom honey
4 slices peeled and smashed
  fresh ginger (the size
  of quarters)

2 scallions with tops, cut
  into 1-inch pieces
2 star anise

Wash and dry duck. Tie a string around its neck skin and hang in an airy place for at least 3 hours. Put a pan under duck to catch drippings. Bring water, honey, ginger, and scallions to boil in a large pan or wok. Lower duck in water and spoon hot honey bath over it, making sure all parts of duck are moistened, even the inside. Simmer in broth 5 minutes on each side, basting with broth frequently. Hang duck 2 to 3 hours over a pan to catch drippings. Preheat oven to 375°. Cut off any loose neck skin. Place duck on a rack in roasting pan. Pour 1 inch water in pan. Roast for at least 1 hour. Lower heat to 300°, turn duck on breast and roast 30 minutes longer. Now turn duck, raise temperature to 375°, and roast 30 minutes. (Total roasting time is 2 hours.) Allow duck to sit 15 minutes before carving. Serve with onion brushes, sauce and mandarin pancakes.

SAUCE

¼ cup hoisin sauce
1 tablespoon water

1 teaspoon seasame seed oil
2 teaspoons sugar

Combine and boil for a few minutes. Serve warm.

MANDARIN PANCAKES

2 cups sifted all-purpose
  flour
¾ cup boiling water

1 to 2 tablespoons sesame
  seed oil

Make a well in center of flour and pour boiling water in. Mix well and knead for about 5 minutes. Let rest about 15 minutes. Divide dough in half and roll into 2 sausage shapes. Divide each sausage shape into 12 pieces. Flatten 1 piece at a time with a glass or rolling pin. Brush flattened piece with oil; place another flattened piece on top and then roll with rolling pin to a 5- to 6-inch circle. Cook in an ungreased crêpe pan or griddle until bubbles appear. Turn over and cook lightly. Wrap in foil. To reheat for serving, place wrapped pancakes in a 350° oven for a few minutes or place in microwave in plastic wrap for 1 minute.

POTPOURRI

ONION BRUSHES

Have a green onion (scallion) for each person to be served. With a sharp knife, feather bottom half of each onion so the onions resembles a paintbrush. The paintbrush onion is used to "paint" the sauce on the pancake. Sliced duck is then added to the pancake. Then enjoy! **HINT:** This seems like a lot of work, but, after you do it once, you will find it really is very easy.

Donna Glass

BEAN AND RAMP SOUP

Ramps are the magical ingredient for Alan and Cheryl Cox's annual feast after the Wheeling Distance Race. West Virginia folklore has long maintained that the wild leeks that permeate the Appalachian woodlands are an excellent spring tonic.

16 pounds navy beans	2 pounds smoked kielbasa
12 ham hocks	12 carrots
1 can bay leaves	1 bunch celery
3 large yellow onions	12 ramps
2 (1 pound) packages smokey link sausages	2 pounds butter
	salt to taste

24 hours before serving soak beans in water. 8 hours before serving place over low to medium heat and add ham hocks. Four hours before serving lower heat to lowest setting; add bay leaves and butter, slice and add onions, smokey links, kielbasa, carrots, celery and ramps. Remove ham hocks before serving. Yield: 10 gallons.

Alan Cox

ROSE JAR

When winter comes, what a delicious aroma will meet you when you lift the cover of your old-fashioned rose jar.

rose petals	1 tablespoon allspice
½ teaspoon nutmeg	1 tablespoon cloves
1 teaspoon mace	1 tablespoon stick cinnamon,
2 tablespoons powdered orris root	broken

Spread rose petals, freshly picked at peak of bloom, in thin layer over screen or rack made of cheesecloth, paper towels or tissues, and keep these in a warm airy place. Stir petals everyday for 2 weeks or until completely dry, crisp and brittle. Measure and mix spices. Using a decortive jar (glass, stone or poreclain), place layer of petals and alternate with spice mixture until jar is filled. Cover tightly.

Ruth Foose

HERB WREATH

A closely woven herb wreath makes a useful gift for an imaginative cook.
It can also be a fragrant decoration in your home.

HERBS THAT CAN BE USED IN WREATH

rosemary	santolina
winter savory	horehound
thyme	blue-green hyssop
lambs ear	silver gray artemisia
gray sage	

DECORATE WITH

whole nutmeg	star anise
cinnamon sticks	dried flowers for color

Take small sprigs of foliage and twist a fine wire or green thread, such as carpet thread, around each bunch and over each other with more thread so that it will hold on a firm background, such as a bent wire coat hanger or straw wreath. Woody herbs can be used to form base of wreath, while others are used to fill in and decorate. **HINT:** Be sure to work with fresh herbs; dry herbs break too easily. Hang completed wreath to dry.

Wheeling Garden Center
Oglebay Park

WREATH

Great for a gift

**3 strips of contrasting
fabric**

polyester stuffing

You may choose any 3 colors of fabric you desire but make sure that you have 2 prints and 1 solid. Cut 3 strips of fabric that are 52 inches long and 6½ inches wide. Fold each strip lengthwise with right sides together and stitch. Turn fabric and stuff with polyester stuffing. Repeat this procedure with all 3 strips. After strips are stuffed, hand stitch them together at one end. Now braid tubes together very tightly and shape into a round wreath, stitching bottom ends to first ends. For a self made bow, cut a strip of material lengthwise on the fold that measures 6½ inches wide and 46 inches long. With right sides together, stitch, forming an angle at each end. Leave a small opening at one end so you can turn the bow. Place bow where ends were joined together. **HINT:** This may be done in Christmas colors or colors that suit your interior design.

Iva White

DEA'S FLOUR KIDS

2 cups all-purpose flour   **¾ cup water**
½ cup salt

Blend flour and salt together with fork. Then slowly add water, mixing continuously until water is absorbed. Then knead dough about 12 times to acquire smoothness. Keep the dough in a covered container so it does not dry out as you work with each piece. Mold bears onto a cookie sheet. Insert wire hook (can use paper clip) into bear and bake in 300° oven for 1 hour and 15 minutes. Bake at a higher temperature for a browner bear. When bears cool, you may paint faces with acrylic paints, or for children, fine tip magic markers are easier. Then glaze bears with a clear varnish. Three coats should insure proper sealing. The more imagination, the cuter they become! Start with piece #1 and mold dough into the shapes shown. Dough will stick easily together if kept moist in covered container as you work. Yield: 1½ to 2 dozen.

Dea Kennen

GINGERBREAD HOUSE

"This has become a family tradition for us. We bake and glue the gingerbread houses separately and two weeks before Christmas our entire families gather for an afternoon of decorating the houses and eating dinner together afterwards. We give the houses as gifts."

This recipe makes 3 to 4 cottages, depending on thickness of pieces.

FIRST STAGE—BAKING

6¾ cups flour
1 tablespoon ground
  cinnamon
1½ teaspoons ground ginger
½ teaspoon salt

1½ cups light corn syrup
1¼ cups packed light brown
  sugar
1 cup butter or margarine

In large bowl, stir together flour, cinnamon, ginger, and salt. In 2-quart saucepan, stir together corn syrup, brown sugar and butter until blended. Stirring constantly, cook over medium heat until butter is melted. Stir this into flour mixture until well blended. Cool until dough is easy to handle. Roll dough onto well-greased (or teflon-coated) rimless cookie sheets. Dust pattern with flour and place on top of dough. (It is easier to handle if all of dough is rolled out at once onto several cookie sheets.) Using a sharp knife or pizza cutter, cut out patterns. Save the extra dough to make logs or tiny animals or trees. Chill 15 minutes before baking. Bake 12 to 15 minutes for large pieces and 5 to 7 minutes for smaller pieces at 350°. Cool on wire racks. **HINT:** House walls should be sturdiest and roof pieces should be thinnest.

SECOND STAGE—ASSEMBLING

Have cardboard base larger than the house ready to put house on. It may be covered with foil.

2 cups sugar

Put sugar in heavy skillet. Start on medium heat and don't turn down; melt sugar quickly because sugar will harden. Stir continually. When melted, glue house together (sides go inside the end pieces). Starting with walls, dip edges of house into sugar syrup glue and place one at a time on cardboard base to form walls of the house. To place roof on house, dip inside edges, excluding top edge, of one roof piece into glue. Brush glue also on the slanting inside edges of end walls. Quickly set first half in place, lining up edge with peak of side wall. Make certain that first half is secure before attaching second piece. Drip glue along meeting edges of roof. Set chimney piece about 2 inches from one end of roof edge. Glue door to one side of opening, leaving ajar. To permit glue to harden, it is best to let is set overnight, or at least several hours.

THIRD STAGE—DECORATING

This is the most fun! Use Christmas candies, candy canes, M and M's, lifesavers, red-hots, gumdrops, licorices and any colorful candy you choose. We have found that when several of us work together and all bring candy, we end up with a wider variety to share.

SUGAR ICING

1 (1 pound) box powdered
  sugar
3 egg whites, slightly beaten

1 teaspoon cream of tartar
drop of white vinegar

Prepare one batch of snow icing at a time. You will need at least two for a large house or several cottages. Beat sugar and egg whites slowly for 1 minute; add cream of tartar and vinegar. Beat on high speed until stiff and shiny. Spread icing liberally on roof. Immediately place desired candy on icing. For larger houses, sugar cookies make nice roof tops. Spread icing on rest of house, one wall at a time, decorating with candy as you go. Cover base with icing and put up fence made out of pretzels, if you wish. Small cookie cutters can make tiny trees and animals for yard. Ice cream cones turned upside down and decorated with snow icing and green glitter are pretty, too. If you are making small cottages, remember to cut out windows before baking. Stained glass windows may be made by putting lifesavers on tin foil and baking so that they run together. Cut out window shape leaving extra for edges and glue behind the window. We have drawn a pattern for a small cottage. You might wish to design larger houses or churches.

POTPOURRI

PATTERN

Cut two of each of pattern pieces. On piece labelled "front and back" windows and doors may be cut out in "front" piece and windows cut out on "back" piece. Pattern piece should be traced then transferred to heavy brown paper. It helps to dust pattern pieces with flour before placing on rolled out dough for cutting.

Lin Companion
Jenny Seibert

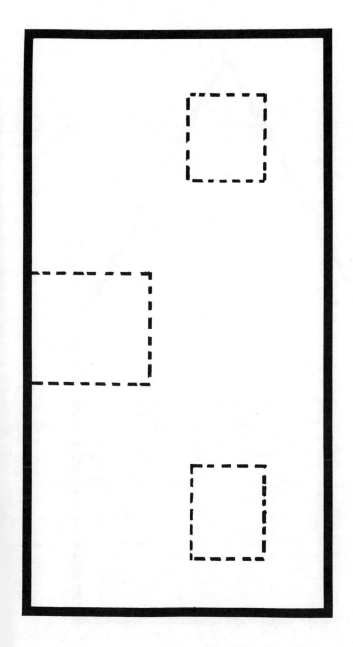

FRONT and BACK—Cut 2

SIDE—Cut 2

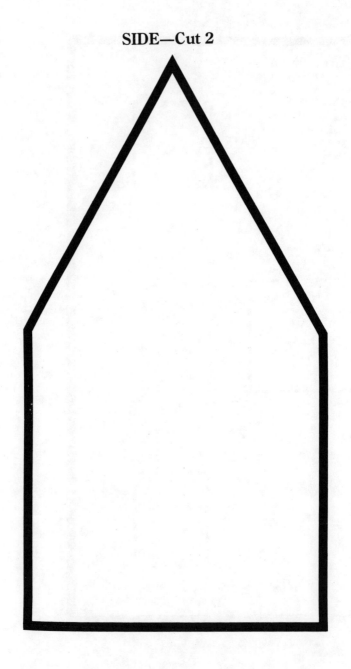

ROOF— Cut 2

BEGINNER'S PIG ROAST

PEOPLE

friendly butcher
friend with electric
  spit big enough for pig

friend who knows how to
  butcher pig
oneself

EQUIPMENT

electric spit and
  electric outlet
4 large pieces sheet metal
  on angle iron to surround
  pit
extension cord
garden hose and water outlet
14 gauge galvanized wire
pliers and wire cutters
3 pairs welding gloves
2 pairs vise grips (optional
  for holding flat metal)
sledge hammer
shovel and mattock
wheelbarrow
garden rake
large pile dry cherry wood
little bit of kerosene
matches
2 really sharp knives
2 pairs new white work gloves
pickup truck to transport
  spit

station wagon to transport
  pig
large folding banquet table
newspaper and plastic cover
  (visqueen) to cover table
garbage bags
phillips and regular
  screwdrivers
splitting maul
concrete block
grass seed
lots of cold beer
sleeping bag for night before
boom box (ghetto blaster) or
  tapeplayers (cassette preferably)
change of clothes
lawn chairs for cookers
fifth of scotch
repertoire of lies and dirty
  jokes

Order pig one month before "pig roast day" from friendly butcher; 1 pound per person, minimum 50 pounds; ask friendly butcher to fill pig's stomach with kielbasa or chicken and to place one clove of garlic in each ham and shoulder. Dig pit 12 to 18 inches deep to fit pig and spit one week before pig roast day; dig supplemental pit, 2'x2'x12 inches, nearby. Gather all equipment for pig roast. Get up early. Hook up garden hose. Two hours before roasting begins, fill main pit with wood to 12 inches above ground and start fire. While one friend watches fire, go pick up pig from friendly butcher who opens store early for you. Put pig on spit rod. Wire pig tightly to spit rod. Put spit rod on spit after flames gone and all coals. Throw switch on motor. Start fire in supplemental pit so will have coals as needed. Watch pig cook. Drink cold beer and supplement with scotch as needed. Roast pig 1 hour for each 10 pounds, minimum of 5 hours. Sheet metal keeps heat on pig. May be longer without. To see if pig is done, cut one shoulder and one ham to bone. If all white, is done. If not, keep roasting until done. One hour before you want to eat, take pig off spit and put on banquet table. Use clean gloves to remove skin. Have smart friend butcher pig. Slice large portions as smart friend butchers. Serve pig while hot. Make sure it doesn't rain. As pig cooks it may slip on spit. Rewire. One day after roast, fill pit with concrete block so you don't have to re-dig pit next year. Cover block with dirt. Plant grass seed. **HINT:** Serve with fresh corn on the cob, fresh sliced tomatoes and green onions, and fresh green beans.

Jim Seibert
as taught by Jim Smith, Kazz
Kasserman and Jack Werner

NOTES

Lagniappe
(Something Extra)

Suspension Bridge, Wheeling, West Virginia

MISSISSIPPI LEMON CHESS PIE

1 (9 inch) pie shell, unbaked
1 tablespoon all-purpose
   flour
2 cups sugar
1 tablespoon corn meal
¼ teaspoon salt
¼ cup butter or margarine,
   melted

¼ cup fresh squeezed lemon
   juice
grated rind of 2 lemons
¼ cup milk
4 eggs

In mixer, combine flour, sugar, corn meal and salt. Add butter, lemon juice, lemon rind and milk. Mix well. Add eggs, one at a time, beating well after each addition. Pour into pastry shell. Bake at 350° for 50 minutes. Yield: 6 to 8 servings.

Julie Squibb

RHUBARB PIE

2 cups sugar
3 tablespoons flour
pinch of salt
2 eggs, beaten slightly

3 cup rhubarb, cut in 1-inch
   pieces
1 double piecrust recipe

Combine sugar, flour, and salt in a large bowl. Add eggs, then rhubarb. Pour into unbaked 9-inch pie shell. Cover with another piecrust and cut openings in top to let steam escape. Bake at 400° for 40 to 50 minutes. **HINT:** Recipe can be doubled. Yield: 6 servings.

Jo Kepner

FLORIDA PIE

Good and unique!

3 egg whites
½ teaspoon baking powder
1 cup sugar
1 teaspoon vanilla

17 Ritz®crackers, crushed
1 cup pecans, crushed
whipping cream for topping

Beat egg whites and baking powder until stiff. Gradually add sugar and vanilla. Fold in Ritz crackers and pecans. Put into 8-inch pie pan. Bake at 350° for 25 minutes. Refrigerate for 12 hours. When ready to serve, top with whipped cream and sprinkle with chopped pecans. Ice cream may be used instead of whipping cream.

VARIATION

This pie can be put into 9-inch pie pan. After baking, strawberries may then be folded into whipped cream and poured into middle of pie. If this variation is chosen, a hollow spot must be made in middle before baking. Yield: 6 servings.

Mrs. R.L. Meek

GRITS SOUFFLÉ

1 cup grits
5 cups water
1 teaspoon salt
3 tablespoons butter

½ pound sharp Cheddar
  cheese, shredded
3 eggs

Heat water and salt to boiling. Add grits and cook for 5 minutes. Add butter and shredded cheese. Stir well and cool. Beat eggs and add to cooled mixture. Bake in casserole at 375° for 1 hour. Yield: 6 to 8 servings.

Lou Crawford

SCALLOPED SWEET POTATOES

8 large sweet potatoes
2 egg yolks
1 cup sugar
1½ cups chopped walnuts
  or raisins

1½ cups milk
1 tablespoon butter
24 large marshmallows

To cooked, mashed sweet potatoes, add egg yolks, sugar, raisins or nuts, milk, and butter. Mix and beat. Bake at 350° for 30 minutes. Just before finished, add marshmallows and brown. **HINT:** Can do ahead. Yield: 6 servings.

Beth Ann Dague

PARMESAN POTATOES

2 (1 pound) cans small
  whole peeled potatoes
½ cup melted butter

¼ cup grated Parmesan
  cheese

Drain potatoes. Place in a 9x9x2-inch square pan. Toss potatoes with butter and cheese. Bake uncovered for 30 minutes at 400°. Yield: 8 servings.

Laura Carter

LEMON CREAMED FETTUCINI

1 (12 ounce) package fettucini
1 cup heavy whipping cream
4 tablespoons butter
½ teaspoon salt
½ teaspoon white pepper
lemon juice to taste
Parmesan cheese

Cook fettucini according to package directions; drain. Warm whipping cream, butter, salt, and pepper. Add lemon juice to taste. Toss with fettucini. Sprinkle generously with Parmesan cheese. Yield: 4 servings.

Dee Dee McCuskey

NOODLES ALFREDO

Excellent served with veal

1 (12 ounce) box fettucini or
   12 ounces medium egg
   noodles
2 cups whipping cream
1 cup butter or margarine
⅛ teaspoon nutmeg
dash of pepper
3 ounces grated Parmesan
   cheese
4 egg yolks

Cook fettucini or noodles according to package instructions; drain and reserve. In an 8- or 10- quart pan on medium heat, bring the whipping cream to a simmer (do not boil). Add butter, nutmeg, black pepper, and Parmesan cheese; heat thoroughly. Beat eggs with wire whisk and then carefully beat in little of hot cheese mixture. Whisk egg mixture into hot cheese mixture until blended well. When mixture thickens, add noodles and serve immediately. **HINT:** Must be done just before serving. Yield: 4 servings.

Mary Lou DeFillippo

ZUCCHINI SAUTÉED PASTA

½ cup margarine
1 tablespoon garlic, minced
1 cup scallions, chopped
2½ cups grated, unpeeled
   zucchini

1 pound spaghetti, cooked
   and drained
½ cup Parmesan cheese

Melt margarine in large skillet. Add garlic and scallions; sauté until tender. Add zucchini and cook over low heat for 6 to 10 minutes until tender (you may need to add a little more margarine). Add spaghetti; toss with zucchini mixture. Sprinkle Parmesan cheese on top and serve. **HINT:** Can be reheated. Yield: 4 servings.

Teresa Brown

HAM, EGG AND RICE SALAD

Great for a picnic or tailgate party

2 cups cooked rice
6 hard cooked eggs, chopped
1 cup diced cooked ham
3 tablespoons finely chopped
   green pepper
1 tablespoon minced onion

½ cup mayonnaise
1 teaspoon salt
⅛ teaspoon pepper
½ teaspoon prepared
   mustard
½ cup sliced Swiss cheese

Combine rice, eggs, ham, and vegetables. Add mayonnaise and mix well. Add seasonings and mix. Toss lightly with cheese. Yield: 5 to 6 servings.

Linda Thonen

24 HOUR LAYERED SALAD

Great for a crowd

1 large head lettuce,
  shredded
½ cup onion, finely chopped
½ cup celery, thinly sliced
1 (16 ounce) can water
  chestnuts, sliced
1 (10 ounce) package frozen
  peas, uncooked
1 cup shredded Cheddar
  cheese

2 cups mayonnaise
3 tablespoons sugar
Parmesan cheese
¾ pound bacon, fried and
  crumbled
3 hard-boiled eggs, sliced
parsley
olives, sliced
tomato wedges

Shred lettuce into a 14x18-inch pan. Layer onion, celery, water chestnuts, peas, and Cheddar cheese. Spread mayonnaise on top of Cheddar cheese. Sprinkle sugar and Parmesan cheese to taste on top of mayonnaise. Cover and refrigerate overnight. Before serving, top with bacon and decorate to taste with sliced eggs, parsley, sliced olives, and tomato wedges. Do not toss. Cut in squares. **HINT:** Must be done ahead of time and can be doubled. Yield: 8 to 10 servings.

Margaret Lee Gibson

FROZEN CRANBERRY–PINEAPPLE SALAD

1 (20½ ounce) can crushed
  pineapple, well drained
1 (16 ounce) can whole
  cranberry sauce

1 cup sour cream
¼ cup coarsely chopped
  pecans

Mix all ingredients thoroughly. Pour into refrigerator tray or muffin tins. Freeze at least 3 hours or until firm. Thirty minutes before serving, remove tray from freezer to refrigerator. **HINT:** Freezes well, can be done ahead of time, and can also be doubled. Yield: 6 to 8 servings.

Phyllis Duncan

FROZEN FRUIT CUPS

1 (8 ounce) package cream
  cheese
½ cup mayonnaise
1 (16 ounce) can fruit
  cocktail, drained

1 cup miniature
  marshmallows
1 banana, sliced
¼ cup maraschino cherries,
  sliced, optional

Soften cream cheese and mix with mayonnaise until well blended. Add drained fruit cocktail, marshmallows, bananas, and cherries. Freeze in 10 paper liners in muffin tins. After frozen, remove salads, still in liners, and store in plastic bag in freezer. Liner can be removed before serving, if desired. **HINT:** Easy to do. Yield: 10 small servings.

Mrs. Edith Kropp

TACO SALAD WITH LEMON—SOUR CREAM DRESSING

SALAD

1 pound ground beef
1 teaspoon salt
1 teaspoon cumin
dash of garlic powder
1 cup chopped onion
1 medium head lettuce

8 ounces tortilla chips,
  broken
4 tomatoes, chopped
2 medium avocados, cubed
8 ounces shredded Cheddar
  cheese

Brown ground beef, salt, cumin, garlic powder, and onion; drain. Layer lettuce, chips, tomatoes, avocados, meat, and cheese.

DRESSING

1 cup sour cream

4 tablespoons lemon juice

Mix sour cream and lemon juice until blended. Spoon dressing over salad. Yield: 4 generous servings.

Diane Montani

HEARTS OF PALM SALAD

1 (14 ounce) can hearts of
  palm, drained
2 medium garlic cloves,
  finely chopped
3 green onions, sliced
2 tomatoes, sliced
1 tablespoon plus 1½
  teaspoons parsley, snipped

¼ cup plus 1 tablespoon
  olive oil
3 tablespoons lime juice
salt
pepper
favorite salad greens

Cut hearts of palm into ¾ inch thick slices. Mix palm, garlic, onions, tomatoes, parsley, oil, and lime juice. Season to taste with salt and pepper. Arrange favorite salad greens on individual plates. Top with palm mixture. Yield: 4 servings.

Diane Montani

TAS-TEA CELERY SALAD

1½ cups boiling water
3 tea bags
1 (6 ounce) package orange
  flavored gelatin
1 (11 ounce) can mandarin
  oranges

1 (8 ounce) can pineapple
  chunks
4 teaspoons lemon juice
2 cups diced celery

Bring water to boil in small saucepan. Remove from heat. Add tea bags; stir well. Let stand 5 minutes. Remove tea bags. Reheat tea just to boiling and pour over gelatin in 3-quart bowl. Stir to dissolve. Set aside. Drain fruits, reserving fruits and syrups. Combine syrups and lemon juice and enough cold water to make 1½ cups liquid. Stir into gelatin mixture. Chill until mixture is as thick as unbeaten egg whites. Stir in celery and reserved fruits (cutting pineapple chunks in half, if desired). Pour into 2-quart mold and refrigerate until firm. Yield: 8 to 10 servings.

Jane McLean

GOOD SHEPHERD'S PIE

TOPPING

2 cups leftover mashed
   potatoes or 3 medium
   potatoes
¼ cup milk

1 tablespoon margarine
½ teaspoon salt
pinch of paprika

Unless you have leftover mashed potatoes, cook potato chunks in fast boiling water until soft. Mash well with margarine, milk, and salt.

FILLING

1 pound broccoli
1 bunch spinach or Swiss
   chard
1 coarsely chopped onion
2 tablespoons oil
1 diced green pepper
1 pound or 4 medium diced
   carrots

½ teaspoon basil
1 bay leaf
¾ cup chopped fresh
   tomatoes or ¼ cup tomato
   paste and ½ cup water
1 teaspoon salt

Cut broccoli into flowers and stems. Peel and slice stems in ¼-inch rounds. Wash spinach thoroughly and cut into bite-size pieces. Preheat oven to 350°. Sauté onions in oil. Add broccoli, green pepper, carrots, basil, and bay leaf. Stir well and add tomatoes. Bring to boil, cover, turn heat to low, and simmer for 15 minutes or until vegetables are just tender. Stir in spinach. Add salt. Put vegetables into 9x13x2-inch baking dish. Spread potatoes over top and bake for 10 to 15 minutes until the potatoes are piping hot. Shake paprika over top before serving. Yield 4 to 6 servings.

Laura Pappas

CORN ON THE COB

For microwave

6 to 8 ears of corn

Clean corn and place in 9x13-inch glass pan. Pour into ¼ cup water in pan; cover with plastic wrap; slit several knife holes to let steam escape. Test after 10 minutes on high. Salt and butter to your own taste. Yield: 6 to 8 servings.

Marlene J. Yahn

241

SPINACH CUSTARD

2 cups milk
3 eggs, slightly beaten
1 teaspoon salt
⅛ teaspoon pepper
2 teaspoons onion, grated

2 (10 ounce) packages frozen
  chopped spinach
1 (2 ounce) jar chopped
  pimento
1 tablespoon butter

Cook spinach and drain well. Scald milk; add eggs, seasonings, and onions. Stir in spinach. Pour into buttered casserole. Dot with butter. Bake at 350° for 40 minutes or until custard is set. Yield: 6 servings.

Mrs. Herbert Kuehn

MARINATED BROCCOLI

2 bunches fresh broccoli
1½ cups cider vinegar
¼ cup cold water
½ cup vegetable oil
2 tablespoons sugar
1 teaspoon salt

1 teaspoon pepper
1 tablespoon dill seed
½ teaspoon minced garlic
ripe olives
pimento strips

Trim off large leaves of broccoli and tough ends of lower stalks. Wash broccoli and cut into serving-size pieces. Arrange pieces in single layer in dish. Combine next 8 ingredients in jar; cover tightly and shake vigorously. Pour over broccoli. Cover and chill at least 12 hours, stirring occasionally. Before serving, remove broccoli from marinade; garnish with ripe olives and pimentos. **HINT:** Must be done ahead. Yield: 12 servings.

Nancy M. Nuzum

COLD MARINATED VEGETABLES

1 (1 pound) can french style
  green beans, drained
1 (1 pound) can tiny peas,
  drained

¼ cup chopped pimento
2 medium onions, finely
  chopped
2 stalks celery, diced

Mix all vegetables in medium bowl and top with marinade. Drain before serving.

MARINADE

1 cup salad oil

1 cup cider vinegar

1¼ cups granulated sugar

2 tablespoons water

Combine oil, vinegar, sugar and water in container and shake well. **HINT:** Marinade may be saved in refrigerator for use again within 4 weeks. Yield: 8 servings.

Donna M. Glass

DILL BREAD

*Makes delicious sandwiches-especially
egg salad or cucumber. Good toasted, too!*

1 package dry yeast

¼ cup warm water (105°
to 115°)

1 cup cottage cheese

2 tablespoons sugar

1 tablespoon instant
chopped dry onion

2 teaspoons dill weed
(or seed)

1 teaspoon salt

¼ teaspoon baking soda

1 egg

2½ cups all-purpose flour,
approximately

1 teaspoon butter, melted

coarse salt or regular salt

Grease well, a round 1½-quart casserole. Put water and yeast in a large mixing bowl and stir to dissolve. In saucepan, heat cottage cheese to 110° to 120°. Add to yeast. Then add sugar, onion, dill, salt, baking soda, and egg. Add flour gradually to make a stiff batter, mixing well. All the flour may not be needed. Cover with plastic wrap and set bowl in a warm place to let dough rise to double, about 1 hour. Stir down. Put in prepared casserole. Cover with waxed paper and put in warm place to rise until double. Greasing waxed paper helps keep it from sticking. Preheat oven to 350°. Bake bread for 40 to 50 minutes. Test with a metal or wood skewer for doneness at center. If bread is getting too brown, put foil over it the last 10 to 15 minutes of baking. When done, remove from oven, brush with butter, and sprinkle lightly with salt. Allow to cool 15 minutes, then remove from casserole to rack. **HINT:** Freezes well. Yield: 1 loaf.

Iva White

LAGNIAPPE

SOUR CREAM ROLLS

Easily made in the food processor

1 package dry yeast
1 tablespoon sugar
½ cup lukewarm water
  (105° to 115°)
¼ teaspoon baking soda
½ cup sour cream, room
  temperature

3 cups bread flour (high
  gluten) (all-purpose may
  be substituted)
1 teaspoon salt
1 tablespoon soft butter

Proof yeast with sugar in the water. Add soda to sour cream and set aside. Let set 10 minutes until foamy. Fit food processor with metal blade. Put 2½ cups flour, salt, and butter into the work bowl. Add proofed yeast and sour cream mixture. Turn machine on and allow to run until mixture balls up on the blade. Check stickiness of dough. If it could be kneaded by hand without more flour, do not add any more. If too sticky, add more flour, 1 tablespoon at a time, processing briefly and checking until just dry enough to knead. (Do not make dough too dry.) Turn on processor and allow dough to revolve around bowl 120 times. This is the kneading. Place dough in greased bowl, cover with plastic wrap, and set in warm, draft-free place to rise until double, about 45 minutes to 1 hour. Punch down. Form into 12 to 18 round balls. Place on greased baking sheet. Allow to double. Bake at 375° for 15 to 20 minutes or until barely golden. **HINT:** Easy and freezes well. Yield: 12 to 18 rolls.

Cookbook Committee

BEER BREAD

This is excellent served hot with main course.

3 cups self-rising flour
½ cup brown sugar (may
  use white)

1 (12 ounce) can light beer

By hand, mix flour, sugar, and beer. Pour into a 9x5-inch loaf pan. Bake at 350° for 1 hour. Test doneness with toothpick. **HINT:** Easy and can do ahead. Yield: 1 loaf.

Beth Ann Dague

ENGLISH MUFFIN TOASTING BREAD

6 cups unsifted flour	¼ teaspoon baking soda
2 packages active dry yeast	2 cups milk
1 tablespoon sugar	½ cup water
1½ teaspoons salt	¼ cup cornmeal

Combine 3 cups flour, yeast, sugar, salt, and soda. In small saucepan, heat liquids to very warm (120° to 130°). Add to dry ingredients and mix well. Stir in rest of flour to make a stiff batter. Grease two 8½x4½x2½-inch loaf pans and sprinkle both with cornmeal. Spoon batter into pans. Sprinkle tops with ½ teaspoon cornmeal. Cover. Allow to rise in a warm place for 45 minutes. Bake in a 400° oven for 25 minutes. Remove from pans immediately and cool. Slice and toast to serve. **HINT:** Easy and freezes well. Yield: 2 loaves.

VARIATION
Whole wheat and raisin. Substitute 2 cups whole wheat flour for same amount of white flour. Stir ¾ cup raisins or currants into dry ingredients before adding liquids.

Joan Stifel Corson

PUMPKIN SPICE MUFFINS

½ cup butter	¼ teaspoon nutmeg
1¼ cups sugar	¼ teaspoon salt
1¼ cups pumpkin	1 cup milk
2 eggs	½ cup chopped pecans
1½ cups flour	½ cup raisins
1 teaspoon baking powder	cinnamon and sugar for
1 teaspoon cinnamon	topping

Have all ingredients at room temperature. Cream butter, sugar, and pumpkin until smooth. Add eggs, blending well. Sift flour, baking powder, and spices and add alternately with milk to egg batter. Do not over mix. Fold in nuts and raisins. Sprinkle a little cinnamon/sugar on top before baking. Bake in greased muffin tins at 375° for 25 minutes. **HINT:** Can be frozen and reheated. Yield: 2 dozen muffins.

Jo Clarke

STREUSEL COFFEE CAKE

Everyone always wants this recipe—easy and delicious!

2 cups graham cracker
  crumbs (approximately
  15 graham crackers)
¾ cup chopped nuts
¾ cup brown sugar, firmly
  packed
1¼ teaspoons cinnamon

¾ cup butter
1 (18 ounce) package yellow
  cake mix
1 cup water
¼ cup vegetable oil
3 eggs

GLAZE

1 cup powdered sugar

1½ tablespoons water

Preheat oven to 350°. Grease and flour a 9x13x2-inch pan. Combine crumbs, nuts, brown sugar, cinnamon, and butter. Mix and set aside. Mix the cake mix, water, oil, and eggs in a large mixer bowl on low speed until moistened. Beat 3 minutes on medium speed, scraping sides occasionally. Put ½ batter into pan; sprinkle with ½ crumbs. Top with remaining batter in an even layer. Top with remaining crumbs. Bake 45 minutes in a 350° oven or until toothpick inserted in center comes out clean. Cool. Combine glaze ingredients, adding more water to reach consistency for drizzling over cake. **HINT:** Easy and freezes well. Yield: 24 to 30 servings.

Cookbook Committee

BUTTERMILK PANCAKES

2 cups flour
1 teaspoon baking soda
1 teaspoon salt
2 tablespoons sugar

2 eggs, slightly beaten
2 cups buttermilk
2 tablespoons melted butter

In a 3-quart mixing bowl, sift together flour, baking soda, salt, and sugar. Make a well in center and add eggs, stirring to moisten flour mixture. Combine buttermilk and melted butter. Add all at once to flour mixture, stirring until flour is moistened. Add up to ½ cup more buttermilk, if too thick. Pour scant ¼ cup of batter onto a hot buttered griddle. Cook until pancakes are dry around the edges and bubbles appear on the surface. Turn; cook other side until golden brown. Several pancakes may be cooked at the same time. Yield: 4 servings.

Etta Rice

CHICKEN MARGARITA

Nancy Welsh Howley, wife of outstanding former WVU and Dallas Cowboy linebacker, is a Wheeling native as is her husband, Chuck.

8 individual boned breasts
  of chicken
flour
2 eggs
4 tablespoons water
salt and pepper

olive oil
6 tablespoons butter
½ cup vermouth
½ cup dry sherry
8 slices mozzarella cheese

Beat eggs with water. Dip each breast in flour, then in beaten egg. In a heavy skillet, heat ½ inch olive oil until oil sizzles. Brown chicken breasts well on both sides, and drain on paper towels. In a clean pan large enough to hold all pieces of chicken, melt butter, sprinkle with salt and pepper, and add wine and sherry. Cook over medium heat, stirring continually, until sauce is concentrated. Place chicken breasts in pan and cook over moderate heat just until chicken is heated through and cheese melts. To serve: Place chicken in a heated platter and pour sauce around. I serve fettucini with this. It's one of Chuck's favorite meals. Yield: 6 to 8 servings.

Nancy Howley

Index

INDEX

249

INDEX

INDEX

INDEX

INDEX

255

INDEX

INDEX

ACKNOWLEDGMENTS

Charles Milton
Stuart Bloch
Ray Byrd
James E. Seibert
Marilyn Mull
Tami Tysk
Don Fusco
Gladys Van Horne
Kitty Doepken
Kathie Briley
Maria Sticco
Nick Bedway
Bill Van Horne
West Virginia Independence Hall
West Virginia University Sports
  Information Department
Nabisco Brands, Inc.
HVR Company
General Pectin Manufacturing Corporation
OPEN PIT (a registered trademark
            of General Foods Corporation)

JUNIOR LEAGUE OF WHEELING, INC.
TREAT YOURSELF TO THE BEST
907 1/2 NATIONAL ROAD
WHEELING, WV 26003

Please send me _____ copies of "Treat Yourself To The Best" at $14.95 per copy, plus $3.00 for postage and handling. (West Virginia residents add $.89 sales tax per book.)

Enclosed you will find my check or money order for $_____.

NAME_____

ADDRESS _____ (NO P.O. BOX #)

CITY_____ STATE _____ ZIP CODE _____

Make checks payable to "Treat Yourself To The Best"

[____]

I would like to see the cookbook at the following store:

STORE _____

ADDRESS _____

CITY_____ STATE _____ ZIP CODE _____

All proceeds of our cookbook are returned to the community through projects of the **JUNIOR LEAGUE OF WHEELING, INC.**

JUNIOR LEAGUE OF WHEELING, INC.
TREAT YOURSELF TO THE BEST
907 1/2 NATIONAL ROAD
WHEELING, WV 26003

Please send me _____ copies of "Treat Yourself To The Best" at $14.95 per copy, plus $3.00 for postage and handling. (West Virginia residents add $.89 sales tax per book.)

Enclosed you will find my check or money order for $_____.

NAME_____

ADDRESS _____ (NO P.O. BOX #)

CITY_____ STATE _____ ZIP CODE _____

Make checks payable to "Treat Yourself To The Best"

[____]

I would like to see the cookbook at the following store:

STORE _____

ADDRESS _____

CITY_____ STATE _____ ZIP CODE _____

All proceeds of our cookbook are returned to the community through projects of the **JUNIOR LEAGUE OF WHEELING, INC.**